CW01521817

Intonation in
and Discou

Studies in language and linguistics

General editors: GEOFFREY LEECH, *Lancaster University*
and
JENNY THOMAS, *University of Wales, Bangor*

Already published:

Intonation in Text and Discourse

Beginnings, middles and ends

ANNE WICHMANN

Longman

An imprint of **Pearson Education**

Harlow, England · London · New York · Reading, Massachusetts · San Francisco
Toronto · Don Mills, Ontario · Sydney · Tokyo · Singapore · Hong Kong · Seoul
Taipei · Cape Town · Madrid · Mexico City · Amsterdam · Munich · Paris · Milan

Pearson Education Limited
Edinburgh Gate
Harlow
Essex CM20 2JE
England

and Associated Companies throughout the world

Visit us on the World Wide Web at:
www.pearsoneduc.com

First published 2000

ISBN 0-582-23475-1 CSD
ISBN 0-582-23474-3 PPR

British Library Cataloguing-in-Publication Data

A catalogue record for this book is available from the British Library

Library of Congress Cataloging-in-Publication Data

Wichmann, Anne, 1946–
    Intonation in text and discourse : beginnings, middles, and ends /
Anne Wichmann.
        p.   cm. — (Studies in language and linguistics)
    Includes bibliographical references and index.
    ISBN 0–582–23474–3 (pbk.). — ISBN 0–582–23475–1 (case)
    1. Discourse analysis.   2. Intonation (Phonetics)   I. Title.
II. Series: Studies in language and linguistics (London)
P302.W53   2000
401'.41—dc21   99–37052
                                                                                        CIP

Set by 35 in Palatino 9$\frac{1}{2}$/12pt
Produced by Pearson Education Asia Pte Ltd.
Printed in Singapore

Contents

Author's acknowledgements

So many people have helped me in so many ways during the writing of this book. My main debt is to Gerry Knowles, who introduced me to intonation in the first place, and whose insights and enthusiasm kept me going.

Colleagues at home and abroad have given me generous encouragement. Students have helped me by asking questions I couldn't answer. Friends and relations have helped by listening, and asking, and listening some more. I am very grateful to them all.

Publisher's acknowledgements

We are grateful to the following for permission to reproduce copyright material:

the author Margaret Stuart Barry for an extract from *The Witch and the Holiday Club*; the BBC for an extract from BBC Radio 3 news report 14.1.1996, and author's agent Jonathan Clowes for an extract from *Through the Tunnel* copyright © 1954 Doris Lessing. Reprinted by kind permission of Jonathan Clowes Ltd, London, on behalf of Doris L. Lessing.

Introduction

'Of course intonation makes a difference too, but . . .'

The focus of this book is the interface between intonation and discourse analysis. It is intended on the one hand for readers with a specialist interest in intonation who would like to know more about its function in discourse. On the other hand it is also for those who work mainly on other aspects of spoken language but who would like to take more account of intonation in their analyses. I so often hear discourse analysts utter a resigned sigh, and a remark to the effect that intonation is important too, but . . . it's so messy / it's so hard to get hold of / I haven't got an ear for it. All I can say is that it *is* messy, it *is* hard to get hold of, and a good ear helps, but it's not entirely without form and void. I hope that what I have to say here will prove useful to all those who study spoken discourse.

In this book I have tried to elucidate both structure and meaning in intonation at the level of discourse. Just as discourse analysis has been traditionally defined as 'structure extending beyond the sentence' (leaving aside for the moment the vexed question of what precisely we mean by 'sentence') so, in concentrating on discourse intonation, this book explores intonational structures and meanings which extend beyond tone groups and 'spoken sentences'.

Although I refer mainly in this book to intonation, I occasionally also make references to 'prosody'. Prosody is the complex set of features which together make up what we commonly perceive as 'tone of voice'. Intonation – or pitch – is just one component. Other features – loudness, tempo and voice quality – also play a part in some of the structures and meanings I have described, but in the main I have restricted myself to describing pitch patterns – the melody of speech.

The interface between intonation and discourse analysis is an area which, despite some notable early contributions (e.g. Brazil et al. 1980), has been largely neglected, and yet it is of central importance for the meaning and interpretation of spoken language. In the last decade or so, most energy in intonation research has focused on the form rather than the function of intonation, and on grammatically integrated units of speech. Consequently, most recent books on intonation are concerned with intonational phonology at or below the level of the syntactic sentence. However, despite sharing a common goal the approaches vary. Cruttenden (1986, 1997), for instance, gives an overview of intonation mainly in terms of the British system of analysis – the nuclear tones and tone groups approach, while Ladd (1996) describes recent developments within an autosegmental framework (see section 1.2.2). In this book I make reference to both these models, but, because of the data I have used, I refer chiefly to the British system, which identifies pitch contours (falls, rises, levels etc.) as the smallest unit of analysis. Since there is still considerable debate about the structure of intonation there is considerable variation in the terminology used, and I endeavour to explain terms wherever the need arises.

There is now a growing interest in the intonation of discourse and there are, as I see it, two broad approaches to the subject. The first approach, motivated to a large extent by the demands of speech technology, focuses mainly on spoken monologue, or short, goal-oriented dialogues, elicited under controlled conditions. Such studies (e.g. Grosz and Hirschberg 1992, Swerts and Geluykens 1993) are mostly experimental, and use instrumental methods of analysis. The other approach focuses on unrestricted, often informal, conversational interaction (e.g. Couper-Kuhlen and Selting 1996): it uses mostly auditory, impressionistic intonation analysis and is firmly situated within the analytical framework of Conversation Analysis (see Chapter 6). I aim to bridge the gap between these approaches, both in the analytical methods I use and in the kind of data I present.

I make use of both auditory and instrumental analysis, thus taking into account what the listener hears and what the computer can measure. Auditory transcription can capture varying degrees of detail: for more phonetic detail I use the so-called 'tadpole' transcription. This represents the speech melody with a series of dots (usually one for each syllable); the degree of salience of each syllable is reflected in the size of the dot, and pitch movement on accented syllables is shown by adding a 'tail' to a dot (hence the impression of a tadpole). I also use the more theoretically motivated system which records, using iconic symbols, only the pitch movements associated with accented syllables (falls, rises etc.). Instrumental analysis, also used in this book, requires a computer and special speech processing software. The recorded speech is digitised, and the fundamental frequency (F0) contour (what we hear as melody) is displayed on the screen as a broken wavy line. The information extracted in this way is useful because it is easily quantifiable. We can measure (in Hertz) the fundamental frequency at specific points in the contour, and from this derive other measures, such as the average F0 over a given stretch of speech.

Most of my observations are based on the analysis of a computer corpus of speech data, and are essentially data-driven. This contrasts, I hope fruitfully, with the more theory-driven approach of those working in the autosegmental framework. The corpus I use is the Spoken English Corpus (Knowles, Williams and Taylor 1996) (see below) from which I have made use of the auditorily transcribed texts and the corresponding sound recordings. The corpus contains mainly prepared but naturally-occurring speech (mostly broadcast), and I have therefore covered some of the neglected middle ground between laboratory speech on the one hand, and the impromptu speech of conversation on the other.

Many linguistic insights, my own included, can of course derive from introspection and casual observation. The act of listening to how people say things (and occasionally in the process forgetting to listen to *what* they say), generates many hunches and intuitions about how intonation works. Corpus data can be used to test these intuitions, but the data can also provide new insights, often of a distributional nature, which are beyond intuition. Both casual observation and quantitative analysis of corpus data can generate new hypotheses, some of which can be tested in controlled experimental conditions. Exploration is thus a kind of cyclical process in which no single method, nor indeed work on a single language, will provide all the answers or even all the questions.

The Spoken English Corpus

The Spoken English Corpus (SEC) (Knowles, Williams and Taylor 1996) is a corpus consisting of 53 different 'texts' of continuous spoken discourse, nearly six hours of speech. It represents a range of types of British English speech but contains mainly prepared monologue spoken in an accent close to Received Pronunciation (RP). The texts are grouped into sections, roughly based on genre. These are:

A: Commentary (e.g. radio reports from foreign correspondents)
B: News broadcasts
C: Lecture (public lecture to lay audience)
D: Lecture (Open University lectures to specialist listeners)
E: Religious (liturgical speech from broadcast religious services, including sermons and prayers)
F: Magazine-style reporting ('chattier' reports on financial news or sports)
G: Fiction (short stories read aloud)
H: Poetry (readings of Betjeman and Newbolt)
J: Dialogue (includes scripted dialogues from ELT text books and a prepared but unscripted dialogue between two EFL teachers)
K: Persuasive text (broadcast charity appeals)
M: Miscellaneous (all scripted monologue)

Reference to corpus texts in this book indicate the category of genre and the number of the text in that category. For example, text SECB04 is corpus text number 4 in category B (News broadcasts).

Although the corpus is small compared to corpora of written texts its value lies in the many parallel versions including the original sound recordings and the detailed auditory transcription. The transcription was carried out by two phoneticians, Gerry Knowles and Briony Williams. They are identified in the corpus and in this book by their initials GOK and BJW respectively. The transcribers were given equal portions of the corpus to transcribe, but there was at least one passage per section which was transcribed by both. These are the so-called 'overlap passages' (about 9% of the corpus) which provided a means of assessing the degree of agreement between the transcribers (see Pickering et al. 1996).

The transcription (for a more detailed explanation see Knowles, Wichmann and Alderson 1996) captures two main aspects of intonation: tones and boundaries.

Tones

Iconic tone marks, based on the 'tonetic stress marks' devised by Kingdon (1958) and still commonly used in the analysis of British English (see Tench 1997), are used to indicate which syllables are accented and what kind of pitch movement occurs on these syllables. There are three simple patterns: falling, rising and level, and two complex patterns: fall-rise and rise-fall. The pitch movement captured by the transcription is that which begins on (or in some cases near) the accented syllable. This is sometimes difficult for untrained listeners to assess. A falling tone, for example, is often preceded by a step *up* in pitch (to enable it to have somewhere to fall from). Untrained listeners often perceive the 'up' *to* the accented syllable more easily than 'down' *from* the accented syllable, and are then inclined to speak of a 'rise' instead of a 'fall'. The deciding factor is where the pitch contour ends. If it ends high or 'suspended' in some way it is usually a rise or a level, if it ends low it is probably a fall. (This is discussed in more detail in Chapter 3.)

Boundaries

Speech is divided into chunks referred to (inter alia) as 'tone groups'. The transcription indicates where the transcribers heard the boundaries between such tone groups. There are two kinds of boundary – minor boundaries, marking groups containing an average of 4–6 syllables, and major boundaries, which mark the end of a sentence-like unit of speech. While major tone groups are determined, in scripted speech, largely by the text, the minor tone groups are more under the control of speakers, who can choose to break up an utterance into smaller or longer phrases depending on the tempo or speaking style. Formal styles tend to produce fairly short tone groups and little variation, while spontaneous speech contains a wide variety of tone group lengths from single syllables to groups of over 30.

The transcription symbols in the SEC also include a number of other symbols, showing, for example, unusual shifts in pitch range and some pauses. A key to the symbols is to be found in Appendix I.

Some examples from the SEC have been cited in order to illustrate a specific local pitch pattern, and in these cases I have replaced the original transcription with a simplified version, highlighting only those features which are relevant. When referring to work in the autosegmental framework I use the basic symbols H and L for high and low tones, together with a small number of diacritics (* and %), which are explained in section 2.2.2.

Overview of chapters

For an integrated study of intonation in discourse we need to have a clear idea of what we mean by intonation and what we mean by discourse. **Chapter 1** contains an outline of the features of intonation which we need to consider, together with a discussion of different models of discourse. I then consider some of the parameters of variation within spoken discourse – broadly subsumed under the term 'speaking styles'.

Chapter 2 looks at the intonation of 'beginnings'. It deals first with an aspect of what is commonly referred to as 'paragraph intonation', namely the way in which a speaker indicates the 'beginning' of a unit of text analogous to a paragraph in writing. Using a number of different spoken texts, I show that, as the complexity of the internal structure increases, so the notion of a 'spoken paragraph' becomes harder to explain. I show that using knowledge derived from the oral reading of simple texts we are able to infer from a performance of more complex texts something about a reader's interpretation of the text, whether we are dealing with the performance of an expert adult reader or the performance of a 10-year-old.

In addition to exploring the well-documented 'topic reset', the high pitch which signals a new topic, I identify a pitch pattern operating over a whole phrase which functions as an intonational discourse marker. The notion of an 'intonational opener', described here as it occurs in the formal scripted speech of the SEC, is to be found again in Chapter 6 where I discuss conversational interaction. Finally in this chapter (2) I summarise recent findings which show the effect of topic initiality on the timing of pitch contours. Using instrumental analysis of both 'real' and experimental data we can see that a new topic causes the pitch peak on the first accented syllable not only to be extra high but also to be extra late. This section is a good example of the way in which corpus analysis and experimental studies complement each other in a fruitful way.

In **Chapter 3** I examine the notion of 'finality' – the sense of 'closure' which we sometimes hear in intonation. I explore the SEC for the distributional features of falling tones which indicate intonational closure, showing clearly that the orthographic sentence and the 'spoken sentence' by no means always coincide, even in the most formal varieties of read speech.

A quantitative study of transcription practice in the SEC reveals a number of different ways of 'closing', melodic sequences which I call 'cadences'. I identify a number of more or less common 'cadences' and also some stylistically marked variants. From studies based on the auditory transcription I then move to closer instrumental analysis of different kinds of falling tones. A perception experiment shows that falling tones can be realised in different ways to signal varying degrees of finality. This is an important observation which I return to later, in Chapter 6, to explain a variety of perceived meanings, particularly 'attitudinal' ones.

After looking at the way in which intonation can signal major disjunctures by indicating degrees of initiality and finality, in **Chapter 4** I turn to the cohesive function of intonation, where we see how a 'depressed pitch reset', a downgraded accent, can have an anaphoric function, linking a new spoken sentence to a previous one. I also examine the phenomenon of another cohesive device, tonal parallelism, showing that it extends over longer and more prosodically complex stretches of speech than other accounts have recognised. Finally I re-examine the intonation of parenthesis, showing that this too is subject to more variation than is generally described.

Chapter 5 takes up again the idea of paragraph intonation, but this time in search of *global* pitch features which characterise a unit of discourse internally, and not, as in Chapters 2 and 3, those features which mark its boundaries. I consider first the various approaches to modelling 'declination', the tendency of pitch to gradually fall in the course of an utterance and also its counterpart across higher units of discourse – 'paragraph declination'. The widely observed trend of supradeclination, generally thought to be to some degree at least of physiological origin – a gradual 'going flat' in the course of a paragraph or text – is shown to obscure many other effects on pitch range both between and inside sentences. These effects are shown to be linguistically motivated – by meaning and meaning relations.

Finally in **Chapter 6** I focus on the intonation of conversational interaction. I first consider the difficult issue of identifying prosodic units in spontaneous, unscripted speech, and show that the rhetorical relationships between these units, whether 'spoken sentences' or larger units of discourse, are signalled in a way similar to what we have seen in scripted speech. Here too we find intonation being used to mark both disjuncture and cohesion. I then turn to examine the role which intonation plays in organising the interaction itself. I draw together the results of a number of studies which deal with the intonation of turn-taking, and show how general principles of 'initiality' and 'finality', described in earlier chapters, also operate in conversational interaction. I show how the intonational opener, presented in Chapter 2, is used strategically in conversation to create conversational space for long turns, either operating independently as a prosodic discourse marker, or intensifying similar markers in the text. Drawing mainly on the work of Couper-Kuhlen (e.g. 1996) I move on to describe the way in which intonation and other prosodic features can signal the degree of cooperativeness between speakers. Finally I attempt to address the elusive 'attitudinal intonation', and propose that at least *some* attitudinal labels belong to the area of speaker meaning, which are best dealt with in the framework of pragmatics.

CHAPTER ONE

Analysing spoken discourse

The purpose of this chapter is to outline the various issues involved in studying the intonation patterns of spoken discourse. The subtitle of this book, 'beginnings, middles and ends', reflects an assumption that all texts, including spoken texts, have some kind of internal structure. We need therefore to say what we mean by a spoken text or discourse, and consider some ways of analysing its structure. A book on 'Discourse intonation' necessarily involves some account of what is meant by intonation and prosody. I will introduce as much as I feel is possible or necessary to understand later sections of the book. Finally, we must also consider the fact that speech, just like other dimensions of language, can vary according to its purpose and the context in which it occurs, and I will discuss some of the kinds of variation that need to be taken into account when studying spoken language.

1.1   A historical perspective

The use of prosody to signal global structures in spoken texts is currently of great interest because of its potential applications in technology. But an awareness of the role of prosody in structuring spoken text is much older. We find evidence of it, for example, in books published in England in the latter part of the 19th century and the early part of the 20th century. These books were concerned with speaking as an art form. They aimed to train speakers in the art of performance, whether for the public stage or for the intimacy of private gatherings. (Both the stage and the Victorian drawing room were accustomed to the dramatic monologue and the recitation of poetry.) One aspect of the training was the eradication of 'slovenly' pronunciations, often quite normal features of connected speech. Vowel reduction in words like *and, for* or *to* was discouraged: it was clearly suitable for the street but not for the stage. These books also devote much space to speech phenomena which we would now term prosodic or suprasegmental – speed, pausing, loudness and melody (intonation). All these, but especially speech melody, are components of the most elusive and yet clearly most important carrier of effective and persuasive performance, which used to be known as 'modulation'. Brewer (1912) in a 'practical handbook of the

7

elocutionary art' explains modulation like this: 'What light and shade are to a picture, and changes of key to a piece of music, modulation is to speech. What accent is to the syllables of a word, and emphasis to the words of a sentence, modulation is to a composition as a whole' (p.83). Only through modulation can the speaker establish 'a sympathy between the speaker and his audience' (p.83). Modulation 'constitutes the chief charm and perfection of elocutionary excellence' (p.84). It was easier, however, to describe the effect of such excellence than to say what the speaker actually had to do. Ultimately it was seen as a gift rather than anything which could be learned. 'Modulation in delivery is . . . entirely a matter of cultured taste and feeling . . . it may be improved by cultivation, but its essential basis, viz., an organ of exceptional quality, can no more be obtained by human effort that can heroic proportions by a man of meagre frame' (p.84).

Such books contain useful insights and, given the practical constraints of the time, acute observations. But, as Crystal points out, they also contain 'a bizarre mixture of social value-judgement, half-truth, pseudoprecision and idealism' (1969: 33). These days we are able to describe the prosody of whole texts in a more systematic way. Firstly, we have the technical means of storing and analysing the speech signal. Secondly, we have a more sophisticated theoretical framework within which to analyse suprasegmental phenomena. And thirdly, we have the benefit of a generation of text-linguistics and discourse analysis: in other words, we have a much clearer view of prosody, and a much more sophisticated idea of the complexities which constitute a 'text'. Effective 'modulation' is not simply an 'art'.

1.2   Prosodic resources

In order to describe how prosody is exploited as a cue to coherence and segmentation of texts it is first necessary to say something about the resources available. The term prosody has meant different things at different times. From its origins as the study of Greek and Latin versification, it has come to refer (especially in British phonetics) collectively to the linguistic patterning of pitch, loudness, timing (including pauses) and voice quality, in other words to speech patterns which operate above the level of the phoneme. (In American phonetics this is generally known as suprasegmental phonology, and the term prosody is reserved for the 'grammar' of intonation.) Not all these prosodic components are included in abstract models of sentence intonation, but all may play a part in the signalling of discourse structure. Voice quality, for example, although often beyond the speaker's control (as an individual characteristic or as a reflection of emotion), can be modified for communicative purposes (breathy voice for intimacy, so-called 'creak' for finality). Pause also has a discourse function, in addition to its grammatical function and its role as a reflection of mental processes (Brown et al. 1980, Couper-Kuhlen 1993, Passoneau and Litman 1993 (cited in Hirschberg 1993)). Timing is a crucial issue in the analysis of speech, from the relative durations of segments and syllables to overall speech rate (the number of syllables spoken per second) or articulation rate (the number of syllables per second of actual speaking time, i.e. excluding pauses). I am not aware of studies which deal specifically with the rhetorical use of speech rate, but it most certainly plays a part in the structure of discourse, as has been observed by Brown et al. (1980), Butterworth (1975), French and Local (1986) and Lehiste (1980). The same is true for loudness: while it is referred to incidentally in some studies of discourse intonation it has not to my knowledge been studied specifically for its role in discourse. Most models of intonation define units (variously known as tone groups, intonation units etc.) which presuppose a close connection between pitch, timing and loudness. To some extent, however, these systems only operate together in certain kinds of data. For this reason, and because there is enough to be said about pitch alone, I shall restrict my observations to one feature, namely intonation, or melody.

1.2.1 Intonation[1]

The melody of speech consists of a more or less continuous, constantly changing pitch pattern, similar to the tune played on a musical instrument, but not restricted to a conventional set of notes in a scale. It is created by the vibrations of the vocal folds during the voiced parts of speech. The frequency of these vibrations is measured in cycles per second or Hertz (Hz). Speech sounds are complex, and consist of many different vibrations at different frequencies. The frequency with which the complex pattern of these combined vibrations is repeated is known as the *fundamental frequency*, abbreviated to F0 ('f zero' or 'f nought'). The F0 of an utterance, what we hear as melody, can be displayed on a computer screen as in Figure 1.1.

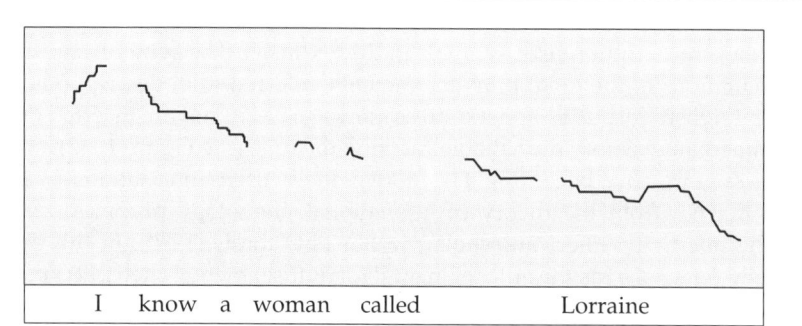

| I | know | a | woman | called | Lorraine |

Figure 1.1 Canonical F0 contour of an isolated spoken utterance, illustrating the way in which pitch typically falls during an utterance ('declination').

Changes in F0 are what we perceive as changes in *pitch*. Since perceived pitch and F0 are not related in a straightforward way the terms are normally kept separate, but I shall use the more familiar term 'pitch' unless the distinction between perception and production is particularly relevant.[2]

A far more important difference between acoustic events and perception is that we, as knowers of a language, learn to hear some differences and ignore others. It is part of our knowledge of a language which causes us to distinguish between linguistically significant and not significant acoustic information. This is of course equally true for our perception of vowels and consonants. Differences between speech sounds are not discrete physically, but in a sound system we know, we may *hear* them as discrete. As with other areas of linguistics, including discourse, as we shall see later, there are many different views on how to formalise the underlying system or systems. Some are language-specific, and more recently there have been attempts to develop a system which can be used to compare different languages. (See section 1.2.2.)

1.2.2   Models of intonation

In most current models of intonation there are two main elements: first of all that of pitch, and secondly the way spoken language is broken down into 'phrases' and the nature of boundaries between them.

1.2.2.1   PITCH

In the British tradition of intonation analysis, the most significant part of the overall contour is assumed to be certain pitch *movements* on or associated with prominent syllables. We identify a number of different patterns of movement: falls, rises, fall-rises and rise-falls (and in some versions of the system, levels). These are often referred to as 'tones' or 'nuclear tones'.

Tones can be represented graphically in a number of ways, and as Cruttenden (1997: xv) points out, the transcription systems are analogous to broad and narrow transcriptions in segmental phonetics. The narrow transcription most commonly used is the interlinear 'tadpole' transcription, usually above the text. The broad transcription uses symbols in the text itself. The symbols are stylised representations of the tonal pitch movements, referred to in descriptions of the Spoken English Corpus as 'tonetic stress marks' (TSMs), and are inserted into the text immediately before the syllable carrying the tone (see Figure 1.2(2) and (3)).

The system now becoming far more widely used internationally is one which derives from the theory of intonational phonology proposed by Janet Pierrehumbert, an American scholar, in her PhD thesis (1980). In this system, generally referred to as the autosegmental (or autosegmental-metrical) approach to intonational phonology, the pitch movements of the British system are decomposed into underlying pitch *targets* on two (abstract) levels – high and low (see Figure 1.2(4)). Thus a *fall* in the British system would be regarded as a sequence of two 'tones' H (high) followed by L (low). The tone most closely associated with the accented syllable is additionally marked with a star (*), so that the falling tone becomes H*L. A revised version of Pierrehumbert's 'two-level' theory (early American analyses required five levels (Pike 1945)) forms the basis of the ToBI (Silverman et al. 1992)[3] system of transcription, which was originally devised as a system for labelling computerised corpora of speech, and is now being developed for different languages to provide some standard means of comparison.

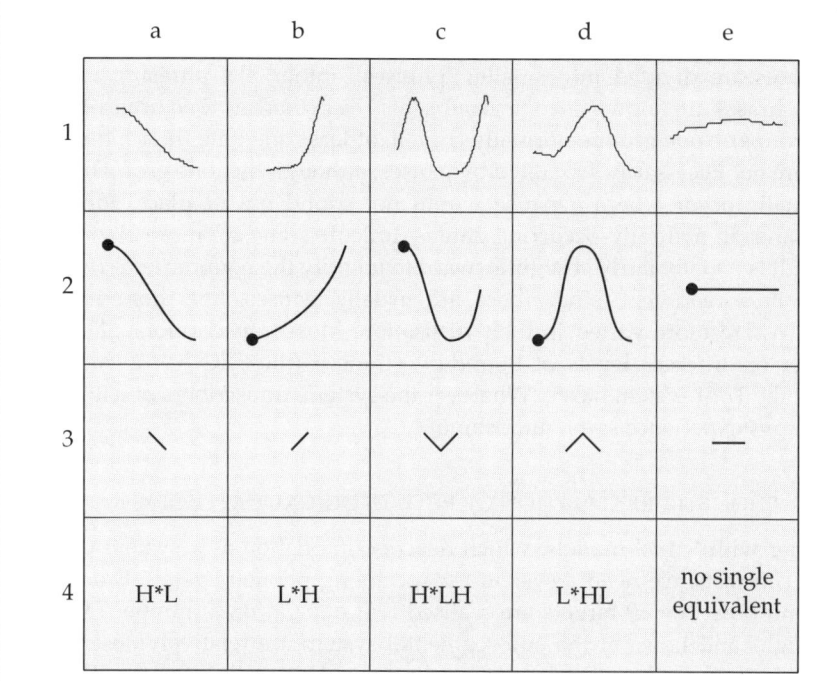

Figure 1.2   Different representations of tonal pitch contours:
(1) F0 contour of typical tones
(2) tadpole transcription of tones
(3) iconic symbols as used in SEC
(4) Autosegmental representation of tones (H*L, L*H, H*LH, L*HL).

The two systems cannot be mapped onto each other quite as easily as the above might suggest (see Roach 1994), but most tones (pitch movements) as in the British tradition can also be expressed in terms of tonal configurations (see Ladd 1996: 82). As Ladd (1996: 45) argues, 'the basic taxonomy of the British tradition is not for the most part rendered obsolete by [the autosegmental model] . . . only cast in a new light. There is no necessary contradiction in recognising both the functional unity of "nuclear tones" . . . and the phonological separateness of their component parts.' Cruttenden (1997) also points out that most recent work on the meaning or function of intonation (e.g. Pierrehumbert and Hirschberg 1990) carried out within the autosegmental approach actually deals with the meaning of tone *sequences* e.g. H*L (fall) or H*LH (fall-rise), rather than of individual tones.

The Spoken English Corpus, from which I draw much of my data, was transcribed using the British system of tones (see Introduction). I shall therefore refer here mainly to pitch configurations in terms of the falls, rises etc., of the British system and to the equivalent autosegmental configurations, e.g. H*L, L*H, only when there are useful points to be made by doing so.

1.2.2.2 PHRASING

The other crucial aspect of intonation is the way in which all but the shortest of utterances are divided into smaller 'phrases', rather like phrasing in music. These phrases are known as tone groups (also elsewhere as tone units or intonation groups). Tone groups normally contain at least one tone (hence the name). They are not necessarily separated by pauses, although the tone group boundaries usually occur where a pause would not sound out of place. Identifying boundaries in naturally-occurring data is difficult: some are more obvious than others. It is usually fairly straightforward to identify the boundaries *between* sentences in a read text, since these are usually pauses, but those *inside* the sentences are more varied in their realisation. Most transcriptions allow for a number of different levels of boundary strength (the SEC has 2: major and minor; the ToBI system has 5). Whatever the system, transcribers of natural data will aways experience some uncertainty.[4]

1.2.2.3 PHONETIC REALISATION OF PHONOLOGICAL CATEGORIES

Together with 'emic' models, which describe intonation as a system of meaningful contrasts, we need a system for specifying phonetic detail. Exactly how high and how low F0 targets are realised will depend on a number of factors. The Highs and Lows of the autosegmental system are relatively abstract, and the realisation of H and L depends on independent scaling factors. The autosegmental system regards pitch range specification as a local issue, prompted by local events such as emphatic stress, topic beginning, or syntactic boundary strength. Some other models relate F0 to more global components such as an underlying, gradually falling, reference line (the phenomenon known as 'declination'). The British system incorporates some of this variation into the system itself (e.g. high and low falls). The degree to which such specification should be part of the 'grammar' and how far it is a separate component remains controversial.

An extra complication involved in describing the underlying phonology of intonation is that the same channel also carries much paralinguistic, or even non-linguistic information – sex, age, emotional state (see Ladd 1996: 1), and, for that matter, (lack of) sobriety. However, the fact that pitch range variation is an area of debate leaves the field open to investigate, in a fairly pre-theoretical way, the variation of pitch range observable in naturally-occurring data. How do individual, local realisations of F0 targets relate to linguistic meaning, and what is the apparent domain to which these local phenomena relate?

1.2.3 Instrumental and auditory analysis

Studies of intonation differ considerably in their approach, and in particular in the type of analysis they use, whether purely instrumental, or based on auditory transcription or a combination of both.

To a certain extent the choice between auditory and instrumental analysis of intonation has until recently been a practical rather than a theoretical issue. The advances in speech technology, while not necessarily the motivation for all intonation research, at least benefit us as consumers. The ability to display acoustic information on the computer screen, gives us access to certain measurements which previously could only be guessed at. Using a stopwatch to measure pauses, for example, is (or should be) a thing of the past. Exactly how high a perceived pitch excursion is (in terms of F0) can now be measured and set against other measurements. The physical shape of a pitch contour over an utterance can now be displayed automatically, where previously we would have to draw a wavy line, or a series of 'tadpoles' (see Introduction). For some aspects of the study of discourse intonation, instrumental analysis is essential: measurements of average pitch range, for example, or relative change are otherwise far too cumbersome. Automatic analysis can also make larger quantities of data available than time-consuming auditory analysis will allow. Finally, the same principles which underlie instrumental analysis also make it possible to manipulate speech data (changing the pitch contours of a recorded sentence, for example, in order to test changes in perception). In this respect at least, technology provides vast possibilities for research .

Instrumental analysis also has its limitations. Some types of data are not readily amenable to instrumental analysis, such as overlapping speech in natural discourse. An instrumental analysis is also not necessarily more 'correct' than an auditory one. We need to remember that physical events and perceived linguistic structures are not necessarily directly related. Just as in music, the absolute duration of a pause in milliseconds, for example, may be less relevant than its relation to perceived rhythmic beats (Couper-Kuhlen 1993).[5] A 'level' tone in the British system may be anything but level if we look at the F0 contour on a computer screen. In addition, the computer makes no distinction between events which are linguistically significant and those which are not. It cannot easily tell us which syllable a pitch peak is *associated* with, only where it occurs physically in the segmental string. Finally, since each speaker uses a slightly different pitch range, direct comparisons between speakers cannot easily be made instrumentally. Pitch patterns have to be normalised (e.g. in terms of musical intervals) before such comparisons can be made.

Both methods of analysis have their advantages and their limitations. There is in my view no question of preferring one to another. Both have a unique contribution to make, and in fact the most interesting insights often occur where there is an observable mismatch between perception and physical reality.

1.3   Modelling spoken discourse

The term 'discourse' when applied to speech is often taken to mean exclusively conversation. Applied to writing it tends to refer to whole texts. I use 'discourse' in this book mainly to refer to the speech of one speaker – whether reading aloud a primarily written text or speaking spontaneously. In Chapter 6 I will examine conversational interaction in its own right.

Most descriptions of intonation to date apply to individual utterances, usu-ally sentences read aloud. But just as written texts are not merely strings of isol-ated sentences, spoken texts are not merely strings of isolated utterances. We are for the most part intuitively aware that all texts, spoken and written, consist of sentences or utterances which clearly belong together and form meaningful, coherent units, units which in turn constitute the text as a whole. These units of text or discourse are often referred to as topical units, reflecting the assumption that a unit is coherent because it is recognisably *about* something.

In written texts, the *boundaries* between meaningful subdivisions of text, in other words where they begin and end, can be highlighted typographically by the setting of paragraphs. A glance at a printed page shows us how the text is divided up, simply by means of indentations, headings, subheadings, and white spaces. The *internal* unity of printed paragraphs is also reflected typographically, in the use of punctuation marks such as the full stop, the comma (to varying degrees), the colon and semicolon,[6] which show that while successive elements may be syntactically independent they nonetheless relate to each other in some way.

The hearer of a spoken text, however, has no access to the visual, typographic cues to coherence and segmentation (punctuation, headings, paragraphs, indenta-tions etc.) which are available to the readers of written texts. In the absence of typographic cues, listeners processing speech in real time have to rely on other cues to identify coherence relations between utterances, and major breaks in that coherence, such as the boundary between two topic units. Some of these cues are prosodic, and it is this 'discourse' prosody which is the subject of this book.

Why do we need independent discourse models? It is difficult to identify the prosodic correlates of structural shifts or topic change in speech without an element of circularity, a problem already noted by others (Brown 1977, Swerts 1994). If we assume, for example, that topics of a spoken text are those units which speakers choose to highlight as such prosodically, then how can we say with confidence that a certain prosodic phenomenon is a topic marker, when we have identified those topics on the basis of prosody in the first place? To avoid this charge of circularity, we must find some independent measure of what constitutes at least a *potential* topic shift in a text, whether or not the speaker chooses to treat it as such. We must relate prosodic patterns and events to an analysis of the text which has been arrived at independently. Text analysis, text linguistics, discourse analysis: all these are fields of research in their own right. Most go far beyond the requirements of the intonation researcher, but they nonetheless offer a more systematic framework than the often intuitive and impressionistic analyses on which many intonation studies are based.

Once we have established the intonation cues to discourse structure on the basis of an independent analysis of that structure, we may use that knowledge to identify discourse structure where it is less evident in the text itself, either because necessary cues are absent or because existing cues are ambiguous. In other words, we can use our prior knowledge of discourse prosody to *infer* the discourse structure intended by the speaker.

1.3.1   Models of text and discourse structure

Just as there are a number of models of intonation, there are also many different approaches to the analysis of text and discourse. Some of these provide a post hoc analysis of a given text, written or spoken, focusing on the higher level units intended by the writer or speaker. These I call propositional models, since they are mainly concerned with propositional meaning. Cognitive models focus instead on how units of narrative are stored in the memory. A different, formal, approach to modelling attempts to explain how listeners interpret text structure as they are hearing it, in other words how they process spoken text in real time.

1.3.1.1   PROPOSITIONAL MODELS

Literate adults are intuitively aware that spoken and written texts can usually be subdivided into smaller units, and also that the units hang together or cohere internally in some meaningful way. These units of meaning are often referred to as 'topics', and thus reflect a concern not so much with identifying where the discourse segments change, but more with what they are 'about'. In other words, the identity of a discourse segment lies in the global proposition contained in it. A number of studies on spoken 'paragraphs' or 'topics' rely on a more or less subjective sense of 'aboutness'.

Propositional models of discourse, which attempt to identify discourse segments in terms of (macro-)propositions, and to define the rhetorical relations between them, are in the tradition of 'story grammars' (Propp 1968, Thorndyke 1977) and deal for the most part with the structure of *written* texts. This is the approach of van Dijk (1977) who sees texts as a sequence of meaningful subunits, as high-level propositions or macro-propositions, linked by references to time, place and people. These macro-propositions are also referred to by van Dijk as 'episodes', the rhetorical function of which depends on genre. Halliday and Hasan (1976: 327) express a similar view. '. . . the presence of certain elements, in a certain order, is essential to our concept of narrative: a narrative has, as a text, a typical organisation, or one of a number of typical organisations, and it acquires texture by virtue of adhering to these forms.' A story, for example, may contain episodes such as *setting, experience, complication, solution*. A scientific report may contain *design, methods, materials* and *results*. These functional units are related to one another structurally in a recursive hierarchy. 'The narrative rules and categories, abstractly defining the narrative expressed by the discourse . . . may be recursive. Narratives may be embedded under various categories of a higher level narrative' (van Dijk 1977: 154). This recursivity allows for example for a story to occur within a story.

Van Dijk thus deals with the meaning relations between topics by applying propositional logic at a macro level. He makes a clear distinction between the grammatical concept of a sentence or sequence of sentences and the propositional content. 'Macro-structures . . . are much less directly related to actual sentences because they are higher level properties of sequences of propositions' (1977: 150). This is important for studies in prosody, since a sentence is not strictly a unit of speech, and since even in the reading of written texts, prosodic 'beginnings' do not always coincide with conventional sentence boundaries. He also claims that these propositions at the macro-level are 'discontinuous', since at the sentence level there will be frequent reference to time, place and people which may form a link between topics. 'Characterising properties of times, places, backgrounds, characters, etc. may be given throughout the whole story, thus either conditioning or explaining certain actions and events' (1977: 154). These he sees as operating at a lower level, in contrast to the high level sequence of 'macro-propositions' or 'topics'. This view differs (I think) from more formal models (see below) in that it allows certain utterances / sentences to remain outside the organisation of macrostructures, or in some way as transitional elements between them. This is clearly useful in dealing with spontaneous speech, which, as we shall see, does not always contain clearly identifiable topic boundaries. Even such familiar utterances as 'Here is the news' do not fit comfortably inside a recognisable discourse segment, and are more easily analysed as transitions between segments.

Propositional models tend not to be used explicitly in intonation research, since many researchers, motivated by the needs of speech technology, are primarily concerned with modelling the way in which a listener processes text in real time, and for this purpose such subjective, top-down models are not appropriate. They do however form the basis of some functional analyses such as 'game moves' in the analysis of (usually domain-specific) interaction. For example, a goal-oriented dialogue (asking for information, giving instructions or directions) can be divided into sections which each have a specific function (Carletta et al. 1995). Such models also provide a useful framework for the analysis of performance by professional readers, for example in the performance of fictional narrative. Here we are not dealing with sight reading (i.e. impromptu reading aloud) but a highly prepared interpretation of the narrative, which may demand a sophisticated insight into the complexities of the text.

1.3.1.2 COGNITIVE MODELS

While the kind of text analysis described above, generally focusing on written texts, is helpful when analysing oral reading, the segmentation of spontaneous narrative must not be assumed to follow the same model. Werlich (1983) suggests that text structure is related to different forms of cognition. For example, 'narrative' is related to our perception of time while 'description' is related to our perception of space,[7] a view which reflects that of Chafe (1979) who argues that although the higher level episodes may be in the consciousness of the writer / speaker, they are not necessarily the units in which texts are stored mentally, by the reader or hearer. He proposes a basic unit of memory – the 'focus'.

> As one moves from focus to focus or from thought to thought, there are at certain points significant breaks in the coherence of space, time, characters, events and worlds. Such breaks lead to conspicuous hesitations and are identified as paragraph boundaries in written language. People seem not to store episodes as such, however, but rather to store coherent scenes, temporal sequences, character configurations,

event sequences, and worlds, all of which interact with each other to produce greater or lesser boundaries when some or all of them change more or less radically.

(1979: 180)

The way in which we structure memories of stories is therefore not necessarily the same as the rhetorical structure of the original, and a spontaneous narrative based on remembered events is also likely to reflect the 'foci' proposed by Chafe. This generates a structure which consists of parallel strands, like a musical score, and the oral narrative moves from strand to strand.

1.3.1.3 FORMAL MODELS

Discourse processing has to do with the reception of texts, whether by reader or listener, but my concern here is chiefly with the way in which *listeners* process spoken texts. This occurs in real time, and may not reflect the structure which is in the mind of the speaker. Most recent studies of discourse prosody are concerned to model formally what the listener does, rather than what the speaker intends. The models focus more on local *boundary* signals rather than the content or function of discourse segments, or the rhetorical relations between them. Grosz and Sidner (1986) in their computational model of discourse structure, acknowledge the existence of higher level structures, but exclude them from their model because, they say, although *speakers* may have such rhetorical relationships between text segments in mind, the *hearer* does not necessarily perceive them (p.202). Since their model is concerned with discourse structure from the hearer's point of view, in other words a hearer's real-time processing of discourse, this approach may be justified.

On-line processing of text structure, i.e. how a listener decides whether an utterance is a continuation of an internally-coherent text unit or whether it marks the beginning of a new unit, is known to depend on a number of strategies. These are used at any point to decide whether the current utterance is a continuation of the current 'discourse segment', the beginning of a new segment and simultaneously the end of the previous segment, or the beginning of an embedded subsegment. There can be several layers of embedding. Some decisions, especially those concerning the level of embedding of segments, can only be made with reference to the purpose or goal of utterances. If, for example, a new segment begins after the utterance: 'I will now describe a number of ways of making an omelette' it should be clear that the new segment is subordinate to the previous one. This is known as the 'domination constraint'. If the purpose of one segment 'dominates' the purpose of the new segment, the first segment cannot be closed (or 'popped off the stack'). There is therefore still a subjective, propositional element in this model, namely in the identification of utterance goals. Other strategies, which I will not deal with here, involve inferences based on the use of tense and aspect, and underlying rules governing the resolution of anaphoric reference (see for example Allen 1995). Such strategies look for cues to the *internal coherence* of discourse or text units which can be found in the surface phenomenon of cohesive ties. The 'ties' which create this cohesion are described by Halliday and Hasan (1976). They include anaphoric and cataphoric reference, lexical substitution and ellipsis. The cohesive devices in a text link related parts together, and are fundamentally semantic resources. They create coherence of meaning.

The most familiar strategy, however, is that which uses words and expressions as cues to the *boundaries between* discourse segments. Such cues vary in part according to the type of text; in other words they are to a certain extent genre-specific.

- In conversational interaction we typically find discourse particles such as *well, now*, which indicate shifts in the topic structure and generally introduce a new segment. Particles such as *incidentally, anyway* can indicate the beginning or end of a digression.
- In more formal, prepared speech we might expect to find more explicit cues to text structure: *in the first place, secondly* etc.; *to digress for a moment; I now turn to . . .*
- In written and spoken narrative we commonly find segment boundaries signalled by adverbials of time and place (*the next day; meanwhile; at the other end of the street*) or by explicit (not pronominal) references to protagonists. All these signal a shift in the underlying narrative framework of time, place and persons.

There are clearly many different ways of analysing texts. Which model we use depends to some extent on whether we are interested in what speakers do or what listeners use. If we are concerned with modelling the real time processing of spoken discourse then formal models are appropriate. 'An argument has a linear sequence and a hierarchical composition, and the transition from one position or level to another is determined by local cues encountered during a single left-to-right traversal of the material' (cover blurb – Reichman 1985). These local cues include surface features (cue words and phrases) reference phenomena (anaphor, cataphor) and inferences derived from the perceived purpose of utterances. These models (Grosz and Sidner 1986, Hobbs 1990, Reichman 1985) are applied in intonation research mainly to the analysis of coherence relations **inside** macro-structures and the identification of macrostructures, rather than to the rhetorical relations between the macrostructures themselves.

If we are not so much concerned with how listeners process spoken texts in real time, but wish on the other hand to investigate the way in which a skilled reader performs a previously constructed text, in particular literary texts (e.g. broadcast short stories, poems, talking books) then we may need recourse to a higher level, rhetorical model of the text. Only then are we in a position to claim some motivation other than artistic licence for some intonation patterns.

1.3.2 *Modelling conversational interaction*

So far I have focused on the structure of monologue, read or spontaneous. I now turn briefly to conversational interaction which is also of considerable interest to those working on prosody.

Conversation can be analysed from a number of different angles. It can be analysed semantically in terms of its topic structure, it can be analysed structurally as a sequence of turns, adjacency pairs etc. (Sacks et al. 1974), or functionally in terms of 'interactional acts', 'game moves' (Carletta et al. 1995; Francis and Hunston 1992) or at a macro level with 'openings' and 'closings' (Douglas-Cowie and Cowie 1997). The study of prosody in conversation must therefore take into account the fact that prosody has more than one 'discourse' function, including (i) to reflect the coherence relations and coherence breaks present in any text, and (ii) in addition, to organise and construct the interaction itself – turn ceding, floor holding, interruptions, backchannel etc.

Past work on the prosody of conversation has tended to concentrate on its role in interaction management, particularly turn-taking cues and interruptions (Beattie, Cutler and Pearson 1982, Cutler and Pearson 1986, French and Local 1986). However, Reichman (1985), whose model focuses on the role of an utterance in the overall argument structure of conversational interaction, does not regard this as a central concern. In her view, turn-taking rules are 'less linguistic conventions than simply conventions of interpersonal behaviour' (1985: 9). Turn-taking is 'restricted to linear conversational development. It has no way to explain . . . the large proportion of discourse that is non-linear and non-sequential – the frequent shiftings, suspensions, and resumptions of topic that we find in natural dialogues' (1985: 9–10). It is precisely these non-linear aspects of conversation which have been the focus of attention in the most recent work on prosody in conversation (Couper-Kuhlen and Selting 1996), but of course the requirements of the argument and the requirements of interaction management overlap. It is difficult to treat them totally separately.

Given the growing interest in prosody in dialogue, however, we should remember that conversation analysts are wary of models such as I have described above. 'In contrast to much text and discourse analysis, which tends to regard spoken data **ex post factum** as a finished product or the "behavioural realization of a preplanned cognitive unit" (Schlegloff 1982: 71), conversation analysts stress that discourse must be treated as being accomplished over time' (Couper-Kuhlen and Selting 1996: 28–9). In other words, dialogue is emergent discourse, collaboratively achieved. For the analysis of prosody in conversation, we need an understanding both of how utterances relate to the give-and-take of interaction, and of how they contribute to the emerging discourse as a whole.[8] For the most part in this book I am concerned with monologue. In Chapter 6, however, I deal specifically with the intonation of conversation.

1.4   Speaking styles

Language is subject to variation depending on the user and on the situation in which it is being used. This holds equally for speech and writing. Most studies of lexical and syntactic variation in speech and writing are carried out within a sophisticated framework of 'context of situation'. This is not yet the case in the study of prosody, where one finds only occasional references to different kinds of discourse. Two common distinctions are made in the study of discourse intonation. The first is that between **monologue** and **dialogue** (or text and discourse), i.e. the text of a single speaker or the jointly constructed text of multiple speakers. This is a practical distinction to make for some purposes. Clearly, any study of prosody used for the management of interaction requires interactive data; the analysis of topic or argument structure on the other hand can be carried out on both monologue and dialogue. A further distinction, although a much more problematic one, is that made between **spontaneous** and **read** speech. References in speech research to 'speaking style' usually refer to this distinction, which is one of mode.

The read/spontaneous distinction as it is commonly used conflates two different parameters. We can distinguish between speech which is scripted (read) or unscripted, and each of those styles can be more or less spontaneous. Reading at sight is not the same as reading a well-studied text. Speaking freely from detailed notes is not the same as conversing informally. Degrees of preparedness can apply equally to monologue and dialogue. A fluent monologue can be completely unrehearsed, while an apparently spontaneous response of a politician to an interviewer's question may in fact be well-rehearsed and often repeated. Let us therefore consider some of the variation found within each of the categories *read (scripted)* and *spontaneous (unscripted)*.

1.4.1   Reading

Reading aloud does not differ only according to how much it has been rehearsed. Brazil et al. (1980) make the important distinction between ways of reading: '. . . He (the reader) has two entirely different options: he can either enter into the text, interpret it and "perform" it as if he himself were speaking to the listener, saying as it were "this is what the text *means*"; or he can stand outside the text and simply act as the medium, saying "this is what the text *says*"' (1980: 83). At the most 'aesthetic' end of the scale we have highly stylised performance, to be judged in part at least by aesthetic criteria. Recitation of prose and poetry was regarded as an art form in Victorian times, and today we have the modern equivalent – talking books. A British journalist wrote of them recently 'How do we judge their performances? Certainly it is an art. Too much vitality and you bludgeon your listener, too little and you bore.'[9] This is reading as entertainment, not simply for information. At the other end of the scale we have what we might call the 'citation' form of the text. This would be the style used if someone said 'just tell me what it says on this instruction leaflet, will you? I haven't got my specs.' The role of the reader is clear: to pass on someone else's message. One is not required to invest any more of oneself than one's ability to decode the text and convert it into speech.

With all its variety, oral reading is very much part of our oral 'ecology'. Abercrombie's dismissive reference to 'spoken prose' (1965)[10] was rightly aimed at those who assumed it to be the only form of speech worth studying, but we cannot therefore ignore it altogether. We must not forget, however, that it is a skilled activity. This is a disadvantage for read-aloud laboratory speech, particularly in the case of texts longer than a single sentence, since on the whole people are not very good at reading aloud. Most people read aloud rarely, and to do it well requires considerable skill. Hours spent listening to students' carefully collected recordings of themselves, friends and relations reading aloud, convince me that the number of readers on which research studies depend, far exceeds the number of those who can be relied on to read well,[11] particularly at the level of discourse. In a study carried out by Esser (1988) an interesting difference was noted between the reading of professional and amateur readers, particularly in their ability to signal text structure. 'Only the professional reader is consistent in his use of high key at the five paragraph beginnings' (p.27). Professionals are paid highly for this skill – if everyone could read aloud well, newsreading would not be so prestigious, and we would not need professional actors to read talking books.

1.4.2 Unscripted speech

Unscripted speech differs in a number of ways from (skilled) oral reading. Depending on whether it is to some degree prepared or rehearsed, or entirely spontaneous, it will to a greater or lesser extent display syntactic and prosodic disfluencies – hesitations, repetitions, incomplete utterances. These are symptomatic of the fact that unscripted speech is simultaneously process and product, while oral reading is the performance of a scripted, i.e. pre-formed text. Pauses, for example, can reflect the structure of the text, just as they do in reading, but in unscripted speech they also reflect the mental processes involved in creating it. This can make intonation analysis difficult, particularly if we are operating within a framework designed for syntactically impeccable sentences.

Spontaneous, unplanned speech must also be viewed differently in terms of topic structure. If it is a narrative text, relating past experience, it will reflect the way in which experiences are stored mentally rather than the way stories are constructed by a writer. If it is a dialogue we must be aware that the topic structure is a collaborative affair, created in real time, and any model of analysis applied post hoc must take this into account. The prosodic marking of topic structure also differs from that in read speech. In spontaneous speech we do not always find clear prosodic boundary signals at syntactic and topical breaks which we expect in read speech. We find, for example, that pauses at clause boundaries occur *after* rather than before a conjunction, and the long pauses we expect at major discourse boundaries may be absent altogether. Instead of signalling a clear break, the speaker may drift gradually from one focal unit to the next, giving us a topic transition phase rather than a topical break. Indeed, we can often only infer from a prosodic 'beginning' that there must have been an ending.

1.4.3 Other speaking styles

Dialogue, like scripted and unscripted monologue, takes many forms, determined by the situation in which it occurs, the participants, and the relationships between them. The kind of dialogue at the most spontaneous end of the continuum is probably informal conversation between friends. Here we find equal rights to turn-taking, interrupting, and few limits on the kind of contribution which can be made. Other kinds of dialogue, such as interviews, pose greater restrictions on the participants. The rights to control the topic, and the rights to question and to answer are not symmetrically distributed between participants, and the interviewee may have rehearsed answers to predictable questions. Some dialogues are particularly constrained in terms of topic. Telephone requests for travel information, telephone numbers and roadside assistance, to give a few examples, all constitute dialogue of a special kind – goal oriented, highly domain-specific and much more predictable in their form and content than casual conversation.

1.4.4   Conclusion

Finally we can distinguish between public and private speech. Interactional behaviour exhibited in private may be constrained by the conventions of a public arena. Media interviewers are trained, for example, not to give too much back-channel feedback. An interviewee, aware of wanting to sound as articulate as possible, may consciously suppress filled pauses (*um*s and *er*s). A politician wishing to avoid the interruptions of an aggressive journalist may develop techniques of dispensing with any end-of-sentence pauses that might offer an opportunity to interrupt, pausing only mid-phrase where an interruption is less likely.

As we have seen, there are many different kinds of speech, or speaking styles, varying according to a number of contextual parameters. I have discussed here only a subset of these parameters, summarised in Figure 1.3.

speech event:	monologue *vs.* dialogue
	public *vs.* private
	goal-oriented *vs.* unconstrained
mode:	scripted *vs.* unscripted
	rehearsed *vs.* spontaneous

Figure 1.3   Some of the factors determining what is generally referred to as 'speaking style'.

There are many other contextual factors, such as speaker-hearer relationships (including power relationships) which may also be crucially important. Future research in discourse prosody will have to consider very many more dimensions of variation than is currently the case.

1.5   Summary

The search for an adequate description of the prosody of speech is not a recent one. It was already the subject of numerous publications in the 19th century, and probably before. In some respects we have made considerable progress since then. We now have a much more sophisticated framework for analysing intonation, both auditory and acoustic, and we know more about what intonational and other prosodic resources are available to speakers. We also know a lot more about the nature of spoken discourse itself. It is rare, however, for studies of discourse intonation to combine views of intonation and discourse of equal sophistication. In the following I will endeavour to show that this is a prerequisite if we are to fully understand either.

Notes

1   It is not possible in this book to provide a complete introduction to the intonation system of English. Those who would like such an introduction are referred to various existing works. These include Cruttenden (1986, 1997), Tench (1997) for a comprehensive overview of the British system of analysis, Couper-Kuhlen (1986) for a survey of a variety of different models including acoustic analysis, and Ladd (1996) for an account of recent developments in intonation theory derived from metrical and autosegmental phonology.

2   There are a number of models of how perceived pitch is related mathematically to fundamental frequency but the most frequently used is that which relates F0 to semitones. For each octave that we hear, the F0 is doubled. Thus we hear the step of 100 Hz to 200 Hz as an octave, and also 200 Hz to 400 Hz, and 400 Hz to 800 Hz. That means that the higher the frequency, the more it must change for us to perceive the same pitch interval.

3   ToBI = Tones and Break Indices. The transcription system marks both pitch levels ('Tones') and boundary strength ('Break Indices').

4   This is of course a phonetic view of tone group boundaries. In phonology, boundaries are abstract entities which are the logical consequence of assuming that intonation has a structure, and are not necessarily phonetic events. Phonetic breaks occur where the underlying structure **allows** it (Ladd 1996: 10).

5   According to Couper-Kuhlen (1993), rhythmic relationships between speaker turns, and pitch matching are clearly perceptual phenomena which are related only very indirectly, if at all, to measurable acoustic phenomena (see Chapter 6).

6   The colon signals that the following element constitutes an elaboration or explanation of what has gone before, while the semicolon signals a sequence of related items of equal status.

7   The forms of cognition Wehrlich refers to are: spatial perception, temporal perception, comprehension, judging and planning.

8   The most important aspect of the CA approach is in the nature of the evidence. Any claims made about the discourse function of intonation phenomena are derived solely from the interactive behaviour of the participants themselves.

9   Lucy Maycock in *The Observer*, 12.1.97.

10   'What linguistics has concerned itself with, up to now, has almost exclusively been – spoken prose' (Abercrombie 1965: 4).

11   Experimental work lends itself more readily to investigating low-level phenomena, since higher level structuring is more evident in the speech of a professional speaker.

CHAPTER TWO

Beginnings

An isolated simple sentence read aloud has a typical pitch pattern: it starts high and ends low. If we read a list of unconnected sentences aloud, the pattern will be repeated, each sentence with the same falling pitch pattern, beginning and ending at much the same pitch each time. For the listener, one of the clearest indications that a new sentence is beginning is the sudden shift up in pitch from the end of one sentence to the beginning of the next. This step up in pitch for a new beginning is known as a pitch 'reset', since it is thought to reset declination – the typical tendency of pitch to fall in the course of an utterance[1] (see Figure 1.1).

Most texts read aloud do not usually, however, consist of single sentences or even lists of sentences. Sentences are normally grouped together in a meaningful way to create larger units. Speakers are able to signal by means of intonation the organisation of units of discourse around a single topic. Observing this, Yule (1980) proposed the existence of the 'paratone' – a prosodic unit which spans a topic or sub-topic in speech, roughly equivalent to a paragraph in writing. The way in which speakers use intonation to group sentences in a paragraph-like way is often referred to as 'paragraph intonation'. (See also Chapter 5.)

Early notions of paragraph intonation were discussed extensively by Lehiste (1975),[2] who showed that the most common prosodic correlate of a new topic or 'conceptual paragraph' is an extra high pitch reset. She also considered whether such features also served as perceptual cues to discourse structure. Her first reported experiment (1975) showed that speakers started a sentence on a higher pitch at the beginning of a paragraph than if the same sentence occurred elsewhere in the paragraph or was spoken in isolation, and that this was used as a cue by listeners to identify the start of a new topic. In later studies of natural conversational data, Brazil et al. (1980), Brown et al. (1980) and Yule (1980) all made similar observations regarding the prosodic marking of beginnings. 'A new start is marked phonetically . . . by the speaker speaking high in his pitch range and speaking loudly' (Brown et al. 1980: 26). (The notion of paragraph intonation as a global rather than a local feature is discussed in Chapter 5.)

We can get a sense of the nature of topic reset by comparing the pitch contours of a topic initial sentence and a topic-medial sentence as in Figure 2.1.

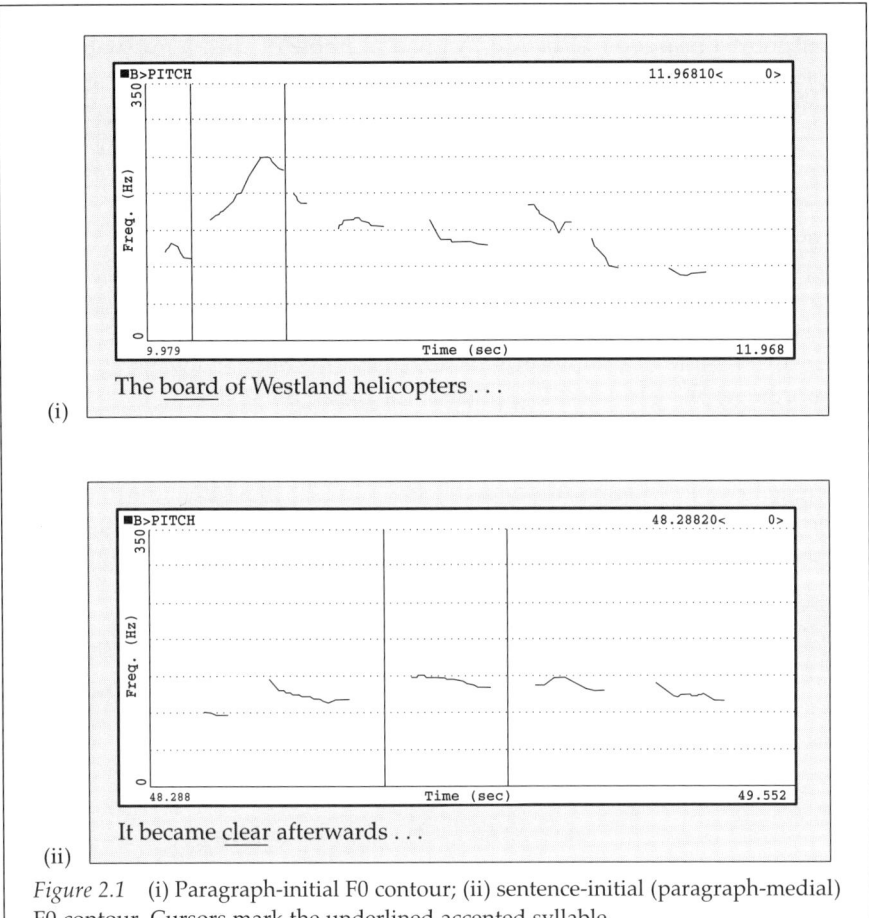

Figure 2.1 (i) Paragraph-initial F0 contour; (ii) sentence-initial (paragraph-medial) F0 contour. Cursors mark the underlined accented syllable.

The phenomenon of paragraph intonation is by now well-documented. Many studies have shown that readers start a new paragraph by using (among other things) an especially high pitch at the beginning of the first sentence. More recently this phenomenon has been referred to as 'topic reset', and in many studies the terms 'topic' and 'paragraph' are used interchangeably as if they were synonymous. This is clearly an oversimplification, but for the moment I will not attempt to distinguish between them.

2.1 Paragraph intonation in oral reading: 4 case studies

2.1.1 Case 1: A news summary

I have already pointed out (Chapter 1) that the study of prosodic cues to discourse structure, or topic structure, suffers from problems of circularity. To illustrate topic resets we therefore need to start with simple texts – those with an uncontroversial topic structure. A good example of such a text with a very simple, unambiguous topic structure, is the news broadcast. News items are prototypical topics, each completely separate from the other. No forms of co-reference, anaphoric or cataphoric, link one news item with another. News broadcasts are therefore a convenient place to start looking at some aspects of discourse prosody in action.

The news summary to be considered (SEC B04 – see Appendix I for full text with prosodic annotation) lasts 5 minutes and contains nine news items (including the final weather forecast) or nine different 'topics'. Predictably, each news item begins with an extra high pitch reset. This can be seen in Figure 2.2.[3] The text is divided into major tone groups which mostly, but not always, correspond to an orthographic sentence. The pitch of the onset, the first accented syllable in each major tone group (measured in Hertz), is shown as a point on the graph. Each linked group of points represents one news item. (The three isolated points belong to linking sentences, discussed below.) In each news item the initial pitch of the first sentence is high in the speaker's range, around 250 Hz, while almost all other sentence beginnings start lower, below 200 Hz.

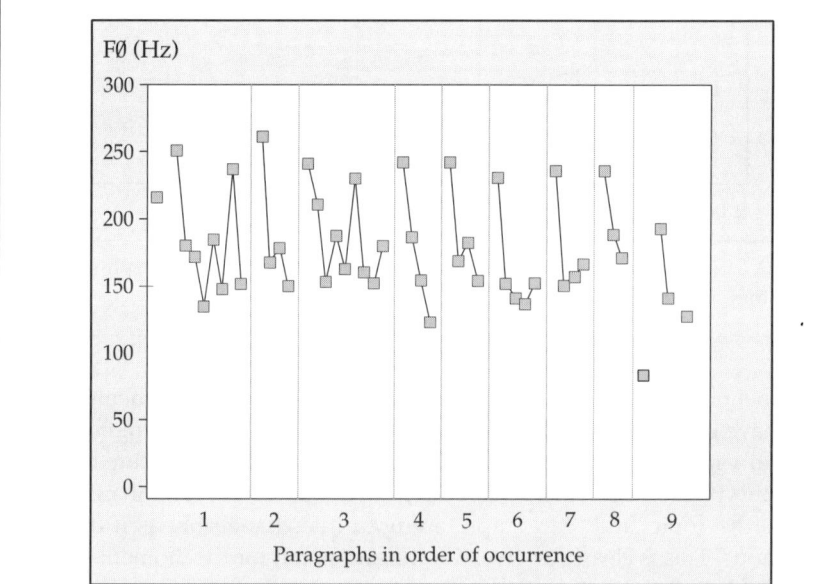

Figure 2.2 Major tone group onsets: This graph shows the height of onset of each major tone group in a news summary (SEC B04), in order of occurrence.

Even this simply-constructed text, however, displays apparent anomalies. The first anomaly concerns the unexpectedly low initial pitch of the two utterances (the first, and the fourth from last) which are represented on the graph in Figure 2.2 as isolated values. The first point on the graph is a little lower than the second. This is surprising since one would expect the beginning of the whole text to be the highest reset of all. For a possible explanation we need to look at the text itself. The broadcast does not actually begin with the first news item; the very first sentence of the text *Now it's one o'clock and this is . . . in the newsroom with the BBC news summary* is a metatextual comment rather than belonging to any one news item, and as such might be regarded as an introduction to the main body of the text. There is therefore a difference in status between this stretch of text and the subsequent 'topic units'. The final unit (the weather forecast) also begins with a metatextual comment *And finally the weather* rather than with the forecast itself, and this utterance does not have the same high onset as the item which it introduces. The pitch of the prehead *And* is much higher, and there is a marked step down to the accented syllable in *finally*, which is unusually low, very close to the speaker's base line. This drop to a low pitch is a typical 'coming to the end' phenomenon, often marked in the transcription with a downward pointing arrow (the 'down-arrow'). (See also section 4.2.) The third isolated point on the graph represents the closing metatextual comment *And that's the news at . . .*

Some formal analyses of the structure of this text (e.g. Grosz and Sidner 1986, see section 1.3.1.3) would place the news items as lower in the discourse hierarchy than the introductory sequence. This should make the beginnings of the news items themselves perceptually less salient than the introductory and closing remarks. This is not the case in this text. The pitch patterns we actually find here relate much more easily to a model of text structure in which topics are discontinuous, and linked by transitional references to time, space and people.

The second anomaly concerns pitch resets which are relatively high, even though they occur on sentences *inside* a news item. (News items 1 and 3.) Looking at the text we find that these are in fact independent sub-units which are inside the topic and which the speaker has highlighted with a fairly high reset, almost as if they were new topics, but with onsets not quite as high as those at the beginning of the news item.

2.1.2   Case 2: A news report

The next text is more complex. SEC B01 is a news report and therefore longer than the summary in B04. The length of individual news items is much more variable, and the broadcast is interspersed with reports from other journalists, so that a number of speakers are involved. Comparing pitch heights across different speakers is problematic since each will have his or her own characteristic pitch range. To be able to make comparisons, only the contributions by the main newsreader have been included here, and those by other readers and on-the-scene reporters omitted. The pitch of sentence-initial accented syllables is plotted in Figure 2.3. As in Figure 2.2, the points which are joined together represent the onset pitch of all major tone groups or spoken sentences in one news item or 'topic'. The figure also identifies meta-text and opening and closing headlines. The overall pattern of topic resets is still visible in this text, but it is less consistent than B04. Unlike the prosodically downgraded metatextual 'frame' in B04

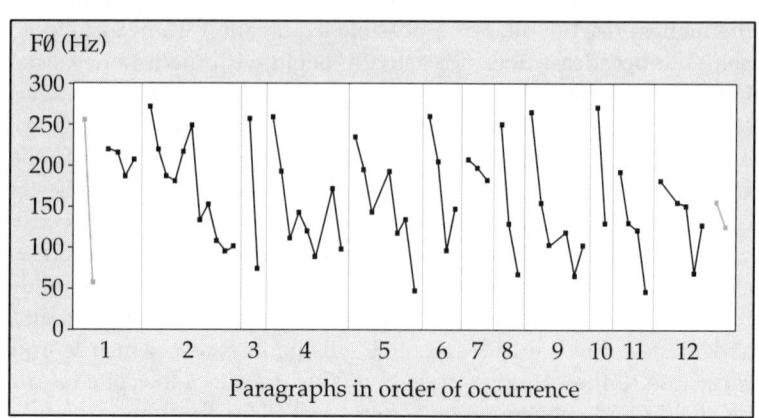

Figure 2.3 The height of each 'sentence beginning' (major tone group onset) in a news report[4] (SEC B01). Sections 1 and 12 contain the opening and closing head-lines, preceded and followed respectively by metatextual links.

(Figure 2.2), the introductory metatextual link to B01 begins at a pitch similar to that of news-item beginnings, but both groups of headlines are downgraded in relation to the main news reports. In some of the longer items (2 and 4) there is evidence of further resets for subtopics within those items, suggesting that there is possibly a hierarchy of resets corresponding to the level of embedding within a topic. However, despite the greater complexity of this text, and the intervening contributions by other reporters, the paragraph divisions are clear: the main newsreader consistently begins a new item with a pitch higher than that of any subsequent sentences in the same item.

2.1.3   Case 3: A short story

The news broadcasts described above are primarily spoken texts. They are of course scripted, but intended to be spoken. However, if they were to be pro-duced in written form – as Teletext for example – we can assume that the topics (news items) we have identified are likely to correspond fairly closely to ortho-graphic paragraphs. In such texts we can safely assume that 'topic' and 'para-graph' are more or less identical. However, we now move to a very different kind of text, the oral performance of a primarily written text, and here we find that the printed paragraphs only account for a small part of the reader's prosodic topic signalling.

   The reading I will discuss here is (one assumes) a highly rehearsed perform-ance, publicly performed, and with an aesthetic rather than an informative purpose. It is the broadcast performance of a short story (slightly abridged) by Doris Lessing: *Through the Tunnel* (SEC G01). The gist of the story is as follows: a small boy discovers the existence of a tunnel which runs under water through a large rock in the sea. He dives down to investigate, determined to find the entrance and eventually to hold his breath long enough to swim through it, in imitation of the local children who play there. His first attempt is thwarted by his inability to see well under water. He persuades his mother, unaware of his plans, to buy him some goggles, and then returns to investigate further, this time successfully. Having trained himself to hold his breath long enough he embarks, alone, on the dangerous dive. The underwater tunnel is longer than he had anticipated . . . !

This is a long text, and I have selected only a short passage, quoted in section 2.1.3.2 below, to show how the reader responds, or more frequently does not respond, to the printed form of the text.

In Figure 2.4 (upper half) the sentence onsets of a small section of the text are plotted in groups corresponding to 6 printed paragraphs. There is little evidence of topic-initial resets coinciding with these paragraphs. However, the reader does occasionally begin a sentence with an extra high pitch (above 300 Hz), and these are the points where the listener perceives a topic shift, but they are not consistent with paragraphs. The question of course is – are they consistent with anything, or are they simply idiosyncratic, random variations in an 'artistic' performance? As I will illustrate below, they are in my view evidence of a systematic interpretation of the text. If we take each high onset as the beginning of a 'speech paragraph' we can regroup the points marked on the graph. These

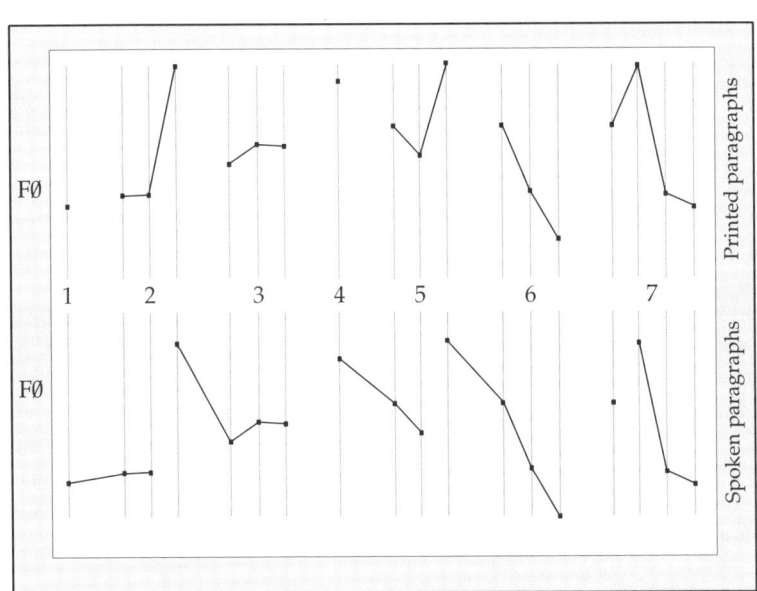

Figure 2.4 Sentence beginnings in a short passage from a short story (SEC G01). (i) Grouped according to orthographic paragraphs; (ii) re-grouped to indicate spoken paragraphs.

speech paragraphs, identified by marked pitch resets, are shown in the lower half of Figure 2.4. There are three shared boundaries, at the end of printed paragraphs 3, 6 and 7. At no point, however, do we find a complete correspondence between a printed paragraph and a speech paragraph.

With a performance of this kind, we can clearly not rely on orthographic paragraphs to predict where a professional reader will choose to segment the text. Although the printed text is laid out in paragraphs, the reader does not necessarily treat them prosodically as such. And yet in studies of discourse prosody the terms *paragraph* and *topic* are often treated as synonymous (e.g. Bruce 1982, Kreiman 1982, Schaffer 1984). To what extent is this justifiable?

2.1.3.1 TOPICS OR PARAGRAPHS?

Paragraphs may reflect linguistic units but are essentially typographical units. They are motivated in part by considerations which are aesthetic rather than linguistic: 'Short paragraphs provide convenient resting places during reading and aesthetically pleasing contrasts between print and white space' (Quirk et al. 1985: 1624n). There is nonetheless an assumption that, to some extent at least, a paragraph will constitute a coherent textual unit of some kind: 'a paragraph enables a writer to show that a particular set of sentences should be considered as more closely related to each other, and that those grouped in one paragraph are to be seen as a whole in relation to those that are grouped in the paragraphs preceding and following' (ibid: 1624). Finally, there is an assumption that 'no grammatical units extend beyond their limits' (ibid: 1624).

To what extent therefore can these grammatical, textual and aesthetic considerations be satisfied at the same time? First of all it is usual that a printed paragraph is coterminous with a grammatical sentence. Secondly the paragraph is usually motivated by some kind of semantic discontinuity, often signalled (see above) by adverbial phrases of time, place ('The next morning . . .'; In another part of the town . . .') or by the introduction of a new character. In experiments (e.g. Stark 1988) designed to find out what motivates paragraphing, such surface cues play an important part. These are the cues to Chafe's 'significant breaks in the coherence of time, space, characters, events, worlds' (1979: 180). (See longer quotation in section 1.3.1.2.) All these strands of discourse operate concurrently, overlapping, and a paragraph may be motivated by a break in one, several or all of these strands. Paragraph breaks are not necessarily 'correlative', that is, even if one begins with a shift in the temporal coherence it may not necessarily end for the same reason. The length of a paragraph is dictated mainly by aesthetic considerations. This means that a suitable coherence break will be chosen or ignored depending on how close it is to the previous paragraph break.

2.1.3.2 SPOKEN VS. WRITTEN PARAGRAPHS

Brown and Yule, in their analysis of discourse, insist that topic structure is not inherent in any text, but a construct of the speaker or the writer. '. . . it is speakers and writers who have topics, not texts' (1983: 68), but we do not always have independent access to speakers' and writers' intentions. Since we already have good evidence that high pitch resets can be a sign of topic shift, we must assume that the reader of this story, Elizabeth Bell, found some textual motivation for her pitch resets other than printed paragraphs.

To appreciate the textual motivation for this performance we need to see the versions side by side. In the left-hand column the text appears as in the published printed form (marking the abridgement). In the right hand column we find the 'speech paragraphs'. The reader's most important deviation from the printed paragraphs occurs at the end of the second paragraph. The sentence 'But the salt was so painful . . .' is no longer at the end of one section but at the beginning of the next.

printed version	spoken performance
. . . They swam back to the shore without a look at him.	*They swam back to the shore without a look at him. He swam back to the big rock, climbed up and dived into the blue pool among the fanged and angry boulders. Down he went until he touched the wall of rock again.*
He swam back to the big rock, climbed up and dived into the blue pool among the fanged and angry boulders. Down he went until he touched the wall of rock again. **But the salt was so painful in his eyes that he could not see.**	*But the salt was so painful in his eyes that he could not see.* *He came to the surface, swam to the shore and went back to the villa to wait for his mother. Soon she walked slowly up the path swinging her striped bag, the flushed naked arm dangling beside her. 'I want some swimming goggles', he panted, defiant and beseeching.*
He came to the surface, swam to the shore and went back to the villa to wait for his mother. Soon she walked slowly up the path swinging her striped bag, the flushed naked arm dangling beside her. 'I want some swimming goggles', he panted, defiant and beseeching.	*She gave him a patient, inquisitive look as she said casually, 'Well of course, darling.' But now, now, now! He must have them this minute, and no other time. He nagged and pestered until she went with him to a shop.*
She gave him a patient, inquisitive look as she said casually, 'Well of course, darling.'	*As soon as she had bought the goggles, he grabbed them from her hand as if she were going to claim them for herself, and was off, running down the steep path to the bay. He fixed the goggles tight and firm, filled his lungs, and floated, face down, on the water. Now he could see.*
But now, now, now! He must have them this minute, and no other time. He nagged and pestered until she went with him to a shop. As soon as she had bought the goggles, he grabbed them from her hand as if she were going to claim them for herself, and was off, running down the steep path to the bay.	*Under him, six or seven feet down, was a floor of perfectly clean shining white sand, rippled hard and firm by the tides . . .*
He fixed the goggles tight and firm, filled his lungs, and floated, face down, on the water.	
[text abridged[5]] Now he could see.	
Under him, six or seven feet down, was a floor of perfectly clean shining white sand, rippled hard and firm by the tides . . .	

At the beginning of *But the salt was so painful* ... the reader makes a marked pitch reset, suggesting a new topic. In addition, her voice quality becomes more tense, and she also changes from a slow to a fast tempo.[6] The marked prosodic break at this point is is not only inconsistent with the printed paragraph; it also introduces a major break at a non-standard sentence boundary – before the conjunction *but*.

The orthographic paragraphs reflect the temporal structure of the story at this point. They divide the text into a chronological sequence of actions (*He swam* ... ; *He came* ... ; *She gave* ... ; *But now* ... ; *He fixed* ... *Now*). If we wish to account for the spoken paragraphs, other than dismissing them as a mistake or an idiosyncrasy, we need some other analysis of the text which can accommodate its complexity. Van Dijk's (1977) functional account of text structure (see Chapter 1) is helpful here. If we return to his concept of 'episodes', we see that a story can have functionally defined 'episodes' such as *setting, experience, complication, solution*. The section of text beginning *But the salt was so painful in his eyes* might, in these terms, be seen as a 'complication' within the story, followed by a 'solution'. The narrative describes the boy's search for the underwater tunnel. The *complication* arises that he cannot see under the water. The *solution* is to buy goggles. He can then continue his search.

In the printed text the 'complication' (requiring a solution) is incorporated at the end of a paragraph (see Figure 2.5(i)). The reader, however, does it differently (Figure 2.5(ii)), treating the complication and solution together. This allows the two related episodes (complication / solution) to be separated prosodically from the main narrative.

(i) [... NARRATIVE/complication]   [SOLUTION]   [NARRATIVE ...]
(ii) [... NARRATIVE]   [complication/SOLUTION]   [NARRATIVE ...]

Figure 2.5   The textual organisation of a section of a short story (SEC G01) according to (i) the printed text; (ii) the spoken performance.

The 'complication and solution' section is internally coherent as a small narrative episode, both contained in and separate from the main story. The justification for this interpretation is clear if we omit the whole sequence from the text. The surrounding text is perfectly coherent when the 'complication–solution' sequence is omitted as in (a) below, whereas this is not so if we omit the corresponding orthographic paragraphs (b). The reader, unlike the typesetter, treats the whole complication episode as a kind of large 'parenthesis', ensuring that the superordinate unit of text remains coherent, and she does this prosodically by introducing a topic reset on 'salt'.[7]

(a) Down he went until he touched the wall of rock again. (*complication/ solution*) Under him, six or seven feet down, was a floor of perfectly clean shining white sand, rippled hard and firm by the tides . . .

(b) Down he went until he touched the wall of rock again. But the salt was so painful in his eyes that he could not see. (*solution*) Under him, six or seven feet down, was a floor of perfectly clean shining white sand, rippled hard and firm by the tides . . .

We see here a marked difference in the orthographic organisation of the text and the reader's interpretation of the story. The organisation of the printed text is coherent at the low level of narrative shifts in time, place etc. The spoken performance is coherent at the level of the rhetorical relationships between the macro-units of discourse.

In summary, it seems highly likely that orthographic paragraphs indicate not the boundary between one clearly definable 'episode' and another, but a point in a text where one or more of the 'coherent scenes, temporal sequences, character configurations, event sequences and worlds . . . interact with each other to produce greater or lesser boundaries when some or all of them change more or less radically' (Chafe 1979: 180). Paragraphs are thus not entirely irrelevant to the study of reading intonation; indeed, many amateur readers respond only to such visual cues to text structure. Professional readers, however, interpret their texts in a more sophisticated, less linear, way. Paragraphs alone do not account for their expert 'modulation'. Topics are units of meaning and not orthography.

Such literary texts are inherently far more complex in structure than the news summary of the previous example. A group of ten readers asked to identify topics, or topic boundaries, in the written versions of this text found it difficult to agree. I doubt whether they would have had the same difficulty with the news broadcast. The fluidity of topic structure in a text such as *Through the Tunnel* allows the skilled reader some scope for interpretation, choosing to highlight some discontinuities in the narrative and play down others. Apart from asking the individual reader what his or her intentions were, the only access we have to an individual interpretation is through the prosody. An awareness of prosody thus gives us an important tool with which to analyse speech performance.

This is of course not the kind of text which needs to be catered for in most speech technology applications. However, it highlights the weakness of the orthographic paragraph as a cue to complex discourse structure. This is particularly true of the kind of literary texts we find as talking books, where we expect readers to give highly interpretive professional performances, and as we shall see from the next text, even of the kind of text we expect young emergent / learner readers to perform.

2.1.4 Case 4: Children's oral reading

The following is a further example of a text where printed paragraph and topic structure do not coincide. It is an extract from a children's book, used in an unpublished study (Turnbull 1995) of children reading aloud. A particularly skilled 10-year-old reader in this study produced a marked pitch reset not at the beginning of a paragraph as expected, but at the beginning of the second sentence in that paragraph.

The text[8] is set out below in the left-hand column with the original paragraph divisions, and in the right-hand column, the spoken version set out in 'speech paragraphs'.

printed version

'I am never going to go to school again!' said the witch. 'Never ever.'

George, the witch's long suffering cat, looked put out when he heard this. He was the sort of cat who liked to be on his own. When the witch was out, he could prowl around the house doing evil things. He could nose into cupboards and drawers and sniff at the witch's belongings. He could claw big holes in the hearthrug; snootch under the settee, and lick inside the pans. But most of all, he could crunch up the furniture when he was hungry. He got smacked of course, but he was well used to that, so it didn't matter.

The witch ignored George's sulky looks and rummaged out her school uniform. She hung it up on a coat hanger and examined it. . . .'

spoken version

'I am never going to go to school again!' said the witch. 'Never ever.' George, the witch's long suffering cat, looked put out when he heard this.

He was the sort of cat who liked to be on his own. When the witch was out, he could prowl around the house doing evil things. He could nose into cupboards and drawers and sniff at the witch's belongings. He could claw big holes in the hearthrug; snootch under the settee, and lick inside the pans. But most of all, he could crunch up the furniture when he was hungry. He got smacked of course, but he was well used to that, so it didn't matter.

The witch ignored George's sulky looks and rummaged out her school uniform. She hung it up on a coat hanger and examined it. . . .'

I infer from the pitch reset on *He was the sort of cat* . . . that the young reader perceived a topic shift of some kind. There is every justification for this. The extract above is the first passage of the whole book, and begins for rhetorical reasons *in medias res*, with a conversation, albeit rather onesided, between a young witch and her cat. The description of the cat, beginning in sentence two, contains necessary background information about the cat, information which in a more conventional narrative might well have preceded the action. Here it is a digression, to explain precisely why the cat is not overjoyed at the idea of being supervised all day. The text segment interrupts the current action, which continues in paragraph three.

The logic of the orthographic paragraph divisions rests on the alternation of focus from witch to cat and back to witch. It also gives the dramatic introductory statement the isolation which allows a young reader to savour its implications. The logic of this particular performance, is to separate the description from the 'dialogue' (assuming that 'sulky looks' can be counted as a contribution to the conversation). This is comparable to the interpretation in the previous section. The skilled reader highlights the rhetorical function of text segments, while the orthographic paragraphs (and probably most unskilled readers) follow a more linear sequence of shifts in time, place or, as in this case, protagonists.

This study used young readers' prosody as an indication of how they processed the text, and the scope of the units they recognised. It has been shown (Perera 1989) that as children learn to read they process text first in units of one word, then in word groups and phrases. The processing of higher level structures and the meaning relationships between them has to my knowledge not been investigated. It is surprising that a ten-year-old should allow the rhetorical structure of a text to override the much more obvious divisions on the printed page. There are several possible explanations: it may be that this is a performance anomaly which has nothing to do with the reader's interpretation of the text. It could also be that this young reader is highly skilled and very sophisticated in recognising text structure in this way, resulting from a familiarity with narrative conventions. Another possiblity is that our response to typographical layout is a skill acquired later in the development of literacy. The children in this study, although skilled, occasionally ignored full stops and capital letters at sentence boundaries, suggesting that sensitivity to typographic conventions is independent of the ability to interpret texts, and that a young reader uninfluenced by the layout may be able to respond more readily to narrative structures which are at odds with the layout.

2.2 Titles, headlines and openers: the 'citation contour' as a topic marker

The previous section was concerned with a very local phenomenon – the way in which a marked upward expansion of pitch range, the high resetting of declination, indicates the beginning of a new topic in speech. There is, however, a further intonational device which speakers use to indicate a new topic, one which involves a complete intonational contour and not just a local shift in pitch range (see also Wichmann 1998).

The complete contour which I refer to here is the canonical intonation contour (see Figure 1.1) which we associate with a sentence spoken in isolation, in what we might call its citation form. This 'citation contour' is of course not uniquely the property of a sentence. One of the most familiar uses of the complete citation contour, other than for sentence-completion, is for reading aloud titles and headlines, which are perhaps prototypical discourse organisers of written text. If we elicit an oral reading of a narrative we can predict with some certainty that the title, and any subsequent headings, will be realised with a citation contour fairly low in the speaker's range, and ending in a very final-sounding fall (Figure 2.6(a)). What is interesting here is that although the title is complete in itself, it is not an isolated utterance but part of a text, of which it marks the beginning, not the end. The 'finality' or 'closure' associated with the completed contour therefore has to be re-interpreted by the listener as a *beginning* of some kind, or at least a boundary which simultaneously closes any previous discourse segment and signals that something new is about to begin.

A title is a conventional signpost, restricted to written texts and their oral performance (Figure 2.6(a)). There are, however, other less formal story 'openers'

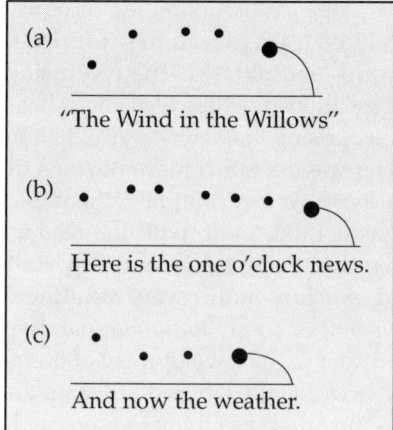

Figure 2.6 The citation contour (canonical 'sentence intonation') functioning as a title and headline.

– introductory sequences which prepare the listener for the text to come. We find these routinely in contemporary broadcast speech (Figure 2.6(b) and (c)).

Titles, openers and metatextual comments are all examples of explicitly sign-posting major topical units of text. There is evidence, however, that the citation contour associated with explicit openers can also operate independently. In this case, the contour can become associated with a sentence element which, unlike openers, is not syntactically independent.

2.2.1   Topic marking in read speech

The pattern we find in read speech – possibly stylistically marked – is that the citation contour is associated with the first noun phrase of a new topic.

The first examples come from news broadcasts in the SEC. The citation contour, ending in a low fall (symbolised here with ↘), is associated in each case with the first noun phrase subject of the sentence. Despite their syntactically non-final position, the falling tones at the end of these NPs have two important characteristics which make them particularly 'final': firstly they begin fairly low in the speaker's range, and secondly they have a low endpoint close to the speaker's baseline, the pitch usually assumed to be reserved for the end of an utterance (Figure 2.7) (see Chapter 3 for more discussion of 'finality').

(1) **The Confederation of British ↘Industry** has said the Chancellor should . . . (SEC B04)
(2) **The unions at Ford ↘Motors** say the company's hourly paid workers appear . . . (SEC B04)
(3) **A major security re↘view** has been ordered . . . (SEC B02)

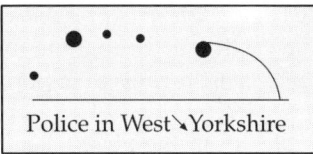

Figure 2.7 Citation contour on the first Noun Phrase of a topic-initial sentence (News broadcast, SEC B01).

(4) **A big ↘rescue operation** was mounted in central London late last night . . . (SEC B01)

(5) **Police in West ↘Yorkshire** say they're investigating a fire . . . (SEC B01)

It is important to note that in each case the NP in question is the subject of the sentence. Others have already noted that it is common to find an initial noun phrase subject followed by a pause (Fang and Huckvale 1996), and/or a tone group boundary (Altenberg 1990). In each of the examples above, however, the noun phrase has another important function. In addition to being the subject of the sentence, it is also the beginning of a new topic – here a news item. The phrase therefore has a grammatical function within the sentence and at the same time constitutes a topic shift in the text as a whole.

The examples given so far might suggest that this is a stylistic mannerism restricted to radio journalism. Certainly, the majority of examples I have found in the SEC come from that genre. There are others, however, which suggest that the device may not be restricted to a particular type of text. The following example (see the pitch contour in Figure 2.8) comes from a broadcast reading of a fictional short story. (Tone group boundaries are also marked here.)

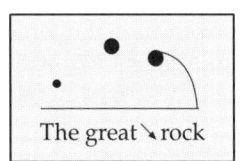

Figure 2.8 Citation contour on the first Noun Phrase of a topic-initial sentence in a short story (SEC G01).

(6) **The great ↘rock** | the big boys had swum through | (SEC G01)

The prosodically highlighted noun phrase marks a shift in the narrative just as in the previous examples, but this intonational device is in fact a rare example in the text. There are a number of possible reasons for this: the topic structure is inordinately more complex in this short story than in a news broadcast, and many shifts in the narrative begin with an expression of time or place rather than with the subject of the sentence. It may be that the function or information status of the highlighted sentence constituent is as important as its initial position in the sentence.

Below are further examples from the SEC, taken from a broadcast lecture. In each case the highlighted noun phrase is the subject (or part of the subject) of the sentence, and occurs at a major shift of topic.

(7) ... below | I painted the three pillars of society | army | church and school ||

Harry ⟍Kessler | a left wing ⟍aristocrat | and ⟍art collector || saw this painting in Grosz' studio ... (SEC D01)

(8) ... the art which is being visibly shattered | by the explosions of last week ||

This in⟍sistence | on life | ... (SEC D01)

The first of these is a particularly marked example since each subsequent appositional NP imitates the same contour.[9] In fact the effect of turning this sequence into a prosodically separate opener is so marked that the transcriber has assigned a major tone group boundary at the end of it, a most unusual occurrence in this corpus.

From the above examples we can see how the citation contour can be used strategically to highlight a topic shift. The contour combines the extra high onset, a high pitch reset typical of topic / paragraph beginnings, with a falling tone, often downstepped, i.e. beginning relatively low in the speaker's range, and falling to a low endpoint. This applies, as we have seen, to titles and to metatextual elements such as story openers, but also to integrated sentence constituents which have no discourse-organising role in themselves. By assigning the citation contour to the subject of the topic-initial sentence, if it is in initial position, the speaker signals that the sentence constituent functions both as an integral part of the text and as an intonational 'opener'. The effect is to project forwards, preparing the listener for a new topic to come.

The use of this device in conversational interaction as an 'opener' or intonational 'routine' (to borrow from Aijmer 1996) will be discussed in Chapter 6. Its use in spontaneous monologue is described in the next section.

2.2.2   Topic marking in spontaneous speech

So far we have been dealing with cases of scripted speech – oral reading for information or for entertainment. In this kind of skilled reading, prosody is a function of the text. At syntactic and topical breaks we expect clear prosodic boundary signals, particularly pauses. In unscripted, unrehearsed speech these boundaries are not always so clear. Spontaneous speech is by definition being created in real time, and many of the prosodic features of the performance will reflect the cognitive processes involved. Pauses, for example, can reflect mental processes involved in creating a text, as well as reflecting the structure of the text itself. Even structural pauses may occur at slightly different places in a spontaneous text. At clause boundaries, for example, we often find pauses (marked (.)) *after* a conjunction and not before it, as we would in read speech.

So we went out and (.) it was quite nice because (.) . . .

Of course, we also find in spontaneous speech the typical filled pauses (*erm* and *er*) and verbal fillers (*you know, you see* . . .) which reflect the ongoing planning processes involved.

So what about topic marking in spontaneous speech? Swerts et al. (1996) suggest that topic boundaries in spontaneous monologue are still marked with longer pauses than at lesser boundaries, often either side of a filled pause. This study was based on elicited data: the subjects were asked to describe a number of paintings. The speakers focused on different aspects of the picture in turn, and when they felt that each aspect had been exhausted they tried to think of another one. In other words they were involved in an open ended activity, but constrained partly by the task of interpreting and describing the picture in front of them. There is no intrinsic hierarchy in such a description – it consists of a linear sequence of foci motivated by the requirement to find something to say. It is thus hardly surprising that there is a considerable pause between sections.

When people talk spontaneously about their own experiences, they are verbalising a series of events and observations which are already stored in their heads. They are recreating past experience, not interpreting the present. As Chafe suggests, these stored episodes include sequences bounded by time, space and people, which overlap. Putting parallel memories into linear sequence often causes the speaker to digress, explain, elaborate, and the result is a complex hierarchy of structures at several levels of embedding. The speaker is concerned more with *how* to tell the story than *what* to say.

A very common feature of this kind of narrative is that the long pauses we expect at major discourse boundaries may be absent altogether. Instead, the most salient features of topic shift are often the high pitch reset and acceleration in tempo of a new beginning. The previous topic does not end, it fades away – the voice becomes quieter, slows down, and pitch range narrows. So the transition from one topic to another in this kind of speech is often a gradual one and it is difficult to identify a precise boundary. We often only infer from a prosodic 'beginning' that there must have been an ending.

This apparent indeterminacy may be compensated for by the frequent use of discourse-structuring elements in the text. Explicit discourse organisation in spontaneous speech occurs typically by means of discourse markers, and also by means of 'conversational routines' (Aijmer 1996) and 'meta-talk' (Schiffrin 1987). Some of these sequences have an organising function at a local level, while others operate more globally, signalling the beginning of major units of discourse. All occur in initial position, are syntactically detachable, and have forward or backward pointing deictic function.

The following extract is taken from an elicited monologue[10] in which the speaker was encouraged to recount events in her life over the past few months, which she did with enthusiasm and at length. This extract contains a major topic shift in the narrative.

> Anyway so (.) at the wedding Pete was no (.) stranger to (.) em to the Vikings[11] and (.) in fact gave an excellent speech and (.) afterwards it was quite funny it was extremely hot it was a very hot day (.) er and these Vikings had been fighting for about (.) an hour or so and they were absolutely (.) s . . . well they were so hot they were steaming

There are a number of surface features of discourse organisation in this text: *anyway* signals the end of a digression, and *so* indicates the (explanatory) purpose of that digression. *Afterwards* signals a temporal shift and is followed by a typical opener *it was quite funny*. It is not yet clear at this point, however, whether this is a global shift in the narrative or a minor shift within the sequence interrupted by the digression. The presence of the conjunction *and* could suggest the latter, but it soon becomes clear that a major new part of the story is beginning.

The prosodic indications of this topic shift are not straightforward. Towards the end of the current topic (. . . *gave an excellent speech*) the speech becomes slower, but there is not a structural pause. The pitch range becomes narrow, fairly low, but does not fall to the speaker's baseline. Unlike in oral reading, there is no clear finality signal, and no clear disjuncture.

The suggestion of a topic shift comes from a number of signals. First there is an acceleration of tempo on *it was quite funny*, but the pitch is still not markedly higher, suggesting that the shift is a fairly minor one. Then there is a very high pitch reset on *it was exTREMELY hot*. This sounds more like a major shift in the narrative but since there has been no clear ending, and given the meaning of the word itself, we might equally ascribe the pitch excursion to emphasis. The final signal, which resolves retrospectively the rather indeterminate end to the previous topic, is the use of the intonational 'opener' described in the previous section. The whole sequence *it was extremely hot* is realised with a complete citation contour (see Figure 2.9), which is then echoed with a slightly reduced pitch range on the next sequence *it was a very hot day*. Note the very low endpoints on both *hot* and *day*. After a lengthy stretch of narrow range, suspended somewhere in low to mid range, characterising the tail of the last topic, we now have a very strong sense that a new topic is being initiated. The effect of the repeated citation contour is thus twofold: firstly it resolves retrospectively the rather indeterminate end to the previous topic, and secondly it projects ahead to the beginning of

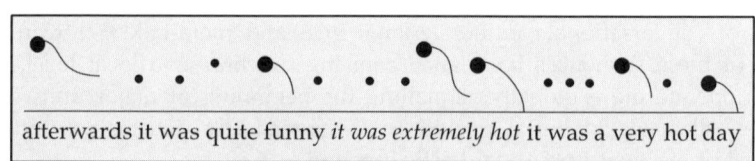

afterwards it was quite funny *it was extremely hot* it was a very hot day

Figure 2.9 Auditory transcription of a topic transition in spontaneous monologue.

something new. In so doing it takes on a backward as well as a forward pointing function.

2.3 Phonetic issues surrounding initiality

2.3.1 How high is high?

We have now established that a topic beginning is signalled by an extra high initial accent. Exactly how high is another issue. As I said in Chapter 1, current intonation models treat the idea of high and low as abstract values, and specify variation in pitch range separately. Pitch range specification (also known as accent scaling) relates mostly to sentence-length utterances, and is partly an attempt to model the phenomenon of declination, the tendency for pitch to fall in the course of an utterance (see also Chapter 5).

There has been little attempt until recently to include in such models of pitch height any structures longer than a sentence. This is because, with a few exceptions, discourse prosody was for a long time of interest mainly to those who wished to describe in a fairly pre-theoretical way what happens in unconstrained natural data. More recently, however, there have been more tightly controlled experimental studies of discourse prosody. Those working in speech technology (speech synthesis and recognition) have begun to recognise the limitations of sentence-based intonation models for generating natural-sounding texts, or for recognising them, and in particular for designing interactive computer speech systems. This perceived need has stimulated research in the area of discourse intonation, but of a different kind. For inclusion in synthesis systems, much more precise quantification is required and the results must be amenable to formal modelling. This change in emphasis in the research into discourse prosody is reflected in the number of papers published using experimental techniques.[12]

2.3.1.1 RELATIVE PITCH HEIGHT

Partly as a result of the current need for precise modelling, an apparently simple and uncontroversial phenomenon – topic reset – gives rise to the theoretically controversial question – how high is high? Pitch (or rather fundamental frequency) can be measured in absolute terms – cycles per second – but since individuals vary considerably as to the actual pitch range they exploit, absolute values provide us with little linguistic information. The linguistic use of pitch can only be expressed in relative terms. The pitch at a particular point in an utterance, for example the highest pitch on a stressed syllable, can be measured either in relation to the pitch of some other point in the same utterance, or in relation to some more stable point such as the speaker's habitual base line.

So far I have compared the pitch height of beginnings by relating the height of one sentence onset to another, and not to any fixed value. There is also a view, rarely published but often discussed informally, that listeners have an intuitive feel for a speaker's own voice range, and are able to judge the height of a syllable not only in relation to surrounding syllables but also with reference to the speaker's voice. How listeners do this is not clear, but it is possibly on the basis of voice quality, which varies to some extent with pitch. We know, for example, that a creaky voice often occurs at low frequencies. It could be that the shape of the spectrum (which we hear as a component of voice quality) tells the listener where speakers are in their own voice range. A recent study (Swerts and Veldhuis 1997) found some evidence for this, but exactly which aspects of voice quality co-vary with pitch is not yet clear.

Ladd (1996, Chapter 7), discusses the theoretical issues surrounding these two ways of describing pitch, i.e. either in relation to the speaker's voice or in relation to the surrounding utterance. He reports experimental evidence for what he calls a 'normalising' view of pitch range (i.e. describing range in terms of the speaker's voice).

2.3.1.2 INDIVIDUAL PITCH PREFERENCES

One argument for a 'normalising' view of pitch height is the observation that 'speakers have a preferred pitch level at which they tend to begin tone units, usually around the middle of the voice range' (Couper-Kuhlen 1986: 101). This refers to unstressed syllables (pre-head syllables) at the beginning of minor tone groups, the stretch of speech roughly equivalent to a phrase, but references made incidentally in other studies seem to suggest that individual speakers may also have a preferred pitch for the first accented syllable of whole utterances, depending on the position of the utterance in the text. Figures quoted by Brown et al. 1980, for example, imply a fairly constant absolute F0 value for different sentence onsets, in this case between topic onsets (major paratones) and other sentence onsets in between.

> We shall . . . distinguish between major paratones, which follow topic pauses and are characterised by very high peaks **(in the speech of 22BS by peaks at around 200 cps)** and minor paratones which follow contour pauses and begin with lower peaks **(typically for 22BS between 160 and 180 cps[13]).**   (1980: 71) (my emphasis)

This pattern is also visible in the SEC, Text B04 (the news summary referred to in section 2.1.1). The sentence onsets in the text are not evenly distributed, but cluster in two parts of the speaker's overall range. Those sentences beginning a new topic (news item) start at a pitch in the region of 240 Hz, while the first accented syllable in other sentences occurs mainly around 140–150 Hz (Figure 2.10).

This speaker seems to have at least two favoured 'keys', which we might categorise as 'high' and 'default', from which he selects an utterance onset pitch. In this text, the majority of the sentences begin with an accented syllable around the middle of the speaker's overall range, which spans between 80 Hz, his lowest pitch, and 250 Hz, his highest pitch. (150 Hz is approximately half way between 80 Hz and 250 Hz., if calculated in semitones.)

It is tempting to see evidence for a further subdivision of topic-medial onsets into 'default' and 'raised', since there is a similar cluster of sentence onsets

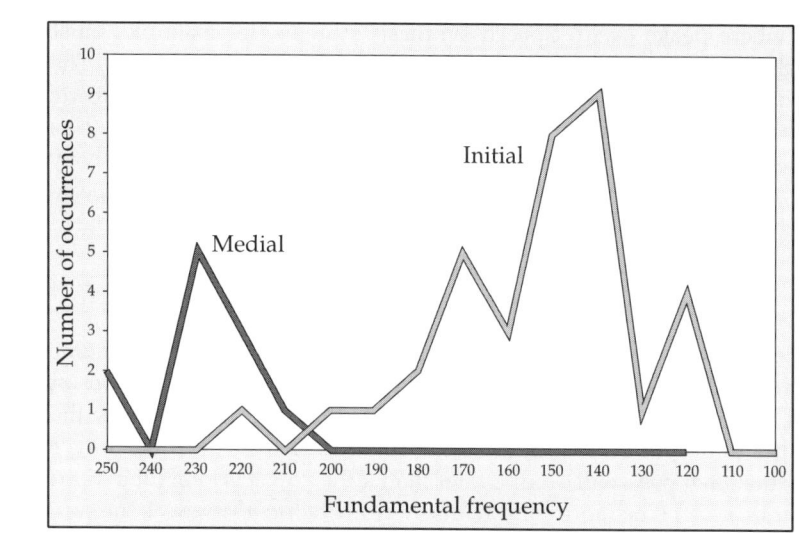

Figure 2.10 The distribution of paragraph-initial and sentence-initial accents in SEC Text B04.

around 180 Hz. Alternatively we might regard anything lower than the default as 'suppressed' and anything higher as 'raised', leaving a final category of 'extra high' for topic onsets. By this means we arrive at a possible four categories of onset:

'low'	– around 135 Hz
'default'	– around 150 Hz
'raised'	– around 180 Hz
'extra-high'	– around 240 Hz

Unfortunately there are not enough values for this to be statistically evaluated, but the data does suggest at least that topic initial onsets belong to a category of their own. The 'high' pitch used to signal topic shifts is high both syntagmatically (in relation to the sequence in which it occurs) and paradigmatically (in relation to a set of choices available to the speaker at any one time).

The idea of fixed target ranges for each speaker does not preclude the influence of declination, but suggests that pitch range relations between different levels of structure are realised phonetically according to certain preferences of the speaker (see Ladd 1996: 279).

2.3.2   *The role of timing*

In addition to the extra high pitch excursions which mark a new topic there is another phenomenon associated with beginnings, and that is to do with the *timing* of the pitch peak. So far we have assumed that pitch peaks in general *co-occur* with accented syllables. It is sometimes necessary, however, to be more precise about where peaks occur. Speech synthesis systems, for example, must have exact alignment procedures to determine the position of a pitch peak. There are many different factors determining the exact alignment of contours, mostly to do with the segmental makeup of the syllable concerned. I will deal with these first, and then show how the timing of pitch peaks is influenced additionally by topic structure. The beginning of a topic has the effect of delaying the pitch peak of the first accent, sometimes so much that it occurs *after* the accented syllable itself.

2.3.2.1 SEGMENTAL AND PROSODIC FACTORS AFFECTING PEAK TIMING[14]

Syllables differ in their segmental makeup: they can contain different numbers of segments, and the segments can belong to different classes: vowels / consonants / voiced / unvoiced / fricatives / sonorants. Both the number and the class affect the timing of an associated pitch contour. If the vowel is short, for example, the pitch peak will occur earlier than if the vowel is long (or a diphthong) (e.g. *hat* vs. *heart*). The more consonants there are before the vowel, the earlier the peak will be, especially if one or more of them is voiced (e.g. *sing* vs. *bring*).

Prosodic context is also known to have an effect: the presence of a tone group boundary immediately after the accented syllable, for example, causes the pitch peak to occur earlier in the syllable, as does the immediate proximity of a subsequent stressed syllable (i.e. where there are no intervening unstressed syllables).

2.3.2.2 THE EFFECT OF DISCOURSE ON PEAK TIMING

In earlier work on discourse intonation in the SEC (Wichmann 1991(b)), I observed in Text B04 that in addition to the high pitch reset at the beginning of each news item, the high peaks often occurred very late in the syllable. Of course, each of the onset syllables (first accented syllable in each sentence) in this text has a different segmental structure – one of the variables impossible to control in naturally-occurring data, so it was not possible to say with certainty that the delay was caused by text structure and not by some other – segmental or prosodic – factors. I have since carried out further studies, together with colleagues (e.g. House and Wichmann 1996, Wichmann et al. 1997, Wichmann et al. forthcoming) to investigate this effect while taking account of all the other known influences on peak timing.

In the natural data we found (Wichmann et al. 1997) that, even when we had factored out all the other underlying timing constraints, the peaks on the first accented syllable of a new topic were consistently later than those at the beginning of a sentence which did not begin a new topic. The peak at the start of a new topic was sometimes so late that it occurred after the accented syllable, on following unstressed syllables. This has already been observed informally elsewhere: 'it is particularly common in accented syllables at the beginning of an utterance to see the high F0 peak aligned in time with the following unstressed syllable' (Ladd 1996: 55).

Another study (Wichmann et al. forthcoming) involved testing the effect of discourse structure on peak timing under experimental conditions, where the segmental make-up of an accented syllable was kept constant, but its position in the text varied. Instead of one text read by one person we now had a text containing four target utterances read by ten people. Subjects were asked to read aloud a text in which the same accented syllable occurred at the beginning of a paragraph, at the beginning of a sentence inside a paragraph, and at the end of a sentence. One of these syllables was the accented syllable in the word enLIGHtenment.

The subjects read aloud texts containing the following sentences:

(i) (Paragraph-initial)
*The **Enlightenment** and its ideas are nowhere more evident than in the great Encyclopaedia published in 28 huge folio volumes between 1751 and 1772.*

(ii) (Sentence-initial but not paragraph-initial)
*The **Enlightenment** was now, although often thought of as a unified system of thought, in fact becoming increasingly diverse.*

(iii) (Sentence-final)
*The movement they created has become famous as the **Enlightenment**.*

Although the biggest difference in peak timing was between the syllables in initial (sentence or paragraph) and final position, there was also a significant difference between the two initial conditions. As we predicted, the peak in the

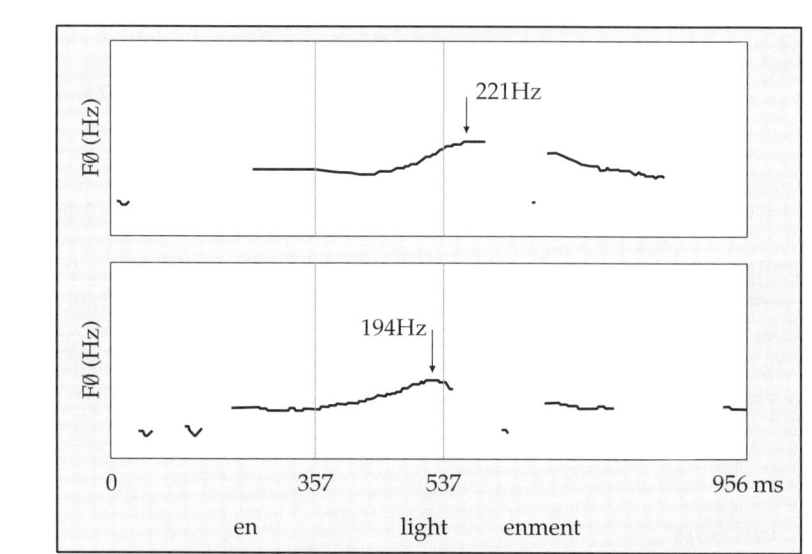

Figure 2.11 Two realisations of the accented syllable in the word 'enlightenment': (i) in paragraph-initial position; (ii) in sentence-initial (but paragraph-medial) position. These show the different alignments of the F0 peak with the accented syllable (marked by cursors).

paragraph-initial onset syllable was both higher and later than in the sentence-(but not paragraph-)initial onset syllable. In this study, as in the previous one, the late peaks often occurred beyond the accented syllable itself.

The difference in timing between the two initial conditions is clearly visible in Figure 2.11. This effect is most likely to be observed in highly professional styles of reading. The original corpus text was read by a professional news-reader, and the readers in the experiments were university lecturers accustomed to 'performing'. They were asked to read the text as if they were recording an Open University lecture, and this elicited careful and expressive reading. As I pointed out in Chapter 1, there is more than one style of reading. The more matter-of-fact way of reading a text, the 'this is what it says here' style, shows less attention to higher level text structures, and this is reflected in a less varied exploitation of pitch range, and a less marked highlighting of topics or para-graphs in general, both in terms of pitch height and in the timing of pitch peaks. It is also considerably more boring to listen to.

2.3.2.3 THEORETICAL IMPLICATIONS: ASSOCIATION VS. ALIGNMENT

The fact that under some contextual conditions the pitch peak can occur outside the accented syllable supports the view expressed by Ladd that the relationship between tones or pitch accents and syllables is one of abstract, underlying asso-ciation and not one of alignment.

> Alignment must be defined as a phonetic property of the relative timing of events in the F0 contour and events in the segmental string. Association, on the other hand, is the abstract structural property of 'belonging together' in some way. The fact of association entails no specific predictions about alignment: if a H tone is associated with a given prominent syllable, we may expect to find a peak of F0 somewhere in the general vicinity of the the syllable, but the peak may be early in the syllable or late, and indeed may be outside the temporal limits of the syllable altogether. (1996: 55)

Interpreting the alignment of pitch peaks as due to contextual factors – position in the sentence and beyond that in the text – also supports the view that, in this respect at least, there is no underlying distinction to be made between nuclear and non-nuclear accents. Such a distinction has been generally assumed in the British tradition of intonation analysis, but was abandoned by the transcribers of the SEC.

2.4 Summary

In this chapter I have described prosodic features observable in naturally-occurring data, both scripted and unscripted, which are associated with discourse-level 'beginnings'. The beginning of a topical unit is marked by an onset which is systematically higher than other sentence onsets. There is also another topic signalling device which consists of realising the first element of a new 'paragraph', whether or not it is syntactically complete, with a 'citation' contour, in other words treating it intonationally as complete.

The concept of 'high' remains a relative one, but the absolute height of a 'topic reset' also appears to be a matter of personal preference with individual speakers. The timing of high peaks is also important: the pitch peak associated with a topic initial onset is delayed so that it occurs towards the end of the accented syllable, or sometimes even to the point of occurring outside the syllable altogether.

In addition to the details of realisation of 'topic resets', I have drawn particular attention to the nature of the units which speakers choose to highlight in this way. In particular I have shown that the conveniently-drawn parallel between 'paragraphs' and 'topics' only holds for certain types of text. The paragraphs in printed texts only reflect one level of discourse structure. Skilled readers frequently override such divisions in favour of more subtle interpretations of the text.

In the next chapter I shall examine some of the ways in which intonational events are modified to express finality: having considered 'beginnings' we will now look more closely at 'ends'.

Notes

1   This chapter is concerned chiefly with the spoken realisation of a syntactic or orthographic sentence. See section 6.2.1 for a discussion of the 'spoken sentence'.

2   This study used laboratory controlled, read speech. The three-sentence 'paragraph' was constructed so that it was cohesive regardless of the order in which the sentences occurred. A similar study was carried out by Bruce (1982) who observed that if a sequence of two related sentences was read aloud, the first began higher than the second. By playing the sentences back in reverse order he found that listeners perceived a topic shift between the two.

3   Here the spoken text has been divided into 'spoken sentences' (major tone groups in the prosodic transcription of the corpus).

4   Only the voice of the main newsreader has been analysed here. Those of other reporters are excluded.

5   This is the only sentence remaining of the original heavily abridged paragraph.

6   Acceleration has been associated with the beginning of tone groups (Cruttenden 1986) and may well also characterise the beginnings of higher level structures, although here both the voice quality and tempo also convey the child's sense of urgency – the roles of prosody in discourse structuring and paralinguistic effect are not always clearly distinguishable.

7   Although the speaker resets her voice to a mid pitch (278 Hz), lower than that on 'salt' at the beginning of the previous episode (salt = 323 Hz), the pitch peak ratio is the same (1.4) each time (peak 2 divided by peak 1 – see Nakajima and Allen 1993, see also Figure 6.2).

8   From: Stuart Barry, Margaret (1988) *The Witch and the Holiday Club* Young Lions.

9   Appositional phrases generally do this.

10 I owe this data to Linda Shockey, University of Reading.

11 The reference is to a club whose members (including the groom and a number of guests at the wedding in question) dress as Vikings and enact Viking 'battles'.

12 To a certain extent the need for tightly-controlled experimental work constrains the type of phenomena investigated, and recent writers on prosody in conversation (e.g. Couper-Kuhlen and Selting 1996b) have called for an entirely new approach. They feel, rightly, that much formal modelling ignores the emergent nature of spontaneous discourse.

13 The abbreviation 'cps' means 'cycles per second', a measure of Fundamental Frequency referred to elsewhere in this book in terms of Hz.

14 There are already a number of other factors known to influence peak timing. In Swedish, for example, timing has been found to be crucial in describing both dialects and the distinction between word accent and sentence accent. Early work on Swedish dialect variation showed that dialect identity was related closely to 'successive, (quasi)continuous displacement of the pitch curves of the accent' (Bruce 1997: 11) In other words, the same pitch contour was associated with an accented syllable in each dialect, but the difference was in the alignment of the contour with the syllable. Timing of tonal events also accounts for the difference between word accent and sentence accent in Swedish. Studies of other languages have uncovered other timing related issues: speech act (statement – question) distinction in Italian, information status in German, attitude in American English (refs. from Bruce).

CHAPTER THREE

Ends

We saw in Chapter 2 that intonation can signal different degrees of 'initiality': the beginning of a spoken sentence, or a written sentence read aloud, is signalled by a pitch 'reset' – a high pitch on the first accented syllable, and the beginning of a larger unit, such as a topic or paragraph, is signalled by a resetting of pitch which is markedly higher than for an isolated sentence. In this chapter I look at finality. I will describe what happens at the *end* of spoken sentences, and then suggest ways in which this 'ending' is modified to suggest greater or lesser degrees of finality.

The nearest prosodic equivalent to a spoken sentence is, in the terminology of the SEC, a major tone group. The major tone group, a term deriving from Trim (1970), has also been described as a 'pitch sequence' (Brazil et al. 1980), an 'extended sentence' (Chafe 1980: 37, cited in Croft 1995), a 'paratone' (Brown 1977) and a 'minor paratone' (Yule 1980). According to Yule, minor paratones have the following underlying pattern:

> the first stressed syllable . . . (is) raised high in the pitch range, followed by a descending order of pitch height on subsequent stressed syllables until the final stressed syllable, which is realised as a fall from high to low. This low pitch followed by a pause marks the end of one paratone amd a shift-up to high on the next stressed syllable marks the beginning of the next paratone. (Yule 1980: 36)

This string of intonation units which together constitute a spoken sentence is recognisable according to Croft by the 'feeling of closure' it signals (Croft 1995). Unlike the tone unit itself, which is believed to be subject to cognitive constraints, the organisation of spoken sentences is thought to be under the voluntary control of the speaker. Chafe, according to Croft, 'suggests that managing closure is a learned skill' (Chafe 1980: 23). But what do we mean by intonational 'closure'? In other words, what do speakers actually do to signal the end of a 'spoken sentence'? In this chapter I will describe some of the patterns identifable in the SEC as 'closures'. I will also examine the kinds of units which skilled speakers choose to close, since the spoken sentence and the orthographic sentence do not always coincide.

3.1 Coming to the end: evidence from the SEC

3.1.1 Falling tones

The most commonly cited signal of finality in intonation is the falling tone. According to Cruttenden we can consider it as 'a nearly absolute linguistic universal that unmarked declaratives have a final falling pitch' (1986: 158). Even the apparent terminal rises in varieties such as Scouse (Liverpool) and Belfast English, can, according to Cruttenden (following Knowles 1975), be interpreted as a kind of fall, distinguished by temporal alignment of the melody, rather than the melody itself.

A study of a small subset of the SEC (Pickering 1996) revealed that nearly 90% of tones occurring before major tone group boundaries are falls. Although this analysis is based on figures from only one of the two transcribers, there is broad consistency between them. Pickering et al. (1996: 71) show that any disagreement on pitch direction is particularly rare, and that there is also consistency in the assignment of major and minor boundaries: the transcribers agree on boundary type in 92% of cases. We can therefore safely extrapolate to the corpus as a whole. The majority (79%) of major tone group boundaries co-occur with the end of an orthographic sentence, in that they co-occur with a full stop or other end-of-sentence marker such as ! or ?. The end of an orthographic sentence in this corpus is thus highly likely to be also the end of a 'spoken sentence' (i.e. a major tone group), and indicated by a falling tone.

There is of course a potential problem of circularity in this analysis. It is possible that the major boundaries were identified precisely *because* they ended in a fall. The boundary criteria explicitly stated by the transcribers do not, however, include tone choice. The major boundaries were identified on explicit phonetic criteria: 'pause, lengthening of a preceding syllable, or a break in the rhythm, but always with the condition that the division must be made at a point that is syntactically possible'[1] (Williams 1996: 51). There are in fact many more falls in the corpus than there are major boundaries, so we must assume that a fall alone could not have been sufficient to suggest a major boundary, and that other criteria, including those stated above, were important. We can conclude, then, firstly that the majority of spoken declarative sentences in this variety of English end with a falling tone, and secondly that a falling tone is a good indication of the end of a 'spoken sentence'.

There are nonetheless some cases where declaratives do *not* end in a fall, and where a spoken sentence is not the same as a grammatical sentence. I will descibe these in the following, with examples from the SEC.

3.1.2 Early closure

3.1.2.1 UTTERANCE-FINAL RISES

The exceptions to the rule that 'sentences end with a fall' are well-known, and are chiefly associated with sentence-final adverbials. Adverbials in this position can end in a rising tone (Allerton and Cruttenden 1974, Cruttenden 1986, 1997), as in the following example. In such sentences, the expected 'sentence closure' occurs at the end of the previous element and immediately before the adverbial.

He's too ill to ↘come, un↗fortunately

This pattern is not restricted to typical adverbials. Sentence-final discourse 'routines' commonly found in conversation are also treated intonationally like sentence adverbials. This is hardly surprising, since these generally function syntactically as adverbials, and are even referred to as 'speech act adverbials' or 'illocutionary adverbials' (Andersson 1975, Mittwoch 1977, cited in Aijmer 1996: 203).

their English actually improved as ↘well | much to my sur↗prise (SEC J06)[2]

In English, a sentence-final rise or fall-rise can also be associated with the non-focal information status of the final element. This is a rearrangement of the more usual ordering of information, with background information first. According to Knowles (1987) 'the retention of the "non-final" pitch movement on the postponed item – common as it is in colloquial English – is not generally found in other languages, and the resulting fall-plus-rise contour may be peculiar to English' (p.189). The reference to the 'colloquial' nature of this pattern explains why the following examples from the SEC are to be found in the more informal, conversational or quasi-conversational texts.

I can't remember↘↗us making a fuss about the weather[3] | when ↘↗we were children (SEC G05)

I suppose ↘they must do some work in the ↗fields (SEC J06)

Oh and he ↘did pass his ex↘↗ams (SEC K01)

. . . anything | rather than the terror of counting on and on into the blue emptiness of the ↘↗morning. (SEC G01)

in the end he only ↘stayed about six ↗months (SEC J06)

3.1.2.2   UTTERANCE-INTERNAL FALLS

We can see that, except under certain circumstances such as those described above, an orthographic sentence read aloud is very likely to end with an intonational 'closure'. We may not assume, however, that such closures do not additionally occur elsewhere. First of all, there are a number of major tone group boundaries in the SEC which are *not* at the end of a sentence, but at some other syntactic boundary, usually a clause. Approximately 19.5% of all major tone group boundaries (Taylor 1996) occur at commas, colons and semicolons in the written text.[4] There are therefore more 'spoken sentences' than orthographic sentences in this corpus. In the following I will examine some of the kinds of units *other than* complete orthographic sentences, which are treated, melodically at least, as in some way closed.

A very common place for a spoken sentence to close, indicated by a falling tone followed by a major tone group boundary, is at the end of a main clause in a complex sentence. For example, before a sentence-final non-finite clause, as in:

> || *the photomontage is a mixture of typography and* ↘ ***images*** || ***including*** *two symbols which strive to suggest effects beyond the limitations of the static image* || (SEC D01)

or before a conjunction (co-ordinating or subordinating), as in:

> | *that Dada's historical significance* | *was an essential impetus* | *to the new art form* | ***of film it*** ↘ ***self*** || ***although*** *he denied individual meaning to Dada works* || (SEC D01)

There are also other closure patterns inside sentences where a major tone group boundary is *not* marked. Intonation research based on relatively simple sentences leads many to suppose that internal closures simply do not occur. And yet falls at minor tone group boundaries are not unusual in the SEC. Pickering (1996) finds that 32.3% of minor tone groups end in a fall. Some of these are high falls, possibly similar to Crystal's (1995) mid fall (see also section 3.2.1), with an endpoint above the baseline and thus non-final in their effect. Many, however, (the exact proportions are not stated) are low falls which drop to the speaker's baseline. Melodically we have here a potential closure, but in the absence of other prosodic features, such as pause and possibly syllable lengthening, it is not enough to cue a major boundary. These all occur at points in the syntactic structure which potentially attract a (minor or major) tone group boundary and possibly a pause. Just one short extract from the SEC yields a number of such cases. (It has to be admitted that this speaker also has a slight penchant for falls.)

1. || *Baader called himself* | ***the*** ↘*Oberdada* | *or su*↘*preme **Dada*** | ***and*** *proclaimed himself president* | *of a world re*↘*public* || (SEC D01)

2. || *The new principles of Dada construction* | *as Huelsenbeck lists them* | *in his nineteen twenty history of Dadaism* | *En avant Dada* | *were* ↗*brutism* | *or* ↘↗*noise music* | ***simultan***↘***eity*** | ***and*** | ***the new medium*** | *of* ↘*collage* || (SEC D01)

In Example 1 we have two closures before the end of the sentence, each between co-ordinated items, in the first case a noun phrase, and in the second case a clause. In Example 2 the co-ordinated NP is part of an extended list. It is a list of three, and normally we would expect two non-final tones followed by a final tone here, but the appositional phrase (*or noise-music*), and the absence of a conjunction immediately after it, creates effectively a four-item list, which is then divided by the speaker into two conjoined groups of two. These last two examples show that some cases of early closure involve using a 'final' fall at a point where a sentence *could* be complete but isn't. This is so common as to be normal. It is certainly not to be regarded as inexpert reading.

Example 3 manages to combine apposition, non-finite clause and final adverbial, each of which prompt early closure (low falls).

3. || *Next up* | *the awesome New Yorker meets James Bonecrusher* ↘*Smith* | *the man* | *who caused a mighty* ↘*upset* | *by knocking out Tim Witherspoon* | *in one*↘*round* | *earlier this* ↘*month* || (SEC F04)

Example 4 is particularly interesting in that it treats a noun phrase as a complete 'spoken sentence', a common phenomenon which I described in section 2.2 (see also Chapter 6). It occurs in particular where the noun phrase announces a new discourse topic, usually in subject position and sentence-initial. Intonation units containing a single NP have been noted before (Croft 1995, Altenberg 1990). However, in spontaneous discourse these NPs tend not to be integrated into larger syntactic units but to be grammatically independent utterances, and have been shown to have a number of different discourse functions including that of topic NP. There are two differences between these observations and those I am making here. First of all the NP is not grammatically independent, and secondly it is not simply given its own intonation unit but that intonation unit ends in intonational closure with a fall to the speaker's baseline. In other words it is being treated prosodically as if it were a complete utterance.

4. || *Alder* ↘*Benjamin* | *in his essay* | *the work of art* | *in the age of mechanical reproduction* | *proposed* | *that* . . . (SEC D01)

We can summarise by saying that, in the corpus, the signal of closure or finality is not associated exclusively with the end of orthographic sentences. Speakers and readers regularly reduce complex syntactic sentences to shorter spoken sentences. Generally these closures occur at points where the utterance is at least potentially complete – such as at the end of a main clause or before a final adverbial phrase or clause. Sometimes, however, the closure signal serves to highlight a single phrase as if it were a complete utterance, usually with a discourse-structuring effect.

3.2   What kind of falling tones are there?

3.2.1   *High and low falls*

In addition to examining *where* falls occur, we must also consider *what kind of* falls occur, and consider the important theoretical issue of whether different falls are variants of one underlying phonological category, or whether they constitute separate categories.

In his *Encyclopedia of the English Language* (1995) Crystal includes three different falls in his list of 'nine ways of saying yes'. (See Figure 3.1 overleaf.)

As we shall see, these three forms capture most of the important contrasts claimed in the literature: there are significant differences in the realisation of both the *starting point* and the *endpoint* of the fall. Differences in starting point will be dealt with in this section. In the next section I will consider endpoints. The semantic gloss provided for these different falling tones is also important: it is difficult to describe different kinds of fall without at the same time discussing what they mean. In general they are considered to share a common function of indicating some kind of finality, and the differences between them are thought to display differences in affect or 'attitude': greater degrees of intensity, emotional involvement or 'commitment' are associated with greater exploitation of pitch range.

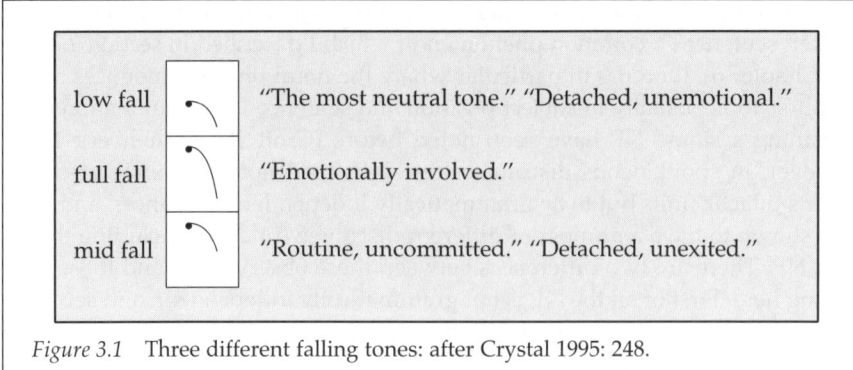

Figure 3.1 Three different falling tones: after Crystal 1995: 248.

The most common distinction, at least in the British tradition (related to RP), is that made between high falls and low falls, a distinction which is also used in the SEC transcription. The low fall is similar to Crystal's low fall, as illustrated above, while the high fall includes both the mid and the full fall in Crystal's terms. While this conventional high / low distinction is useful for pedagogical or other practical purposes, there is less certainty about its phonological validity. The general view seems to emerge that the distinction is ultimately arbitrary. It is either a conflation of many more distinctive categories (Crystal 1969) or a convenient but equally arbitrary division of what is in fact gradient (Cruttenden 1986). Some recent autosegmental descriptions, however, continue to incorporate contrasting falls: falls 'with and without downstep' correspond roughly to low and (not very) high falls (Gussenhoven and Rietveld 1991).[5] In the following I shall therefore examine some accounts of this contrast.

The idea of contrasting forms of falls has a long tradition in (British) English intonation analysis. Armstrong and Ward (1931) identify two complete 'tunes' in English intonation, each one implicitly (as is evident from their examples) coextensive with a complete sentence. Tune I ends with a falling contour, and Tune II ends with a rising contour. There are two kinds of Tune I, one a 'variant' of the other. The normal one ends with a falling contour which starts towards the lower third of the speaker's range,[6] while the 'emphatic' variant closes with a contour which begins in the upper third of the range. Both fall to the base-line, and appear identical, at least in stylised form, to Crystal's full and low falls. In his early work on English intonation, Palmer (1922) subdivides 'tunes' into constituent parts, including nuclear 'tones'. He writes of a low fall and high fall as a conditioned variant and intensified variant respectively (cited in Tench 1997: 244). Only one person dispenses completely with the idea of different categories of falls: Kingdon (1958). His analysis contains three tones with a final rising contour – high rise, low rise and fall-rise – but only one fall, which, he says, indicates that the utterance is 'decided and final' (1958: 9).

It is clear, then, that when talking about 'different falls' we must decide whether we are discussing them from a theoretical point of view, or from a practical (including pedagogical) point of view. Cruttenden (1986) is the only writer hitherto to make this theoretical vs practical distinction explicit. While conceding the tendency of some to 'treat the difference in the height of falls as gradient and the difference between them as gradient' (p.100), he finds it nonetheless useful to distinguish high and low falls. Unlike most, however, he goes on to examine the meanings which such distinctions are able to convey. To both categories of fall he ascribes the basic underlying meaning of 'finality' or closure. The difference between them he claims is one of affect.

> Both falling tones involve a sense of finality, of completeness, definiteness and separateness when used with declaratives; hence both tones are more common on sentence final intonation groups than on sentence non-final intonation groups. The low fall is generally more uninterested, unexcited and dispassionate, whereas the high fall is more interested, more excited, more involved . . .
>
> (Cruttenden 1986: 100)

By suggesting the common meaning of 'closure', Cruttenden probably excludes falls (like Crystal's mid fall) which have a non-low endpoint, and generally sound unfinished or non-final. By putting differences down to what is generally seen as paralinguistic (affect), he implies that what is categorical is linguistic and what is gradient is paralinguistic. This is a theoretical issue which is clearly bound up with the theoretical status of pitch range, on which, as Ladd (1996) points out, the jury is still out.

The SEC transcribers made a pre-theoretical decision, but one which had a firm basis in earlier descriptions of English intonation, to limit themselves to two falls. In fact, as we shall see (in section 3.2.4) attempting to use tonal categories for transcription is one way in which their perceptual adequacy can be tested. And only by discovering the perceptual adequacy of categories can we make progress on the theoretical front.

To summarise, we have a long tradition in the study of English intonation of feeling the need to make *some* distinction between different realisations of falling tones. Whether there are two, three or more distinct categories, or whether the distinction is a gradient one, listeners and users of the language clearly feel that both the starting point and the endpoint of a fall can make a difference in perceived speaker meaning. A low endpoint seems to convey some kind of closure or finality, while variation of the starting point seems to prompt interpretations which can be classed as paralinguistic and gradient. The assumed paralinguistic effects are reflected in labels such as 'emphatic', 'decided', 'involved' and 'dispassionate'. I believe that a more satisfactory interpretation ascribes the difference to degrees of finality or closure, which then, in conversational interaction, is interpreted as 'excited', 'involved', 'dispassionate' by a process of pragmatic inference.

3.2.2 Tails and endpoints

The above discussion of high and low has concentrated on physical differences in the starting point of the fall. But I have not yet discussed the contrast implicit in Crystal's third version of 'yes': the 'uncommitted' *mid fall*. This differs from the others in the realisation of its endpoint: the contour seems to be truncated, somewhere in the middle of the speaker's range.

This is the phenomenon described by Brown (1977: 102) as a fall to '*not-very-low*', and is also to be found elsewhere as a 'half-completed' fall (Gussenhoven and Rietveld 1991), with an endpoint in mid-range.[7] This kind of shallow fall, ending above the speaker's baseline, is sometimes taken in the British system to be a truncated variant of the fall-rise, at least when it occurs in nuclear position, and in the SEC it is transcribed as such. This is consistent with Brown's observation that falls at the end of sentence-final tone groups have a lower endpoint than those at the end of non-final groups. In other words, the truncated fall signals a degree of non-finality, as do fall rises and rises, which are grouped together by Brown et al. (1980) as sharing a 'non-low terminal'.

Phonetically, the end point of an utterance-final fall is widely assumed to be fairly constant for a given speaker. Actually, most references to a speaker's constant endpoint are to a single study (Menn and Boyce 1982) of adult-child interaction, where the endpoint of each adult turn was found to fall to a constant F0 value.

There are of course contextual effects on individual pitch range, but these seem to have a stronger influence on the upper ranges of the voice.

Even those speech environments which have been found to affect the baseline do not necessarily mean that it becomes more variable. Extreme raising of the voice (i.e. to be heard above a noise) can cause a raising of the baseline (Ladd and Terken 1995). My own observations suggest that there are other, non-noisy environments which can also cause some speakers to shift into a style which consistently avoids falling to their natural baseline. Children reading aloud can sound inexpressive and anxious, partly because of a compressed pitch range over all, and partly because the compression involves a raised baseline, which makes their reading sound 'suspended' and uncomfortable. This could mean that they have not yet acquired the skill of 'closing', referred to in the introduction to this chapter. Ritualised or stylised speech (such as the typical 'liturgical' style) can also be seen to derive part of its characteristic sound from an avoidance of utterance-final lows. Final falling tones tend to be realised as level or slightly rising. Of course, it is possible that, in the case of the liturgy, having to perform in public and project one's voice in a large space, produces an effect similar to that of trying to be heard over background noise. In the case of the child reader, the sense of having to perform, and be assessed on the performance, may create a tension which has a similar effect on the voice.

In general then, the lowest pitch of a speaker's utterances is fairly stable. Unfortunately, the observations of Menn and Boyce (1982), supported by frequent observation of isolated sentences, have led to the assumption not only that the speaker's 'low' is constant but also that it is reached *only* at the end of a sentence. This is based on a false assumption that 'spoken sentences' are co-terminus with orthographic sentences. I have illustrated (section 3.1.2 above) that while the end of an orthographic sentence in read speech is highly likely to end in a 'closure', this is by no means the *only* point at which intonational closure occurs. We do not know (I think) whether Menn and Boyce observed an 'utterance-final low' anywhere other than at the end of a speaker turn. If not, either they did not look, or each adult speaker turn consisted of only one 'spoken sentence'. The step from the observations in this study to generalisations about 'sentence-final intonation' are not justified. The phenomenon of a constant endpoint for a given speaker was observed in my own work on the SEC (Wichmann 1993) but the same study shows that the speaker also reached this baseline value at many other points in the utterance.

I have to admit that there is a counter-argument to be found in speech synthesis systems, where it is common practice to incorporate 'final lowering' in the pitch contour. This is usually couched in autosegmental terms, where a falling tone is decomposed into a high tone associated with an accented syllable (H*) followed by a low tone (L), which is then followed by a so-called 'boundary tone', an additional specification of the pitch level at a tone group boundary. This is given the symbol H or L with an additional percent sign. A low boundary tone is therefore represented as L%. The so-called 'final lowering' implies an extra low realisation of the L% boundary tone at the end of a sentence, and when incorporated into the contour makes synthesised speech sound more natural. Nonetheless, it is not readily observable in natural speech. Firstly, the fall to low is certainly not restricted to the end of sentences. In read speech at least, we find that this 'utterance-final' low actually occurs much more often, dividing long orthographic sentences into smaller units which span maximally one finite clause. Secondly, the speaker's habitual end-of-sentence pitch is not necessarily different from the pitch of the L tone in the trough of a fall-rise (H*LH) or from the L* tone at the beginning of a low rise (L*H). It cannot be denied, however, that the inclusion of 'final lowering' in speech synthesis (text-to-speech) systems improves the perceived naturalness of the speech. I suspect the explanation for this lies elsewhere. The low pitch which occurs at the end of an utterance often co-occurs with a 'creaky' voice quality. The extra drop in pitch incorporated into speech synthesis systems may compensate perceptually for changes in voice quality. However, since endpoints are notoriously difficult to measure, this is not easy to demonstrate empirically. Current work on the relationship between pitch and voice quality (e.g. Swerts and Veldhuis 1997) may shed light on this in future.

Hirschberg and Pierrehumbert (1986) in their discussion of finality cues consider the *shape* rather than endpoint of the nuclear tail[8] to be contrastive. They suggest that the tail following a nuclear fall can either continue to fall, which they describe as 'final lowering', or it can level off, in which case final lowering is absent. If the nucleus has no tail (i.e. no trailing syllables), the same pattern is presumably distributed across the voiced segments of the nuclear syllable. The presence or absence of 'final lowering', they suggest, is an indication of the degree of finality of the utterance. Presumably, if there are only two possibilities – presence or absence of final lowering, there can be only two degrees of finality, but the authors do not expand on this.

Their account of the behaviour of post-nuclear syllables reflects, but does not acknowledge, Crystal's earlier (1969) account of the same two patterns. He describes a 'general tendency for syllables . . . to continue the direction of the pitch movement which began on the nuclear syllable preceding . . .' (p.146). In the case of a nuclear fall, this would be the equivalent of 'final lowering'. This, Crystal suggests, is the norm. He allows one other possibility: that the post-nuclear syllables are levelled off: 'The only other possibility is for a **continuance** feature to be introduced into the tail following the kinetic tones, i.e. a syllable on the same level as the preceding syllable . . .' (1969: 146).

3.2.3 Finality and discourse structure

Most of the accounts above refer to relative finality inside an individual utterance. The end of a sentence is assumed to be realised with the most final version of the fall – with low endpoint or final lowering. Some analysts have nonetheless seen the potential for degrees of finality to be exploited at levels above the sentence – in the structure of discourse and the management of interaction.

Brown et al. (1980), for example, consider the endpoint of falls to be an important finality signal in discourse. They distinguish in fact between low and not-low terminals. Not-low terminals include other, more typically non-final, contours such as rises and fall-rises, but I quote their comment here because of its relevance to falls.

> Low terminals are regularly associated with the end of topics, with the end of a turn when a speaker has no more to say on a topic, and with conducive questions where the speaker has a high expectation of the correctness of the assumptions that lie behind his question. Low terminals are also frequently associated with non-finality in topic or turn when a speaker indicates that there is more to come on the same topic by some other means, for instance, incomplete syntax. . . . Not-low terminals are associated with more to come on the same topic, in the same turn, and with non-conducive questions. Not-low is also associated with a range of affective meanings including deference, politeness, vulnerability. . . .   (p.30)

The semantic association claimed here between truncated falls, rises and fall-rises, actually supports the view taken by the SEC transcribers that a mid fall is simply a variation of a fall-rise, and therefore not to be considered as belonging to the same category as the other two falls.[9] Brown et al.'s account does not, however, allow for the occurrence of a fall to low on a syntactically complete utterance which is *not* turn- or topic final.

We are left, then, with truncated falls, functionally equivalent to non-final tones such as a fall-rise, and falls which share a common (low) endpoint. The endpoint itself seems to be fairly constant for each speaker, and is probably physiologically determined; any linguistic contrasts here are therefore to be made not by the endpoint but by the starting point of the fall.

> There are relatively few contrasts which can be made using the endpoint compared with the range of contrasts elsewhere, partly because of the formal indeterminacy which exists at the end of a glide. It is usually immaterial how far a low fall falls, for example, this being largely a matter of physiological vocal range. It is the relative pitch height of the whole tone within the tone unit and the width of the tone which are linguistically the most important features, and the determining factor in this is the beginning-point of the glide.   (Crystal 1969: 213–14)

My concern here is to investigate what these contrasts are, and what they mean (see section 3.4).

3.2.4 High and low falls in the SEC

It is clear from the above that there is as yet no consensus over whether the differences between high and low falls are differences within or between categories. Are the categories of height simply a practical way of coding what is in fact a gradient distinction, much as in the division of the temperature scale as *hot*, *warm* and *cold*? If the difference is gradient and not categorical, then how successfully will transcribers assign such categories to a large amount of real data? Phoneticians trained in an intonation system should be relatively consistent in applying existing categories, but we would expect them to have some difficulty in applying arbitrary categories to a gradient phenomenon.

The transcribers of the SEC, while showing remarkable consistency in most of their transcription practices, have difficulty with the assignment of the agreed categories of high and low falls. In an analysis of the so-called 'overlap' passages in the SEC, those sections of the corpus which were transcribed independently by both transcribers and which make up approximately 9% of the corpus, Pickering et al. (1996) show that the identification of high and low falls is in fact the area of greatest disagreement between transcribers. In what follows I shall attempt to explore the reasons for this disagreement, and what we can deduce from it.

An analysis of all nuclear falls, i.e. all those which occur immediately before a major or minor boundary (see Figure 3.2), shows that one transcriber (BJW) has a distinct preference for high falls, while the other's (GOK) choice is more evenly distributed. If we consider falls occurring at minor boundaries alone, the figures are similar to those overall. However, if we consider only the tone choice at major boundaries, we see that BJW's preference for high falls remains constant, while GOK's choice is now strongly weighted towards low falls.

All boundaries		Minor boundaries		Major boundaries	
BJW 75% high	25% low	BJW 78% high	22% low	BJW 73% high	27% low
GOK 46% high	54% low	GOK 53% high	47% low	GOK 38% high	62% low

Figure 3.2 Percentage of high vs low falls chosen by both SEC transcribers at tone group boundaries of different strength.

The working definition used by the transcribers explicitly defines 'high' and 'low' in relation to what has gone before, and not in terms of the speaker's voice. Changes in height in relation to the speaker's range were deliberately ignored (Williams 1996), in order to factor out of the transcription any range differences predicted by declination. Instead, the categories high and low were selected in relation to the preceding pitch environment.

The tonetic stress marks do not represent the extent of pitch movement, nor the mean pitch of an individual syllable or group of syllables relative to the speaker's normal range . . . a high falling nucleus begins by definition at a pitch level higher than the previous one used, but need not necessarily be located high in the speaker's overall range: in fact, towards the end of a tone-unit such a syllable may well begin at a point fairly low down in the speaker's range. The converse is true for a low tonetic stress mark.   (Williams 1996: 55)

Despite the agreed definition, there are frequent disagreements between transcribers. We can trace this back to the fact that the definition is ambiguous: the height of a fall could be related to that of the preceding *accented* syllable or to the preceding *syllable*, whether accented or not. The difference in transcription is, in part at least, a result of different interpretations of this working definition of high and low falls. One transcriber (GOK) interprets the height in relation to the preceding accent (1), and the other (BJW) in relation to the preceding syllable (2). This is illustrated in Figure 3.3. In such a pitch sequence the transcribers would agree in their assignment of high and low only if (2 > 3 and 1 > 3) or (2 < 3 and 1 < 3).

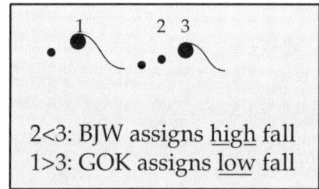

2<3: BJW assigns high fall
1>3: GOK assigns low fall

Figure 3.3   The pitch relations which underly the two transcribers' choice between high and low fall. The pitch relations in this sequence are as follows: 1 > 2; 2 < 3; 1 > 3. The relation 2 < 3 leads BJW to assign a high fall; the relation 1 > 3 leads GOK to assign a low fall.

An instrumental analysis of a sample of nuclear falls in the overlap passage SEC A04 (Wichmann 1991b) shows how this stylised version relates to real speech. The passage contains 15 major tone group boundaries, 11 of which are marked by both transcribers, and the other four by BJW alone. (This is consistent with BJW's overall tendency to mark more major tone groups.) Each of these ends in a fall. Of these 15 falls, there are only four where the transcribers agree on pitch height: two high falls and two low falls. In all the remaining 11 cases, GOK has marked a low fall and BJW has marked a high fall, typical of the preferences shown in the analysis of all the overlap passages. The examples in Figure 3.4 illustrate this. The final fall in each case is marked as 'high' by BJW and 'low' by GOK.

The different interpretation of high and low explains the above discrepancies, but it does not necessarily lead to different transcriptions. There are also some cases of agreement. In Figure 3.5(a) the fall begins higher than both the preceding syllable and the preceding accented syllable. It is therefore a 'high' fall by both definitions. In Figure 3.5(b) there is no intervening unstressed syllable

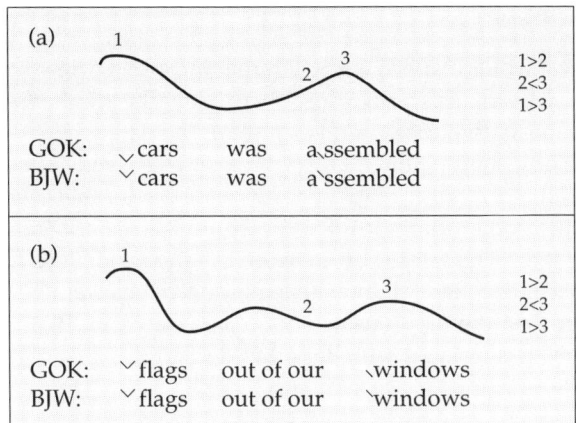

Figure 3.4 Stylised F0 contours of the sequences (a) '. . . cars was assembled' and (b) '. . . flags out of our windows' with the prosodic transcription showing a discrepancy between transcribers.

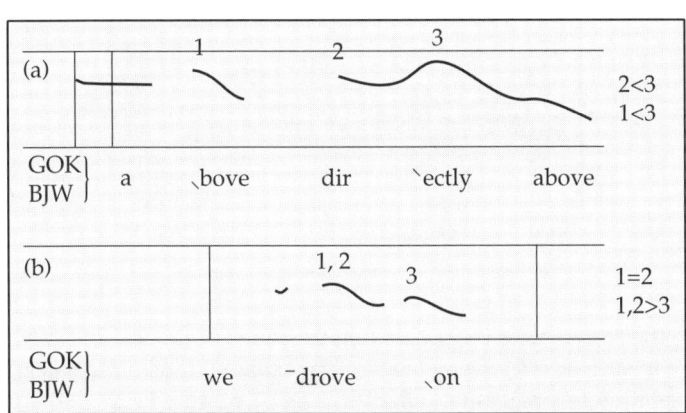

Figure 3.5 Stylised F0 contours of the sequences (a) '. . . above, directly above' and (b) '. . . we drove on', with the prosodic transcription from the SEC showing agreement between transcribers.

between the two accented syllables. The immediately preceding syllable (BJW's reference point) and the preceding accented syllable (GOK's reference point) are now identical. Both transcribers can therefore consistently mark a low fall. We can see then that most of the disagreements, and even some agreements, are the result not of a difference in perception but a difference in definition.

61

3.2.4.1 INCONSISTENCIES: EVIDENCE FOR THE ROLE OF THE SPEAKER'S RANGE

There are, as one would expect, a few internal inconsistencies which show that under certain circumstances both transcribers allow the speaker's pitch range to play a role. There are two cases in this subset of the data where the transcribers appear to be inconsistent (within their own rules). This is illustrated in Figure 3.6. In Figure 3.6(a) the contour is across a fairly wide pitch range. GOK transcribes a high fall at this point although 1 > 3. In Figure 3.6(b) both transcribers agree that *on* is accented.[10] The fall is very narrow in range and close to the baseline. GOK transcribes it as a low fall, which is internally consistent because it begins at a pitch lower than the previous accent on *fair*. However, BJW also gives *on* a low fall, which is inconsistent with her other decisions.

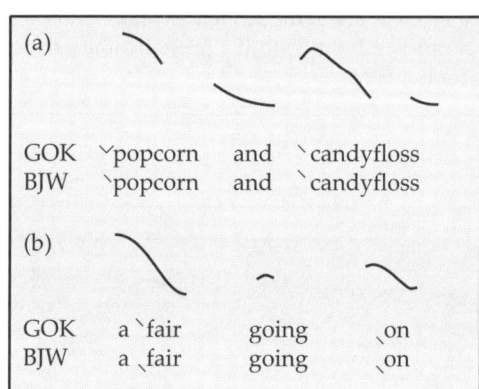

Figure 3.6 Stylised F0 contours showing transcriber agreement but internal inconsistency: (a) '. . . popcorn and candyfloss'; (b) '. . . a fair going on'.

In both the above cases it appears that the range of the fall, or the *height of the fall relative to the base line*, overrides the transcribers' decision to categorise high and low relative to preceding syllables. It is of course not possible to simultaneously mark pitch range and up- or downstep, and yet remain consistent, as Cruttenden points out:

> a low-fall typically involves a step-down from any preceding pre-nuclear syllables and a high-fall typically involves a step-up. But this represent(s) a bit of a simplification. A high-fall will certainly involve a step-up but not all steps-up can be regarded as high-falls: if, for example, the prenuclear syllables are on a very low pitch, the voice cannot help but go up in pitch if it is to accommodate a fall. (. . .)
>
> Cruttenden (1986: 99–100)

This can be illustrated in a stylised fashion as in Figure 3.7. In Figure 3.7(a) both falls must be marked as high, since they both start at a pitch higher than the preceding syllable, but they differ considerably in range. In Figure 3.7(b) the width

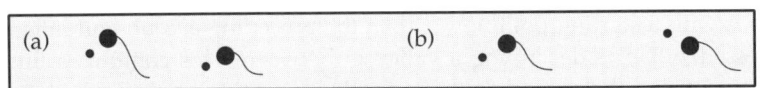

Figure 3.7   Stylised high and low falls: (a) two 'high' falls which differ in their realisation; (b) two similar falls of which the first is 'high' and the second is 'low'.

of fall is the same, but the starting point relative to the preceding syllable is not. The first would thus be a high fall, and the second a low fall.

This brings us back to the same problem which I discussed in Chapter 2: that of the definition of 'relative' pitch. In the transcription of the SEC there are obviously occasions where an intuitive perception of actual height (above the speaker's baseline) interferes with an interpretation based on height relative to what has gone before. The examples above show that neither the overall width of a final fall, nor its starting point relative to preceding syllables can account on their own for the perceptual categorisation of a final fall. The most likely explanation for this in my view is the following. A fall which is markedly high or markedly low in the speaker's range is identified as such by both transcribers. Falls which begin somewhere in the middle of the range are probably perceived as 'neutral', but since there are only two categories available, the decision is based on phonetic observations, namely the height of the preceding syllables. Perhaps a third category – 'default' – might have served as well.

3.3   'Cadences': melodic closure

It is clear from the above that certain types of fall are more common than others, and that they occur not in isolation, but are tied into a sequence of stressed and unstressed syllables. This sequence creates a recognisable tonal, or melodic, progression which can be compared to a musical 'cadence', which is a sequence of chords forming a harmonic unit at the end of a musical phrase, and sounding more or less final depending on the chords and the sequence in which they occur.

Even though the phonological basis on which the transcribers were working remains unclear, we can in fact make good use of the disagreements. From them we can derive some useful phonetic information and judge what kind of realisations of end-of-sentence contours are most common. If GOK's choice of high and low relates to the pitch of the preceding accent, and 62% of the falls he marks at major tone group boundaries are 'low', then we can assume that approximately 62% of falls at major tone group boundaries start lower than the preceding accent. Since BJW relates height to preceding syllable, and she marks 73% of sentence final falls as 'high', we can infer that 73% of nuclear falls at major tone group boundaries start higher than the immediately preceding syllable. Since this syllable is more often unstressed than stressed, we can assume that unstressed syllables between two accents usually 'sag'. Putting the two together we can see that the most common realisation of a fall at the end of a major tone group is with a starting point lower than the preceding accent, and intervening unstressed syllables describing a valley in between. This contour, a final sentence accent slightly lower than the preceding accent, is consistent with the phenomenon of declination, whether modelled as a global trend or local 'downstep' (see Chapter 5). A fall which does not drop lower than the preceding accent, or one which begins considerably lower, departs from the norm and is thus perceived as marked. The default pattern further explains why a configuration in which intervening unstressed syllables are *not* allowed to sag,[11] is perceived as very marked.

I shall first illustrate some of the more common cadences and then turn to those which depart from the norm in some way.

3.3.1 Common cadences

The four most common cadences (closing contours) in the SEC are illustrated in Figure 3.8. The most common pattern in the SEC is that in Figure 3.8(1) in which the utterance- or sentence-final fall (with a low endpoint) begins slightly lower than the preceding accented syllable and slightly higher than any intervening unstressed syllables. This is often transcribed as a high fall followed by a low fall, as the following examples from the SEC illustrate.

(Symbols: ⌐ = rise; ⌐ = high fall; ⌐ = low fall; ⌐⌐ = fall–rise; __ = low level; ⎺ = high level; | = minor tone group boundary; || = major tone group boundary)

the ⌐people of El Salvador | while they may ⎺ache for⌐ peace | have become a ⌐naesthetised to ⌐war || (SEC A04)

and con ⌐solidate | ⌐old ties a ⌐broad || (SEC A11)

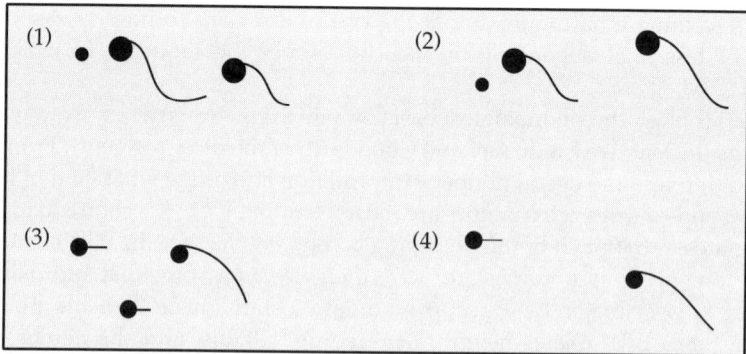

Figure 3.8 Summary of cadences: a stylised representation of the pitch pattern of the last two, or three, accented syllables in an utterance; any intervening unstressed syllables follow the trajectory of the preceding tone.

The high fall (Figure 3.8(2)), often transcribed as a sequence of two high falls, sounds more non-final and is sometimes considered to be marked.

|| ˋsome perks are eˋxotic || (SEC F01)

to be ˋgiven that ˋfreedom || (SEC J06)

ˋthat seems fairly ˋboring || (SEC J06)

you ˋjust couldn't get anything ˋdone || (SEC J06)

In read speech we find a common third version of the cadence (Figure 3.8(3)) – a sequence of high–low–high accented syllables.

__roads have been ⎯blocked | by ⎯floodwater and __fallen ˋtrees || (SEC B01)

what to do with the ⎯carcass | __later this ˋmorning || (SEC B01)

ˋ↗track | to the__nearest ˋstation || (SEC B01)

⎯when is__miracle ˋnot a miracle || (SEC A01)

This alternation of high and low appears to be a feature of the more heavily accented style of reading aloud ('heavy' = here: more accented syllables in a tone group). The low level tones, although technically of equal status, are less prominent than high tones and may be considered as a downgrading of prominence, somewhere in between stressed and accented. For example:

(He was awarded an honorary degree last week) | by the ⎯Roman__Catholic Uni__versity of La ˋPlata | in Buenos ⎯Aires | Argen ˋtina || (SEC A01)

A more spontaneous speaking style (in the following example partly rehearsed but unscripted) tends to prefer not to give any prominence at all to syllables between high pitch accents. This is no doubt also reflected in tempo. For example:

|| but ˋour terms are ˋtwenty weeks ˋlong so in fact | the ˋschooling is ˋtwice what ˋyours is || (SEC J06)

The last, and least common, cadence (Figure 3.8(4)) is a sequence of a high level followed by a low fall. In this pattern the unstressed syllables between the two H* tones (the level and the fall) are not permitted to sag. The suppression of sag, where the final fall begins lower than the preceding unstressed syllable, is the pattern judged most final in the perception experiment described in section 3.4.

it's now ⎯ten past ˋeight || (SEC B01)

(all services) | will be ⎯back to __normal ⎯later to ˋday || (SEC B01)

3.3.2 Stylistic variation

In addition to the cadences I have already described in Figure 3.8 and illustrated above, we find in the SEC a number of variants on the 'normal' cadence, which are restricted to certain speaking styles.

3.3.2.1 THE JOURNALISTIC 'FLOURISH'

The most quirky cadence is a variant of the low level – high fall cadence (Figure 3.8(3)) above. It appears to be a journalistic mannerism, and has an audible 'bounce' to it, caused by unexpected pitch prominence on otherwise unstressed syllables and a subsequent low drop. The tune is illustrated in Figure 3.9.[12]

Figure 3.9   The journalistic flourish – a typical end-of-sentence mannerism.

Some of these cadences are identifiable from the prosodic transcription of the SEC. The transcription system assumes that the pitch of unstressed syllables is predictable. Those which are unusually pitch prominent, but otherwise unstressed, are marked with an up-arrow (↑).[13] The following are some examples from the SEC:

|↑ *a __massive* ↘*credit* || (SEC A12)
|↑ *of __holding a press* ↘*briefing* || (SEC A12)
|↑ *to* ↗*parallel* ↗*those of the fi*↘*nanciers* || (SEC A12)

However, although the presence of the up-arrow suggests a marked step *up* in pitch on an unstressed syllable, in fact the most significant feature of this tune is the subsequent drop *down* to the low stressed syllable. The obtrusion caused by the high unstressed syllable is simply a way of creating a subsequent drop, and is not necessary if the unstressed syllable is high by default, for example when it is the continuation of a high level tone. Thus while the presence of an up-arrow can indicate the presence of such a cadence, its absence does not necessarily mean the absence of the cadence. Listening to the original text it becomes evident that the pattern does in fact occur more often than is indicated by up-arrows, as in the following examples. (* = high unstressed syllable.)

(i) || *in* ⁻*fact it was* *the ↘*bank of* ↘*China* || (SEC A12)

(ii) | ⁻*seems* **to __fade into the* ↘*background* || (SEC A01)

(iii) *as* | **a __prophet of our* ↘*time* || (SEC A01)

(iv) ⁻*airport* | *with* *a __case full of ↘*cash* || (SEC A12)

In (i) and (ii) the unstressed syllable is high by default, since it follows a high level tone. In (iii) and (iv) there is an intervening tone group boundary, and one would normally expect the leading syllables[14] (*a* and *with a* respectively) to return to a default (mid) level. They do not, however, since in (iii) the leading syllable continues a rise in the previous tone group, and in (iv) the leading syllables continue at the high level of the previous tone group. This fact suggests a potential independence of melody and phrasing.

As illustrated in Figure 3.9, this pattern is a variant of the contour in Figure 3.8(3). The difference between the two is ultimately not melodic, but is a difference in time-alignment. In the first version the penultimate peak is associated with an accented syllable, while in this variant the peak is associated with an unstressed syllable. This gives the same sequence of high–low–high, but the first high is associated with an unstressed syllable. Both versions occur within a minor tone group and also across minor tone group boundaries. Regardless of the position in relation to boundaries, the pattern forms a recognisable 'tune', mapped onto a sequence of stressed and unstressed syllables.

For reasons which are not entirely clear, some speakers anticipate the sudden drop in pitch, and then copy the low level tone (or low rise) several times before the terminal high to low fall (Example (i) below). The drop itself can also be iterated (Example (ii) below). Intermediate unstressed syllables are given almost as much prominence as the initial one, so that the whole pre-closing downstep appears to be repeated.

(The high before the drop from high to low is marked in the examples by an asterisk.)

(i) *visits *the __Autumn A ⟋ssembly | of *the __British Council of ⟍Churches* (SEC A01)

(ii) *an *e__vent | un*ex__plained by ‾science or natural ⟍laws ||* (SEC A01)

Treating all these utterances as realisations of the 'same' melody is a problem for intonation analysis. The traditional division into tone groups of equal status makes no provision for melodic units which extend across tone group boundaries. One solution is to treat prosodic structure as distinct from melodic structure (see Ladd 1986, Wichmann and Knowles 1995).

If these are all cases of a 'single linguistic choice' (Ladd 1986: 320–1), whether extending across one or more tone groups, we must assume that speakers plan whole contours, and adapt them to the text as necessary.

3.3.2.2   THE LITURGICAL 'DROP'

Early work by Crystal and Davy (1969) discussed the prosody of liturgical style from the point of view of tone choice (observing a preponderance of level tones) rather than tone realisation. It is true that in liturgical speech we find many more level tones than in more 'normal' speech. This perception could also be the result of a generally compressed pitch range: speakers in a liturgical setting often use a narrow pitch range above an unusually high base line (compared with their normal voice). Whether the top line is very low, or the baseline raised, the compression of range causes pitch movement on accented syllables to be so restricted that utterance-final tones are perceived to be level rather than falling. As we have seen, the final tone is only one component in a melodic sequence. In a 'liturgical' style, it is not only the final tone which is markedly different, but the whole melodic closure sequence. While the default cadence consists of a sequence of two high accents, with intervening unstressed syllables in a 'valley' in between, in a liturgical style the unstressed syllables are not allowed to sag. The pitch of any prenuclear unstressed syllables is raised so that each nuclear syllable is approached from *above*, usually with a step down or drop (Wichmann 1996: 182) (Figure 3.10).

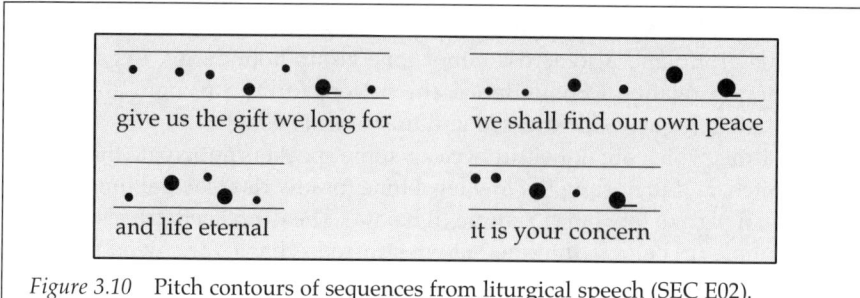

Figure 3.10 Pitch contours of sequences from liturgical speech (SEC E02).

This highly marked behaviour of unstressed syllables – pitched so that accented syllables are approached from above, is not exclusively an utterance final feature. In a 'liturgical' style there is also a tendency to raise any pre-head syllables to be as high as or higher than the onset syllable (Wichmann 1996: 183) (Figure 3.11).

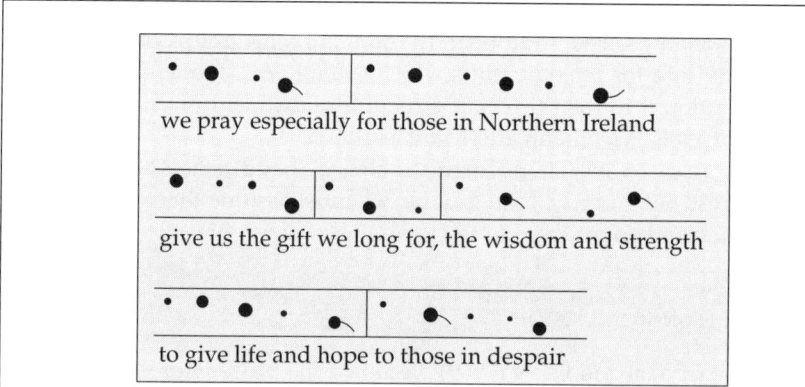

Figure 3.11 Pitch contour of liturgical speech extract (SEC E02) illustrating markedly high unstressed syllables.

A further characteristic of this speaking style is the frequent repetition of 'tunes', or melodic sequences, and since the repeated melody is not always associated with the identical number of syllables, prehead syllables may substitute for onset syllables if necessary (Figure 3.12).

Liturgical speakers are often said to 'intone' the liturgy. This style of speaking may therefore be derived from Gregorian chant, a type of plainsong associated

Figure 3.12 Pitch contour of liturgical speech illustrating melodic repetition (SEC E02).

with Pope Gregory I (c.540–c.604), which prescribed melodic formulae, known as 'tones', for performing readings and prayers.

3.4 Perception of falls – experimental evidence

So far I have described what speakers do. In this section I will consider how utterance-final contours are perceived. If there are categories of falls (e.g. high and low or with and without downstep) they must be assumed to represent linguistically meaningful deviation, otherwise the distinction need not be captured in the phonological system. Experimental research has shown that listeners sense a difference in meaning between different falls and also perceive discrete categories, even when the height of the fall is varied in equal steps (Gussenhoven and Rietveld 1991). However, the concept of a categorical, all-or-nothing, contrast is weakened somewhat in the light of the problems with assigning transcription categories to SEC data. In a perception experiment, first reported in Wichmann (1991a, 1991b) an attempt was made to find out whether variation in the height of sentence-final falls influences the perceived meaning – in this case how final or 'closed' the sentences sound.

In judging finality, i.e. whether or not a speaker has finished, we rely of course not only on prosody but on the content and syntax of the utterance. Sentences such as *'And that is the end of the news'*, or *'Now the next problem is this'* will give a pretty good idea of whether or not there is more to come, independently of the way they are said. In order, therefore, to be as certain as possible that the subjects were judging finality on the basis of prosody alone, the utterances were selected, in a preliminary experiment based on written sentences taken from the SEC, as those which were semantically least marked for finality or continuation.

In the experiment, the pitch contours of the chosen sentences were manipulated so that there were five versions of each, in which the height of the final falling tone varied systematically from high to low. Listeners were asked to judge whether or not the speaker had finished speaking, based on a four-point scale ranging from 'definitely finished' to 'definitely going on'.

The variation in the height of the nuclear fall was intended to reflect the variation observed in the corpus (and the assumptions made by the SEC transcribers), namely that pitch height is perceived relative either to the height of the preceding accent or the preceding syllable. The starting point of the fall was therefore changed systematically in relation to both the preceding accented syllable and to the immediately preceding unstressed syllable.[15] See Figure 3.13.

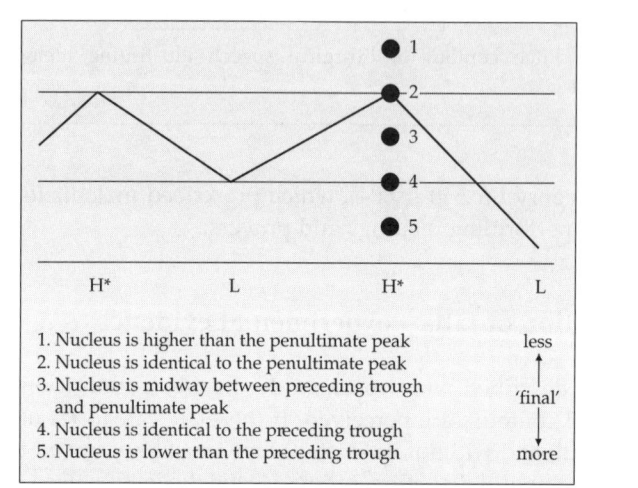

1. Nucleus is higher than the penultimate peak
2. Nucleus is identical to the penultimate peak
3. Nucleus is midway between preceding trough and penultimate peak
4. Nucleus is identical to the preceding trough
5. Nucleus is lower than the preceding trough

less
↑
'final'
↓
more

Figure 3.13 A stylised representation of five different falls, from high to low, created by manipulating original recordings from the SEC.

The listeners' responses show that the height of the starting point brings about a gradual change in the perception of finality (i.e. the perceived likelihood that the speaker has no more to say decreases with the height of the final fall[16]). This seems to provide some evidence that the starting point of a final fall influences the listener's perception of closure. However there is no evidence to suggest that this perception is a categorical one: whether we take the average scores of finality, or the average ranking of the different versions relative to one another, the result is a gradient. This suggests that the finality of a fall is perceived in terms of *degrees* rather than in terms of categories, binary or otherwise, and that these degrees relate to the height of the starting point. It also suggests that falls are able to carry discoursal meaning, contradicting the claim by Lehiste that 'the terminal intonation contour serves a grammatical purpose' (1975: 199). She was looking for intonation cues to higher level structures (paragraphs), and concluded that the final contour was not available for this purpose. She does not explicitly reject possible differences in attitudinal meaning, which would presumably be seen as non-linguistic, but simply excludes other linguistic functions other than syntax.

The observations in this experiment are consistent with the findings of Swerts (1994) who also found that a low fall contributed to the perception of finality.

The 'high' and 'low' falls he observed, and which seemed to have an effect on perceived finality in Dutch, actually differ in the *timing* of the falling part of the contour, rather than in the height of the fall. This is also true of the falls with and without 'downstep' referred to by Gussenhoven and Rietveld (1991). The fall 'without downstep' begins late in the syllable, while the fall 'with downstep' begins early in the syllable. Swerts hypothesised that it is in fact the timing of the fall, rather than its height, which is the cue to different degrees of finality. This would mean that peak timing is a consistent factor in discourse intonation. Just as a late peak in the sentence onset is a correlate of intiality (discussed in Chapter 2), so an early peak in the nucleus relates to finality. This effect in closure sequences has so far been observed mostly at sentence level. The discoursal effect on peak timing in onsets is highly likely to have its correlate in the timing of peaks in (discourse unit) final accents too, but this has still to be investigated.

We are nonetheless left with some unresolved issues. The falling contours used by Swerts (1994) and by Gussenhoven and Rietveld (1991) equate roughly to versions 2 and 3 in the experiment described above. They do not include anything resembling version 1, a fall which begins higher than the preceding accented syllable. The final fall with this much higher starting point, which is so common in the SEC, is not easily incorporated in their systems.

There is one more unresolved issue: the binary contrast between high and low is still very much a part of current intonation models, and Gussenhoven and Rietveld (1991) suggest that listeners do perceive categorical distinctions between falls. The effect of different falls on the perception of how final an utterance sounds, on the other hand, seems to be a gradient one. The aims of the studies were of course different: one was focused on the underlying phonology of intonation, the other was focused on discoursal effect. How the two can be reconciled remains to be seen.[17]

3.5   Summary

This chapter was concerned with the idea of intonational 'closure', represented by the falling tone. First of all I examined the occurrence of *'closure' in relation to syntactic structure*. Typically, the end of an orthographic sentence read aloud co-occurs with intonational closure. However, it is clear that even skilled readers also create spoken sentences which do *not* correspond one to one with orthographic sentences. Conjoined clauses are frequently treated melodically as separate spoken sentences, even if their close relationship is still signalled by features of timing, such as the absence of pause or final lengthening. The intonational closure (falling tone) frequently occurs at a point in the utterance which is at least potentially complete. Some sentence elements, notably sentence-final adverbials, are then appended in such a way that they are heard as an additional but integrated part of the whole utterance.

Secondly I examined the *melodic realisation of closure contours*, including the most common 'default' patterns and some stylistically marked variants. The final falling tone has a fixed low endpoint, but a variable starting point, and should be seen as a component in a melodic sequence – the 'cadence'. The question whether there are discrete phonological categories of fall, such as high and low, or with and without downstep, has not yet been satisfactorily resolved.

Finally I considered the *meaning of falls*. While I accept an underlying meaning of finality or 'closure', I have shown that different kinds of contour have an effect on the *degree* of 'closure' perceived by listeners. Closure, or finality, signals the end of an utterance unit. Perceived degrees of finality can be exploited for discoursal effect, i.e. to indicate the closure of a unit other than the orthographic sentence. This can be a word, a clause, a syntactic sentence, a paragraph, a topic or a text. Finality can also be exploited for interactional purposes, by signalling the end of a turn at speaking. It may also indicate whether the utterance is the last word on the subject or not. It may invite or discourage a response. While I have demonstrated the usefulness of the 'closure' view of the height of falls, I accept that in conversational interaction attitudinal meaning may also be involved, a dimension which I have not investigated here. Be that as it may, it is certainly no longer enough to claim, as Lehiste did, that the terminal contour only serves 'a grammatical purpose'.

Notes

1   'Syntactically possible' is open to interpretation, but it clearly does not necessarily mean exclusively the end of a sentence. It does however mean that any pauses or closure signals at places which do not constitute syntactic boundaries in the wider sense are unlikely to have cued a major boundary, and cannot therefore be derived from the transcription.

2   For simplification, the original transcription of this and other examples from the Spoken English Corpus has been reduced to the features relevant in this chapter.

3   The scope of the pitch movement for a fall-rise can be very similar to that of a fall plus rise. In this example the rise of the fall-rise occurs on the stressed syllable of 'weather':

> *I can't remember↘⤴us making a fuss about the weather*

This is similar to the contour of the fall plus rise in the next example:

> *in the end he only ↘stayed about six ⤴months*

4   We do not have access to all the original scripts for this corpus. The orthographic sentences referred to here are those proposed in the orthographic transcription which was based on the unpunctuated transcribed written text alone, and not influenced by the spoken performance.

5   The autosegmental distinction between pitch accents with and without downstep is not a feature exclusively of utterance-terminal falls. Downstep occurs on other tones too under certain conditions. Gussenhoven and Rietveld's study (1991), which claims to show a categorical difference between downstepped and non-downstepped falls, actually deals with the perceptual distinction between falls which start around the same height as the preceding accent and those which start lower that the preceding accent. This excludes a priori the possibility that there could be falls with a higher starting point. While it is interesting that listeners perceive a categorical distinction between the two falls tested, suggesting that downstep is a phonological category rather than a paralinguistic effect, we are left with the thought that, while the testers found the differences they were looking for, there may be others which they did not think to look for.

6   These estimates are based solely on the graphic representation of their examples and not on any explicit description by the authors.

7   Swerts (1994) suggests that this is a typical pre-final contour.

8   Any unstressed syllables following the nucleus and contained in the same tone-group.

9   Hadding-Koch and Studdert-Kennedy in their experiments (1964), reported in Ladd (1980: 115) may have observed something similar when they found that a synthesised fall which fell to a mid point and then suddenly became less steep was also sometimes perceived by listeners as a rise.

10   The fact that *going on* is given a separate tone group and not treated as the nuclear tail of *fair* is a feature of the journalistic style of delivery. Journalistic style also accounts for the accenting of the final lexical word in Figure 3.4(a).

11   In the system of intonation ('t Hart et al. 1990) developed at the IPO (Institute for Perception Research) in Holland this pattern has been described as a 'flat hat'.

12   An instrumental analysis of this is difficult: the syllables are so short that there is often no visible trace.

13   *The use of the up-arrow in the transcription of the SEC :* In the SEC the basic distinction between high and low is reserved for accented syllables only. There are however two additional symbols which are used for all syllables, whatever their degree of stress: these symbols, the up-arrow and the down-arrow, are used to mark any syllable which is perceived to be higher or lower than 'normal'. These can therefore occur together with tonetic stress marks and also stand alone. Some functions of pitch suppression, i.e. extra-low pitch, are described in Chapter 4. Here we are concerned with the functions of extra-high pitch marked in the SEC by up-arrows.(↑) When the up-arrow co-occurs with a high level, fall-rise or fall, that syllable is already prominent for reasons other than pitch, and the step up is simply greater than that which is implied by the use of the tonetic stress mark alone. When the up-arrow stands alone, it indicates an unexpected step up on a syllable which is otherwise unstressed. Theoretically, pitch obtrusion is considered to be the main perceptual correlate of an accented syllable, in other words a step up in pitch is the reason why a syllable is perceived to be accented. This means that otherwise unstressed syllables, often function words which are extremely short and may contain reduced vowel segments, are not assumed to have any pitch prominence. The fact that some do is not a challenge to the theory of prominence, but a stylistically motivated deviation from the norm.

14   Leading syllables are any unaccented syllables before the first accent in a tone group.

15   The resynthesis of 10 sentences, each in five different versions, produced a set of 50 differ-ent stimuli. A stimulus sequence file was generated in which each stimulus was repeated five times, thus eliciting 250 responses from each subject. In this sequence file the stimuli occurred in random order, and were preceded by a test sequence of 10 occurrences. The total number of responses from each subject was therefore 260 (250 plus test sequence of 10). The first ten responses were ignored in the analysis. The stimuli were separated by a response time of 3.5 seconds.

16   Version 1 = 1.81; Version 2 = 2.43; Version 3 = 2.87; Version 4 = 3.53; Version 5 = 4.43.

17   **The pasta fall**: University students discovered that they could exploit the finality of the falling tone to increase the portions of food they received in the cafeteria. Each day a pasta dish was offered on the menu, intended as a complete dish but often preferred by students with additional vegetables. Catering staff filled the plate with pasta if it was a complete meal, but served a smaller portion if they knew it was to be supplemented with vegetables. Students learnt that if they said 'I'll have the pasta' with a final fall, the staff inferred that they intended it to be a complete meal and filled the plate. The student then added 'and chips (carrots/peas etc.) please', causing a disgruntled caterer to pile vegetables onto an already full plate. (I owe this observation to my colleague Paul Livesey.)

CHAPTER FOUR

Cohesion

So far in this book I have considered the ways in which the edges of intonation contours are modified to reflect major disjunctures in speech. However, it also falls to intonation to indicate the opposite – namely the close conceptual relatedness of successive utterances, and of course of the component parts of utterances themselves.

Cohesion is that property which gives us the sense that 'something is a text and not a random collection of sentences', a sense created by '. . . the use of language forms to indicate semantic relations between elements in a discourse' (McArthur 1992: 230). In written texts, such forms can be grammatical (using reference, ellipsis, substitution and conjunctions), lexical (through the use of synonymy, metonymy and repetition), and typographical (through the use of punctuation). My task here is to consider how cohesion is created in *spoken* texts, and to do this I need to extend the notion of linguistic forms to include prosody.

In this chapter I will deal first with the anaphoric links created by modifying utterance beginnings, and secondly with the cohesive effect of modifying utterance-final contours, a device known as intonational parallelism. Finally I will reconsider the well-known phenomenon of parenthesis.

4.1   Cohesion and intonation

4.1.1   Intonation and information structure: accenting and de-accenting

The view that prosody can have a cohesive function in discourse is not new, and has most commonly been discussed in relation to information status, involving the concept of 'given and new information'. 'Given' information is 'information which the speaker assumes to be already in some way in the consciousness of the listener and which is hence not in need of highlighting' (Cruttenden 1997: 81).

If 'given' information occurs in the position which would by default attract a nuclear accent, that syllable is deaccented and the nucleus occurs on an earlier item.[1]

(I'm going to buy her a toaster.)
But she's GOT a toaster.

In many cases this prosodic pattern compensates for the inflexibility of word order in English, which does not allow the syntactic re-ordering which is possible in, say, German.

(Ich schenke ihr einen Toaster.)
Einen Toaster HAT *sie doch. (a toaster* HAS *she + modal particle = 'but')*

Thus although intonation is only one possible device for focusing attention on a particular part of an utterance, it is a device which is often necessary in spoken English.

The effect of information status – what is given and what is new – on the prosodic realisation of an utterance is assumed to lie primarily in deciding 'which words to accent and which to de-accent' (Hirschberg 1993: 92). However, reducing the salience of given information need not result in de-accenting altogether. Gårding (1982) claims that '. . . downgraded accent may be anaphoric', and this may be achieved through the *choice* of accent, rather than by the decision whether or not to de-accent. A low rise (L*H), for example, is in some contexts less salient than a fall (H*L) (see Pierrehumbert and Hirschberg 1990). Thus the utterance above could be realised differently, with a rise on the final item, but still indicate the same relative given and new status.

(I'm going to buy her a toaster.) But she's ↘ GOT a ↗ TOAster.

If a single lexical item is de-accented, or realised with a low tone rather than a high tone, we have a local cohesive device analogous to grammatical and lexical devices (pronominal reference, lexical repetition etc.). However, it is not only nucleus placement or tone choice inside the tone group that can have a cohesive effect in speech. While nucleus placement reflects information structure inside the utterance, there is also a need to indicate semantic and pragmatic relationships between whole utterances which are not necessarily reflected in surface features of cohesion. This aspect of relatedness or disjuncture between utterance units can be expressed intonationally at the boundaries between the units, and this is my main concern in this chapter. The global pitch effects of the relationships between utterances is discussed in Chapter 5.

4.1.2   Cohesion and 'onset depression'

We already know that speakers indicate the strength of a boundary in a spoken text by adjusting the way in which they realise 'normal' sentence-boundary signals. A particularly strong boundary, such as that at a major shift in a narrative, will display prosodic features indicating the maximum disjuncture, including the 'topic reset'[2] described in Chapter 2. For a new topic the pitch reset, or step up in pitch, which would occur anyway to mark the beginning of an utterance, is boosted to show that it is not only the beginning of a new, grammatically-independent utterance but, more importantly, that it is also the beginning of a new section of the text. If, however, two consecutive independent utterances are very closely related, for example when the second elaborates on the first, the speaker is obliged to produce conflicting signals: on the one hand there is a need to indicate the beginning of a new, grammatically independent utterance, and on the other hand to indicate the close anaphoric relationship which holds between this and the previous utterance. In other words the speaker has to indicate 'new' and 'not new' at the same time.

This has a certain parallel in the *punctuation* of written texts, which has two functions, namely to separate and to specify (Quirk et al. 1985: 1610). The clearest indication of syntactic separateness is the period or full stop. Its function is simply to separate; it makes no statement about the units it separates, other than that they are syntactically independent of one another. It does not give any indication of the semantic relations which may hold between the consecutive sentences. These must be inferred by the reader from the meaning of the text itself. Sometimes, however, the reader can be given some assistance. The colon or semi-colon, for example, can be used in English to separate two syntactically independent clauses but to indicate at the same time a close semantic or pragmatic relationship between them. The colon suggests that what follows it is in some way an elaboration of what precedes it, while the semi-colon is very close in meaning to the co-ordinating conjunction *and* (see Quirk et al. 1985: 1620, 1622). The use of a colon or semi-colon can thus indicate simultaneously 'separate' and 'not separate', or more specifically, syntactic independence and conceptual dependence.

This difficult combination of simultaneous independence and dependence is a challenge to the prosodic realisation of spoken text. It can be achieved by reversing what happens at major disjunctures. The normal sentence reset is not boosted, as for topic boundaries; instead the reset is suppressed so that it is lower, rather than higher, than expected.

This kind of variation in pitch range is usually not reflected in broad prosodic transcriptions such as is used in the SEC. The prosodic annotation is normally restricted to marking pitch movement on accented syllables. However, the SEC transcribers also included in the SEC transcription, in addition to the symbols indicating tonal contours (tones), two symbols – the up-arrow ($\uparrow$) (see also 3.3.2.1 n. 13) and the down-arrow ($\downarrow$) to indicate pitch levels which are either higher than expected or lower than expected. The up-arrow is fairly straightforward: it indicates a step up in pitch which the transcribers perceived to be higher than a subjective 'norm'. The down-arrow on the other hand can indicate two different phenomena. Firstly, it can indicate a marked step *down*, to complement the marked step up signalled by the up-arrow. Secondly, and for my purposes here more importantly, it can indicate a step *up* which is smaller than the transcribers' subjective 'norm'. The down-arrow can therefore be said to mark pitch range compression in general, rather than simply downward pitch excursion.

A number of these down-arrows appear to indicate some kind of prosodic cohesion, and by studying their distribution in the text we can find supporting evidence for this view. The down-arrow cooccurs most frequently in the SEC with the beginning of a tone group, regardless of whether the first syllable is accented or not. As with the topic reset, the depressed reset involves both the height of pre-head syllables and the height of the first accent (Figure 4.1). By deliberately depressing the reset of pitch at the beginning of a single tone group

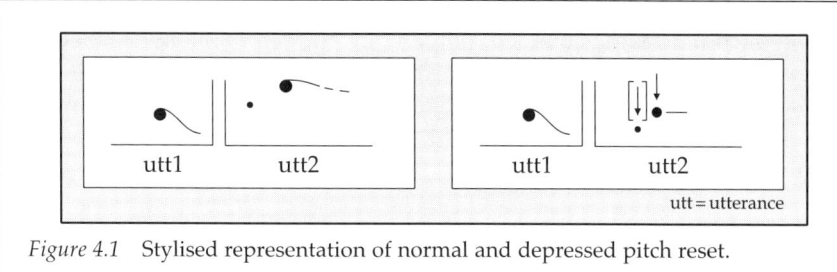

Figure 4.1 Stylised representation of normal and depressed pitch reset.

or of a complete utterance, speakers signal something like 'not going on', or 'this utterance is backward-pointing in its reference'.

4.2 Cohesion in the SEC

The value of a corpus is that it allows one to search automatically for instances of a linguistic phenomenon. In a speech corpus like the SEC this could be, for example, instances of certain tones, or certain boundaries. However, without an additional detailed syntactic and semantic labelling of the text, and an instrumental analysis to complement the auditory transcription, a textually-motivated depression of onset height is virtually impossible to search for automatically. The only guide to unusual changes in pitch height is to be found in the use of up-arrows and down-arrows.

The distribution of the down-arrows in the SEC is shown in Table 4.1. A number of them may simply be idiosyncratic, since they do not seem to correspond to any underlying regularity. They may also indicate more global changes in register, or have a rhetorical function, but so far we must assume that the motivation for these local shifts may not be recoverable. The function of the remainder appears to fall into two broad groups. In approximately 18% of the cases the down-arrow is a feature indicating the approaching end of an utterance. A narrowing of pitch range towards the end of an utterance is predictable, and

Table 4.1 Distribution of down-arrows (↓) in the Spoken English Corpus

uncategorisable	65 (25%)
end-of-sentence closure	46 (18%)
cohesive	148 (57%)
– *sentence boundaries*	
– *phrase/clause boundaries*	
(co-ordination, postmodification)	
Total	259

down-arrows occurring in this position are not remarkable: they suggest simply that the pitch narrowing sounded a little more sudden to the transcribers than they expected. Over 50% of down-arrows, however, occur at the beginning or in the middle of utterances. These indicate an onset depression which functions as a cohesive device, both between and within sentences and it is this function which will be examined here.

4.2.1 Phrase and clause boundaries: pitch depression inside sentences

Ascribing meaning to intonation is problematic if there is no independent evidence either from the text (in monologue) or from subsequent interaction (in dialogue). Sentence-internally it is a little easier, since the functional/semantic relationships between syntactic units *inside* clauses are a function of their grammatical status, and those *between* clauses are often made explicit by the use of conjunctions. The semantic relationships between independent sentences on the other hand are less explicit and open to subjective interpretation. If we can establish intonation patterns which occur systematically where the meaning relations are known, we are then in a position to use intonation patterns to infer meaning (or at least the speaker's interpretation) where this is not known. I shall therefore look first at the occurrence of pitch depression at sentence-internal boundaries, dealing in turn with the subcategories identified above (Table 4.1): before items of postmodification, co-ordination and at clause boundaries. I will then move on to the effect of onset depression between independent sentences.

4.2.1.1   NON-RESTRICTIVE POSTMODIFICATION

The down-arrows co-occurring with postmodification constitute the largest group in the SEC (40% of those occurring at phrase or clause boundaries inside sentences), and appear to be a signal of non-restrictiveness. The postmodifying constituents are of three main types:

- noun phrases in apposition
- relative clauses
- prepositional phrases

The first important point is that there are of course many more of these constituents in the SEC than are marked by a down-arrow. The co-occurrence with a down-arrow can for this reason not be formally related to either the type of constituent (NP, PP, subordinate (relative) clause) nor to a particular function, such as adverbial. Nor is it possible to argue that the down-arrow is directly related to the non-restrictiveness of these constituents. Such an argument would be circular, since it is to some extent the prosody which causes us to perceive a constituent as being non-restrictive rather than restrictive. We can only aim to establish that pitch depression occurs before constituents which are *potentially* non-restrictive. We can then claim that it is the underlying ('additional') meaning of the pitch depression (described below under co-ordination, section 4.2.1.2) that *causes* these constituents to be perceived as parallel items and therefore non-restrictive.

The terms restrictive/non-restrictive refer to the degree of certainty to which the reference of the head can be determined with or without the post-modification. According to Quirk et al. (1985: 1239) 'Restrictiveness ... indicates a limitation on the possible reference of the head ... Alternatively, the referent of a noun phrase may be viewed as unique or as a member of a class that has been independently identified ... Any modification given to such a head is **additional** information which is not essential for identification, and we call it "non-restrictive"' (my emphasis).

I shall discuss this relationship below with respect to the three groups of post-modifying constituents most commonly treated prosodically with a narrowed pitch range and therefore marked in the transcribed SEC by down-arrows: appositional noun phrases, relative clauses and prepositional phrases.

(i) Apposition   In each of the following four examples, the head is uniquely identifiable without the additional information in the appositive. The apposition is therefore clearly non-restrictive and the prosody serves no disambiguating function. In examples (1.i) and (1.ii) the appositional phrase names an already identifiable referent, thus identifying individually someone who has already been identified in terms of his function in an institution. In (1.iii) and (1.iv) the process is reversed: the head is a name (UNESCO, Ben Gurion) and the appositional phrase is explanatory. In (1.iv) the apposition is complex, containing two further postmodifications, one embedded in the other: [of the country [that's ...]]. In each of these examples the appositional phrase is preceded by a down-arrow, signalling a marked depression of pitch height at that point.

1.   (i) *The rector of the University* ↓ *Dr Nicholas Argentato ...* (SEC A01)

   (ii) *The General Secretary of the TUC* ↓ *Mr Norman Willis ...* (SEC B01)

   (iii) *is to withdraw from UNESCO* ↓ *the United Nations cultural and scientific agency ...* (SEC B03)

   (iv) *hijacking from Ben Gurion* ↓ *international airport of the country that's the target of most hijackings, are unknown.* (SEC A08)

(ii) Relative clauses   Not all decisions as to the restrictive or non-restrictive function of a post-modifier are so simple. The following examples show that it can be difficult to determine whether a relative clause is restrictive or non-restrictive.

2.   (i) *away from the philosophical abstractions* ↓ *which had characterised Zurich Dada, and ...* (SEC D01)

   (ii) *deafness is truly the invisible handicap* ↓ *which isolates people.* (SEC K02)

   (iii) *shares in Pentos* ↓ *which carry ten per cent off ...* (SEC F01)

   (iv) *a single pensioner* ↓ *also on ninety pounds a week ...* (SEC F02)

In (2.i) both interpretations are possible. Example (2.ii) is also ambiguous: it could be restrictive, but it is more likely to be non-restrictive, i.e. that the speaker means there is only one invisible handicap, namely 'deafness'. The relative clause could then be rephrased with a co-ordinate clause: '. . . and it isolates people.' In (2.iii) the relative clause is more obviously non-restrictive. The last example (2.iv) contains an ellipted relative clause which, through the inclusion of *also*, clearly has an additive, i.e. non-restrictive function.

So far only one isolated case has been identified in the SEC of an unambiguously restrictive relative clause marked by onset depression. The following is an example of co-ordinated postmodification which is clearly restrictive.

> 3. *is wasting Reith lectures labouring points* ↓ *which are familiar to every first year economics student and aren't important.* (SEC C01)

It is possible that the pitch discontinuity is in this case attributable to the length of the postmodifying sequence. The boundary is less likely to have occurred at that point if the co-ordinated items had been in the reverse order: ('. . . points which aren't important and are familiar to every . . .'). From the evidence from co-ordinated items discussed earlier we might predict a break before the second (ellipted) relative clause. Again this may be a result of the ordering of the units and their respective length. Alternatively, the speaker may be suppressing the pitch in order to indicate a list of two (see section 4.2.1.2).

With the exception of this item, when onset depression occurs before a relative clause, the clause is potentially non-restrictive in the context, and can therefore be treated as a separate, potentially downgraded item (see also section 4.4).

(iii) Prepositional phrases The restrictive/non-restrictive distinction commonly applied to relative clauses is as far as I know not usually applied to prepositional phrases, even though, as Quirk et al. point out, 'A prepositional phrase is by far the commonest type of postmodification in English . . .' (1985: 1274). There are many prepositional phrases in the SEC which are not marked by any unusual (to the transcribers) lowering of pitch level. Those which are preceded by a down-arrow are all adverbials, in (4.ii) and (4.iii) sentence adverbials.

> 4. (i) *sensational coverage* | ↓ *on television* . . . (SEC A03)
>
> (ii) *the last time* | *he addressed striking miners* | ↓ *in South Wales* | *earlier this month* . . . (SEC B01)
>
> (iii) *and I argued* | ↓ *with the help of my fictional colleague Mr MacQuedy* | . . . (SEC C01)

Prepositional phrases functioning as sentence adverbials are often treated as intonationally independent in the SEC. In Chapter 3 we saw that in conversational styles adverbials are often realised with a rising tone after an 'early closure', in other words where the expected falling tone occurs immediately before the adverbial. In more formal read speech the early closure still occurs, but the final adverbial is more likely to copy the same tone, in other words ending with a repeat of the falling tone rather than a final rise. Whichever nuclear tone is chosen, the intonational 'closure' before syntactic closure requires the speaker to retrospectively integrate the adverbial into the previous, apparently complete, stretch of speech. The onset or pre-head depression reflected in the down-arrow may be one of the ways in which a speaker does this, as in the following example.

5. *there's some renewed ↘grumbling | ↓ about Anglican am↘bivalence to the British Council of Churches . . .* (SEC A01)

4.2.1.2   CO-ORDINATION

As we have seen, onset depression occurs before appositive phrases or non-restrictive relative clauses, and other non-defining postmodifiers which have an additive, i.e. non-defining, function inside a sentence. According to Quirk et al., 'Non-restrictive relationship is often semantically very similar to coordination, with or without conjunction, or adverbial subordination' (1985: 1258). It is therefore not surprising that the same prosodic feature should occur between sentence elements which are explicitly marked as co-ordinating, i.e. additive in some way.

The difference between co-ordination and subordination is a gradient one. There are several criteria involved, and these are satisfied to varying degrees and under varying conditions. Quirk et al. (1985: 927–8) suggests a rough grouping of conjunctions into

- those which are most typical of co-ordinate relationships: (*and / or / but*)
- those which are most typically subordinators: (*for / so that / if / because*)
- those which are more co-ordinating or more subordinating depending on the criteria applied. (*nor / so / yet / however / therefore*).

In addition to this last group of 'semi-co-ordinators' there are some items 'which we may call "quasi-coordinators", because they behave sometimes like coordinators, and at other times like subordinators of prepositions' (1985: 982). These are *as well as / as much as / rather than / more than / like*.

In the SEC the down-arrow (↓) occurs frequently at boundaries between clauses and phrases which are co-ordinated or quasi-co-ordinated in this way, as in the following examples.

6.   (i)   *. . . in their first innings were fourteen without loss at lunch ↓ **and** in the second test in Brisbane . . .* (SEC B01)

   (ii)   *. . . last week I showed my hand as the price mechanist that I am ↓ **and** I argued . . .* (SEC C01)

   (iii)   *. . . prospects of help from Brussels ↓ **and** the European Community . . .* (SEC A06)

   (iv)   *. . . any returning Tamil will be slaughtered on the spot ↓ **or** at least arrested and tortured.* (SEC A10)

There is a special case of co-ordination: structural parallelisms such as **lists**, of which there are several examples in the corpus marked with down-arrows. There is a tendency to anticipate a list with a low pre-head syllable.

7.   (i) *... the outside world is seen* ↓ *at best as* ..., *at worst* ... (SEC C01)

    (ii) *... in his view* ↓ *the rituals, priests, and doctrines of Christianity had* ... (SEC D02)

    (iii) *... for example twice one fifth is one third plus one fifteenth* ↓ *twice one ninth is one sixth plus one eighteenth and so on.* (SEC D03)

In this last example (7.iii) the list is only suggested. The first calculation is presented as an independent item, ending in a fall. The drop in pitch before the next item suggests that the speaker could cite a whole list of similar calculations but refrains from doing so, substituting further listed items with 'and so on.'

Pitch depression can also occur before each of the listed items (including the last) as in example (8.i), which in its transcribed form contains a succession of four down-arrows, the first at a sentence boundary, and the subsequent three indicating a list. The next example (8.ii) contains a list of three within a list of two:

8.   (i) *widespread pressure to stay in has been resisted.* ↓ *It's come* ↓ *from the commonwealth* ↓ *from the European community* ↓ *and at home from the house of commons select committee* ... (SEC)

    (ii) *three of the most successful, Hong Kong,* ↓ *Singapore and Taiwan* ↓ *are small, while none of the group is very large.* (SEC C01)

While syntactic co-ordination is often the realisation of semantic equivalence, it is not necessarily the case that all co-ordinate clauses or phrases are semantically symmetrical. This can be illustrated by the many meanings of the most typical co-ordinator *and*: it can for example have a conditional meaning, as in: *Go by air and save time.* Quirk et al. (1985: 930–2) cite this conditional use of *and*, and also the following:

    and = and as a result / and therefore
    and = and then
    and = and in contrast
    and = and yet
    and = and similarly
    and = and also
    and + pronoun = which ('there's only one thing to do now and that is to apologise')

The SEC contains an unexplored number of *ands* carrying a variety of meanings, but all the examples of syntactic co-ordination which are additionally marked with onset depression are of the type 'semantically equivalent'. It is clear, therefore, that the intonation is an expression of a certain kind of meaning relation and not of the syntactic device of co-ordination. It indicates a semantic relationship which may or may not be expressed through syntax. As Bolinger noted, '... if a grammatical explanation is valid, it is probably because of the semantics of the grammatical category' (1989: 247).

4.2.2 Undoing early closure

So far, all the elements with depressed onset are constituents in their own right, but closely related to the preceding constituent – adding to it or modifying it in some way. There is therefore some evidence to suggest that the onset depression is an intonational device to signal this closeness, and that it functions because it minimises the pitch reset normally expected at the beginning of a tone group.

Having the prosodic means of linking utterances is particularly useful when a speaker has realised a complex orthographic sentence as more than one 'spoken sentence'. I described in Chapter 3 the use of intonational 'closure' (especially low falls) at clause boundaries, whether between co-ordinate main clauses or between main and subordinate clauses.

9.   (i) || *tube trains were halted on three lines* | *the Victoria* | *Bakerloo* | *and Central* | *when the current was turned* ⬂*off* | ↓ *and so far this morning* | *services are still being dis*⬂*rupted* || (SEC B01)

    (ii) || *one of the few ways of getting books at a discount* | *they're still retail price maintained of course* | *is to buy shares in* ⬂*Pentos* | ↓ *which carry ten per cent off* | *at shops such as Dillons and* ⬂*Hudsons* || (SEC F01)

    (iii) || *England* | *who were four hundred and fifty-eight for three* | *in their first innings* | *were fourteen without loss at* ⬂*lunch* || ↓ *and in the second test in Brisbane* | *the West Indies were two hundred and sixty-three for five at tea* | ↓ *in reply* | *to Australia's first innings total of one hundred and seventy-*⬂*five* || (SEC B01)

The boundaries in (9.i) and (9.iii) are between two coordinated main clauses, about as close to independent sentences as it is possible to be. It would even be possible to write them as two orthographic sentences, beginning the second with a capitalised conjunction. It is therefore not particularly surprising that the boundary has some of the features of a sentence boundary. The low falling nucleus to the left is a strong finality signal, and the high level onset is a typical initial tone. The link between the two clauses is set up by the depression of the prehead and onset of the second clause, in part by the depression of the first syllable of the second, which in fact also includes a depression of the onset syllable itself, although it is not independently marked with a down-arrow in the transcription. The fact that the boundary is marked in the transcription as a minor tone-group boundary suggests that other strong prosodic boundary features (such as long pause) are absent. In spontaneous speech (where the term 'sentence' is in any case problematic) we might possibly expect speakers to add afterthoughts using a kind of prosodic repair strategy. Reading aloud written texts, however, is another matter. Assuming that professional broadcasters are unlikely to be bad readers, we cannot easily dismiss it as a performance error. The speaker is not repairing a 'mistake', but has deliberately chosen to subdivide the text into chunks, and has modified the boundary features to both separate and link at the same time.

In (9.ii) the sentence elements divided in this way are not equally independent. Here the falling nucleus occurs before a subordinate clause, in this case a sentence-final relative clause. This is a more typical case of early closure, and it occurs at a point where the sentence is *potentially* complete, since it is the end of the main clause.

These examples illustrate the use of depressed pitch reset in 'undoing' finality retrospectively, not for repair, but in a deliberate strategy to show cohesion between segments of text which are syntactically, and sometimes intonationally, independent. The close relationship indicated by the onset depression need not be defined more closely. The nature of the relationship, other than its closeness, is determined by the text. But the depression of pitch reset indicates to the listener that the new constituent is to be understood as pointing backwards in some way – either adding or modifying what has just been said, or requiring restrospective integration in what appeared to be complete.

4.2.3 *Cohesive links between sentences*

The device used for linking phrases and clauses *inside* syntactic / orthographic sentences is equally valuable to indicate close relationships *between* sentences. A series of sentences each with the same sentence intonation is very likely to sound like a list of sentences rather than a coherent text, and a speaker may wish to indicate that although the sentences are syntactically independent, they nonetheless belong together to form a unified conceptual whole. Evidence from the SEC suggests that the same device of onset depression which creates an audible link between related phrases and clauses, also serves to link independent sentences in a text.

10. (i) ‖ *staff* | *on Brent council in London* | *are meeting today* | *to discuss the sacking of three social workers over the death of Jasmine* ⬂*Beckford* ‖ ↓*union leaders* | *have accused the council of making them* ⬂*scapegoats* ‖ (SEC B03)

   (ii) . . . *a House of Commons select committee* | *with a Conservative* *ma*⬂*jority* ‖ ↓*the expected statement* | *in the Commons this afternoon* | *will be made* | *by the overseas development minister* | *Mister Timothy* ⬂*Raison* ‖ (SEC B03)

   (iii) ‖ *so it seems the widespread pressure to stay in* | *has been re* ⬂ *sisted* ‖ ↓*it's come* | ↓*from the commonwealth* | ↓*from the European community* | ↓*and at home* | *from a House of Commons select committee* | *with a Conservative ma*⬂*jority* ‖ (SEC B03)
   [The second, third and fourth down-arrows indicate a list – see discussion of example (8.i)]

   (iv) ‖ *he said that in the Oval Office* | *President Johnson* | *had all three networks* | *running simul* ⬂*taneously* ‖ *he even had a TV in the* ⬂*bathroom* ‖ ↓*sensational coverage* | ↓*on television* | ↓*said Westmorland* | *had a far greater impact on the president* | *than my* *re*⬂*ports did* ‖ (SEC A03)

Each of the above examples has onset depression at the beginning of a sentence which is cohesively linked to the previous sentence. This is reflected in (10.ii) in the definite reference of '*the expected statement*' and in (10.iii) in the pronominal subject '*it's come from . . .*'. Examples (10.i) and (10.iv) contain lexical links: '*networks running*' – '*coverage on television*' and less obviously *staff meeting – sacking – union leaders*.

4.2.4 Conclusion

There is considerable evidence that a depressed onset is a signal of cohesion, which affects both the first accented syllable and any preceding unstressed syllables, illustrated in Figure 4.1. The closeness of prehead syllables to the speaker's baseline creates a restrospective link to the final pitch at the end of the previous utterance. This might suggest an almost iconic link between the pitch pattern and its cohesive function – close in pitch and close in meaning. This interpretation is tempting, but does not hold up when we consider that the same depression also occurs when the previous element ended in a high terminal (i.e. a rising tone). The pitch depression must therefore be seen as a locally-motivated modification which is paradigmatic, rather than a sequentially-motivated attempt to minimise the pitch discontinuity from one tone group to another.

Whatever the phonological explanation for this pattern, we can see that speakers modify intonational 'beginnings' – the pitch reset at prosodic boundaries – both to show conceptual breaks (topic resets as in Chapter 2) and to show the opposite – cohesion.

4.3 Intonational parallelism

As section 4.2 has shown, intonation is capable of indicating relationships between consecutive grammatical units by modifying the *beginnings* of the units, such as the depression of pitch reset at the beginning of parallel or included items. In this section (4.3) I will examine the cohesive effect of modifying the contours at the *end* of such a unit.

4.3.1 Some common parallelisms

In the prosodic realisation of complex utterances we often observe the phenomenon of melodic copying or tonal parallelism. The nuclear tone of one tone group is imitated by that of the next tone group so that we get the impression of a melodic 'rhyme'. A typical example, often quoted, is the intonation of lists. It is said that each item in a complete list has the same (usually non-final, i.e. a rise or a fall-rise) nuclear tone except the last. In the case of an incomplete **list**, each item will have the same nuclear tone (again usually non-final). See examples (11.i–iv).

11. (i) . . . ad ↘venture books ↗mostly | ↗Henty | ↗Kipling | Rider ↗Haggard | King Solomon's ↗Mines | ↗that sort of thing | . . . (SEC G05)

(ii) (*The nine hour operation to move Nemo, the whale, from Clacton to Windsor*) . . . | involved a police ↘↗escort | medical ↘↗specialists | civil ↘↗servants | ten ↘↗frogmen | and a mobile ↘crane ‖ (SEC B02)

> (iii) *here in ↗Washington | in Bei↗rut | and in Jer↘↗usalem |...*
> (SEC B02)
>
> (iv) *Did you have a set ↗text book | or ↗handouts ‖* (SEC J06)

The copying of nuclear tones is also familiar in cases of **apposition** such as the following examples (12.i–iii):

12. (i) *... the most expensive hotel in the ↘↗world | the Nova Park Elysee in ↘↗Paris |...* (SEC F03)

    (ii) *as the managing director | of the Windsor sa↘↗fari park | Mr Andrew Heyworth ↘↗Booth |...* (SEC B02)

    (iii) *the leader of the A↘↗lliance party | in Northern ↘↗Ireland | Mr John ↘↗Kushnahan | has asked ...* (SEC B02)

Tonal parallelism also occurs in conversation, where a turn can consist of a number of utterances each ending in the same tonal 'gesture'. (Examples 13.i–ii.)

13. (i) *Well of course you'd have to pay ↘↗extra | and you wouldn't really have a lot of ↘↗time there | so you wouldn't get to ↘↗see much | and ...*[3]

    (ii) *em | we have | a ↘different | system we ↘also have two ↘terms like ↘you do in the Su↘dan ‖ but ↘our terms are ↘twenty weeks ↘long so in fact | the ↘schooling is ↘twice what ↘yours is ‖ em | and although I have ample ↘time to get through the work I ↘want to get through I have a ↘nother problem | in that | the students just cannot ↘concentrate for twenty weeks ‖ nor can the ↘teachers | it's just too ↘long ‖* (SEC J06)

In extreme cases, the imitation of final contours becomes a stylistic mannerism, a kind of 'automatic pilot' which has little to do with the structure or meaning of the utterance, as in the following poetry reading ('Betjeman reads Betjeman') (Example 14):

14. *with her latest ↗roses | happily en↗cumbered | Tunbridge Wells ↗Central | takes her from the ↗night ‖ sweet second ↗bloomings | frost has faintly ↗umbered | and some double ↗dahlias | waxy red and ↘↗white ‖* (SEC H01)

All the constituents discussed in section 4.2.1 above, mainly co-ordinated phrases and clauses, appositional phrases and postmodifiying phrases, which are marked initially by pitch depression, can also be marked finally by the behaviour of the terminal contour. The last (nuclear) tone of the sequence frequently imitates the last (nuclear) tone of the previous sequence, setting up the kind of intonational parallelism described above.

4.3.2 Models of tonal parallelism

Tonal parallelism as a phonological phenomenon has been described by a number of people in the past, for example as 'co-ordinating sequences' (Palmer 1922), 'tonal reduplication' (Crystal 1969), 'multiple subordination' (Fox 1984), and 'series intonation' (Bolinger 1989). Palmer (1922, cited in Crystal 1969: 237) distinguishes between co-ordinating sequences which have the same nuclear tone, as in afterthoughts and adverbials, and subordinating sequences, which have different nuclear tones such as a fall followed by a rise. Crystal (1969: 241) also notes the tendency in his data for tones to 'repeat each other in the sequence'. This he refers to as 'tonal reduplication'.

Despite the differences in terminology, we are dealing with similar phenomena. The models all aim to account for a succession of two or more nuclear tones which have the same direction (rising, falling etc.) and are either very similar in terms of beginning and endpoints or in overall range. This results in a gradience of 'sameness'. The more criteria are satisfied, the greater the similarity.

This much observed phenomenon has also been referred to by Bolinger (1989) as *'series intonation'* or *'parallel items in sequence'*. Most importantly for my purposes he also refers to its cohesive function.

> 'What is probably more important as a general feature of series intonation is not the particular profile that is used on any one item . . . but the repetition of the same profile. **This is a cohesive device in discourse**.'
>
> (Bolinger 1989: 205) (my emphasis)

4.3.3   Reconciling models with corpus data

With the exception of Bolinger, previous accounts of tonal parallelism make at least two assumptions, firstly that parallelism only occurs between tones which are the same in form, and secondly that it only occurs between adjacent tone groups. I shall deal with each of these in turn, and show that both are at times inconsistent with corpus data: we find cases of perceived parallelism between different tones, and between tones in non-adjacent tone groups.

4.3.3.1   PARALLELISM BETWEEN DIFFERENT TONES

There are of course many examples of perceived tonal parallelism between identical nuclear tones, between a fall and a fall, a rise and a rise etc. There in in fact no way of retrieving automatically from the SEC anything other than this kind of parallelism. By listening to the original recordings, however, we find many other cases of audibly recognisable parallelism which are not recoverable from the prosodic transcription.

(a) High vs low   In some cases the problem is simply that a 'high' tone is perceived to imitate a 'low' tone. The British system distinguishes between high and low variants of the same nuclear tone (see Chapter 3). Does parallelism therefore strictly require a sequence of the same variety, two low rises, two high falls etc.? The example illustrated in Figure 4.2 contains two Noun Phrases in apposition, a typical example of two parallel items on which we would expect tonal parallelism. If we ignore the high/low distinction this is indeed the case, as both items end on a rise, and despite the difference in transcription, the auditory impression is that these tones do imitate each other very closely:

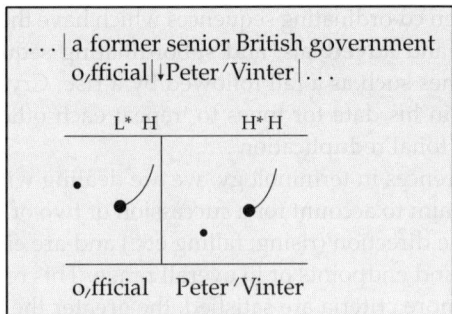

Figure 4.2 Prosodic transcription and pitch contours of an example of intonational parallelism between high and low falls.

As I explained in Chapter 3, the high/low distinction in the SEC transcription is based primarily on 'height' in terms of upstep or downstep, i.e. higher or lower than what has gone before, rather than on a position high or low in the speaker's voice range. As illustrated in Figure 4.2, the first rise in this example is 'low' because it is lower than the preceding syllable, and the second is 'high' because it is higher than the preceding syllable. However, phonetically the rises are very similar. The perceived parallelism is clearly a response to the phonetic realisation of the two rises, and not to their phonological categorisation.

(b) Falls and fall-rises   In the previous example (Figure 4.2) one could argue, as I did in Chapter 3, that the high/low distinction is a convenient one but does not necessarily indicate two phonological categories. In the following example (Figure 4.3) the perceived parallelism is between tones whose phonological distinctiveness, at least in the British tradition, is less controversial, the rise and the fall-rise.

In Figure 4.3(a) we see that the rising part of the fall-rise occurs not on the nuclear syllable itself but on a stressed syllable in the nuclear tail. This is imitated in the next tone group by a simple rise. In Figure 4.3(b) the sequence is reversed; that is, a rising tone is imitated by the rising part of a fall-rise.

A possible way of accounting for this is to decompose the nuclear tones, which in the British system constitute the smallest unit of intonation and are therefore indivisible, into the constituent pitch targets of the autosegmental-metrical model. A terminal 'rise' in this model is represented as the tonal sequence L*H, while the fall-rise is H*LH. To claim similarity between L*H and LH is more elegant than claiming similarity between one entire nuclear tone and a part of another. Tones and pitch targets, however, are abstract categories and the actual pitch of H and L is not specified in the grammar. Even if we redefine parallelism in terms of a sequence of autosegmental pitch targets we must still specify separately that these targets must be given very similar phonetic realisation, in other words they must be perceived to be at the same pitch.

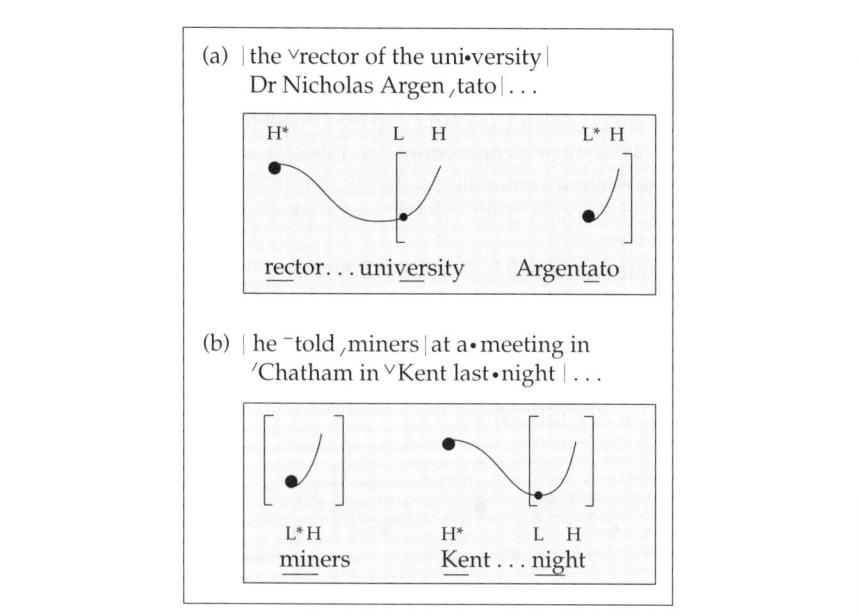

(a) | the ⱽrector of the uni•versity|
     Dr Nicholas Argen ⟋tato| . . .

rector. . . university   Argentato

(b) | he ⁻told ⟋miners|at a•meeting in
     ʹChatham in ⱽKent last•night | . . .

miners   Kent . . . night

Figure 4.3   Intonational parallelism between different tones (fall-rise and rise).

4.3.3.2   PARALLELISM BETWEEN NON-ADJACENT TONE GROUPS

The second assumption made by the models discussed earlier is that parallelism can only be identified between consecutive tone groups, and indeed it is difficult to see how it can be otherwise. To take any two identical tones and claim parallelism is like claiming rhyme in poetry between any two words which happen to have the same syllabic rhyme, whatever their positions. The effect of rhyme is only achieved if the words in question are at comparable points in the text, such as at the end of a line or the end of a metrical unit.

The majority of examples of tonal parallelism in the corpus are in consecutive tone groups, but there are a few apparently anomalous cases where a parallelism is audible despite being between two non-consecutive tone groups (Figure 4.4). These merit some further discussion.

The first example (a) in Figure 4.4 is a complex list from the SEC, with the list items numbered. Because of the length of each item and the heavily segmented reading style, these items could not be contained in single tone groups. There is nonetheless some typical listing intonation, but the parallelisms are no longer neatly between consecutive nuclei, but between (*wake up* + *radio*), (*alarms* + *kettle*), (*car* + *horn*), (*telephone* + *chat* + *family* + *touch*).

The next example in Figure 4.4(b) makes grammatical sense – the parallelism is between the noun and its postmodifier, but the postmodifier is relatively long and is divided into two tone groups.

89

(a) ... something a lot of us take for granted | our hearing ‖ (1) we set our alarms | to wake up | (2) we listen to the radio | as you are doing now ‖ (3) when the kettle whistles | we know the water has boiled ‖ (4) we hear a car coming | and its warning horn (5) or the telephone ringing | and enjoy a chat with our friends and family ‖ just to keep in touch   (SEC K02) (*Numbers 1–5 indicate the items*)

(b) a ⱽfreight train | which had just left Souʹthampton | on its way to ⱽLiverpool | ... (SEC B02)

(c) ‖ ↑ the problem ʽis | that | while there ⱽis an airport se•curity staff ‖ ↓and the ʽLebanese genˏdarmerie|⁻and ˏarmy | have _airport •staffs as ⱽwell ‖ (SEC A08)

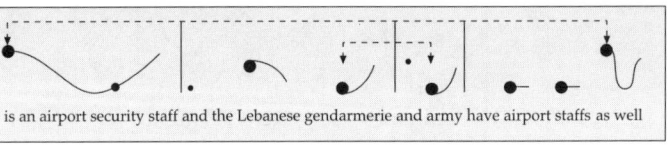

is an airport security staff and the Lebanese gendarmerie and army have airport staffs as well

Figure 4.4   Parallelism between non-adjacent tone groups.

The final example ((c) in Figure 4.4) shows tonal parallelism between co-ordinated items: a fall-rise beginning on ↘↗*is* (*an airport security staff*) is imitiated by the fall-rise on (*staffs as*) ↘↗*well*. According to the transcription, however, the intonational 'rhyme', although between consecutive grammatical elements, is not between consecutive tone groups. To find a way of reconciling these examples with the model of parallelism we must question the equal status of consecutive tone groups.

One way is to allow a recursive hierarchy of prosodic domains, which allows one tone group to be embedded inside another tone group. In example (c) (Figure 4.4) we could perhaps interpret the tone group containing *and army* as a parenthetical, an aside embedded in the middle of a single tone group – i.e. a tone group within a tone group. If we disregard the 'parenthetical tone group' we could be left with a single tone group to carry the parallelism – which would no longer be anomalous:

↘↗ IS *an airport security staff* | *and the Lebanese gendarmerie[...] have airport staffs as* ↘↗ WELL

Given the style of the rest of the report, this seems unlikely. Read texts such as these tend to have tone groups which are relatively stable in length and tend not to exceed more than about 7 or 8 syllables. (Spontaneous speech is different: there is a wide range of tone groups from the very short to the very long.) It therefore seems likely that, even without the parenthesis, this sequence would have been realised as two tone groups.

An alternative way of reconciling these anomalies is to consider a possible separation of the melodic system – the structure of tunes – and the system of phrasing – breaking utterances down into tone groups. The structure of intonational tunes has been discussed by Ladd (1986, 1996: 211) who argues for the existence of overall melodic shapes, containing an obligatory nucleus and a prenuclear constituent which can contain one or more accents. He takes this idea from the British tradition which differentiates between head and nucleus in a tone group, and reconciles it with the American autosegmental system by considering the head not as a 'global shape' but as an iteration of prenuclear accents.[4] Ladd's approach combines the British idea of a tone group having constituents of different status, and the autosegmental models which reduce these constituents to strings of accents. The overall intonation pattern (melodic shape) of an utterance is, in Ladd's view, planned holistically, and local patterns are low-level strategies for progressing through a preplanned tune, or as Ladd puts it, a 'single linguistic choice'.

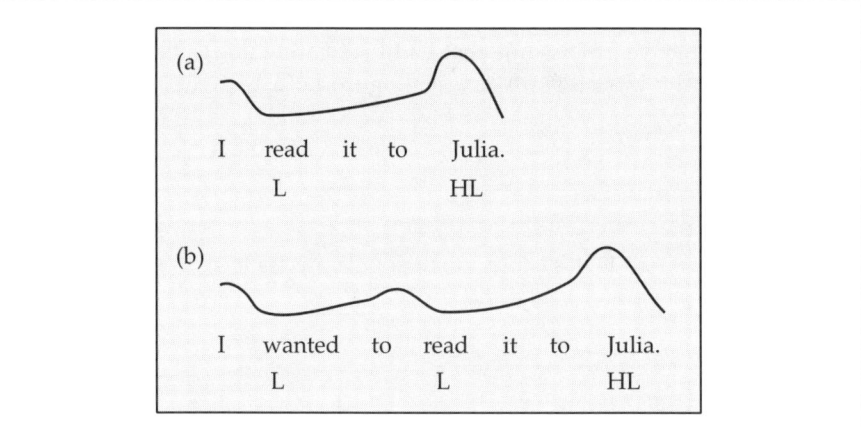

Figure 4.5 Two tunes – a single 'linguistic choice' (reproduced from Ladd (1986: 321)).

Ladd offers an illustration (Figure 4.5) of two contours which he sees as fundamentally the 'same', since the first two accents in (a) and the first accent in (b) are assigned to the same 'head' constituent.

> The traditional overall-shape view, while it unquestionably leads to difficulties in getting from the phonological specification to phonetic detail, nevertheless makes what seems to be the correct pragmatic prediction that the shape of the head reflects a single linguistic choice. . . . Both (utterances) appear to have 'the same' intonation, in the sense that both convey the same pragmatic force suggested by informal glosses. The number of prenuclear accents seems to depend solely on the number of accentable prenuclear syllables, and the type of prenuclear accent . . . seems to represent a single choice, regardless of whether the head contains a single accent or

several . . . Pierrehumbert's analysis has no way to treat the repetition of prenuclear accents as the relatively low-level phenomenon that it thus appears to be.

(Ladd 1986: 320–1)

The independence of tunes and tone groups is not a claim made by Ladd, but in my view it can be argued on the basis of other observations on the occurrence of pauses. While recognising 'whole tunes', Ladd also has to recognise that tunes are sometimes interrupted by pauses. A well-known example is the case of reporting verb groups as in *No, he said,* where we typically find a pause between what is melodically the nucleus and the nuclear tail. In other words we perceive one melodic 'shape' (a nuclear fall with nuclear tail), but two pause-defined groups. The second of the two is anomalous as a tone group since it does not contain an accented syllable.[5] In such cases it becomes clear that while we can take both internal structures and boundary cues into account for identification purposes, we cannot consistently **define** an intonation unit in terms of its internal structure and at the same time in terms of phonetic boundary features (see Chapter 5).

A less familiar example is to be found in another 'tune' described by Ladd. He recognises an overall contour containing a repeated head (similar to the 'Julia' example in Figure 4.5) in the example seen in Figure 4.6(a). By analogy with the previous example we can assume that Ladd is treating this as the same contour as a hypothetical *It was a difficult decision* (Figure 4.6(b)).

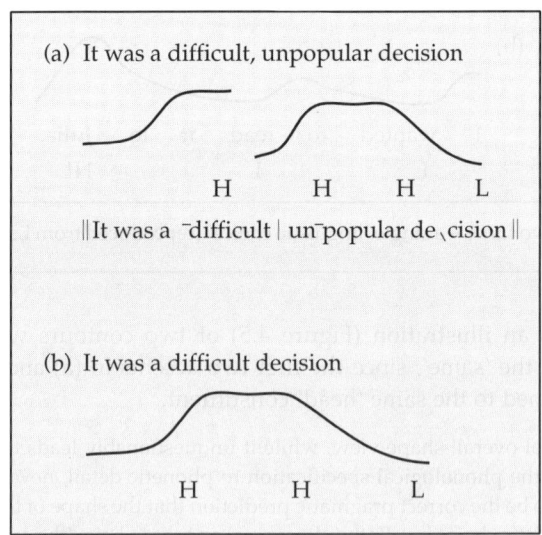

Figure 4.6 An analysis of two hypothetical utterances: (a) It was a difficult, unpopular decision (NB the prosodic transcription is also hypothetical); (b) It was a difficult decision, following Ladd (1986) (see Figure 4.5).

I would claim that this utterance might well contain a pause after *difficult*, particularly if it was being read aloud and the reader responded prosodically to the comma. There would almost certainly be a glottal onset on the first vowel of 'unpopular' to avoid a possible misinterpretation as 'and popular'. Whatever discontinuity is created, the sentence might be transcribed prosodically as in Figure 4.6(a). If this is so, we must allow one coherent tune to be spread over more than one tone group.

Prosodic transcription always runs into difficulties when temporal and melodic discontinuities do not coincide. In spontaneous speech, intonational contours are often interrupted by hesitation or 'planning' pauses. In formal scripted speech, the 'heavy' intonation – close proximity of accented syllables and short tone groups, can force a speaker to break a coherent contour into small chunks. It is therefore possible that the 'tone groups' marked in the SEC and also those in corpora of spontaneous speech, such as the Corpus of spoken American English (Chafe et al. 1992), are not all of equal status – some represent coherent melodic groups, others represent rhythmic groups, and some represent both.

Let us return now to the problem we started with – the anomalous parallelism in Figure 4.4(c). If we apply Ladd's suggestion that some accents can be iterated (as shown in Figures 4.5 and 4.6) we might interpret the 'parenthetical tone group' *and army* melodically as the iteration of a prenuclear tone (low rise), and therefore belonging to the same melodic contour which carries the nuclear parallelism, but marked by the transcribers as a tone group because of other prosodic discontinuities. A similar analysis of Figure 4.4(b) would interpret the postmodifying clause as one coherent 'tune', but with a discontinuity of some kind between the head and the nucleus.

4.3.4   Conclusion

I have shown here that cohesion through parallelism extends over longer and more prosodically complex stretches of speech than other accounts have recognised. However, recovering parallelisms from a prosodically-transcribed corpus such as the SEC is difficult. The transcription is intended to contain mainly phonological information rather than phonetic detail, but both are required for the identification of parallelism: melodic imitation lies in the phonetic realisation of contours which are phonologically of equal status. The examples illustrated here, based on auditory identification, raise interesting questions about the grammar of intonation. However, we should not lose sight of the main function of parallelism, which, as Bolinger pointed out, is as an important cohesive device in speech.

4.4   Parenthesis – a reassessment

The previous section (4.3) examined the way in which some kinds of grammatical units are commonly realised prosodically to indicate a close parallel or additive relationship with what has gone before. Many of these units – such as co-ordinate phrases and clauses, and postmodifiers, are also typical of the kind of units which can be treated as 'asides' or intonational parenthesis. In this section (4.4) I would like to suggest that the prosody of 'parenthesis' as it is typically described, is simply an extreme form of this kind of additive treatment. I would also like to show that there are many other ways of treating an utterance or part of an utterance as parenthetical: the prevailing view of its prosodic realisation, and indeed the concept of what constitutes parenthesis is far too narrow in current intonational research.

4.4.1 The intonation of parenthesis

The intonation features associated with parenthesis in speech have been described by a number of people in the past, including Armstrong and Ward (1931: 27ff), Bolinger (1989: 186ff), Cruttenden (1986: 129), Crystal (1969: 144, 160) and Kutik, Cooper and Boyce (1983). These accounts are consistent in their claim that the most common intonational feature of parenthesis is a pitch-range which is lower and narrower than that of the matrix utterance (Figure 4.7).

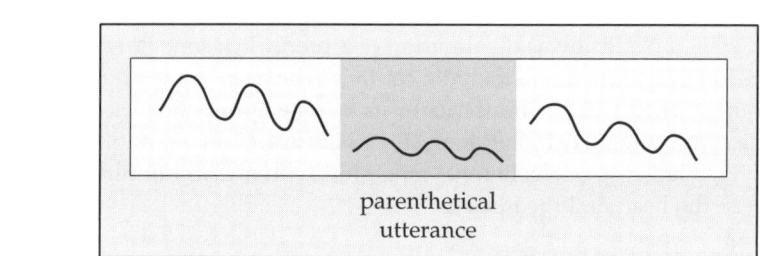

parenthetical
utterance

Figure 4.7 Stylised representation of the prosody of parenthesis – an utterance which is lower and narrower than the matrix utterance.

Bolinger (1989: 186ff) decomposes this pattern into three main prosodic features of parenthesis:

- the parenthetical is lower in pitch than the matrix sentence,
- it is set off by pauses, and
- it has a rising terminal.

Bolinger's account differs from the others in several useful ways. He points out that any of the three features he describes can be suspended and that the application or suspension of the features depends on the length, syntactic makeup and 'nature' of the parenthetical. This is the only account to my knowledge which suggests that not all parentheticals behave alike. He also ascribes a function to each of the features: the lower pitch signals 'incidentalness', the pauses indicate separateness, and the rising terminal functions as a link back to the frame sentence. In his view the presence or deletion of pauses may relate to the length and syntactic makeup of the parenthetical. (Presumably very short parentheticals need not be separated off by pauses.) According to Bolinger, the pitch level of the insertion '. . . depends on the nature of the parenthesis. If it is a question its pitch may well be higher than that of the frame sentence . . . Similarly with a parenthesis offered as a strong appeal or rebuttal . . . If the speaker intends the parenthesis as an essential direction to the hearer to take the frame utterance in a particular way . . .'. Referring to the options in respect to nucleus behaviour he claims that the 'terminal rise may be reduced or suspended depending on the degree of nexus, which in turn depends on discourse factors and to some degree on the point at which the insertion is made'.

This less rigid view of what constitutes parenthesis in speech reflects well some of the variety to be found in the SEC. Finding examples, however, can be a potentially circular business. Parenthesis in intonation is a way of *treating* a word, phrase or clause, and is not necessarily inherent in the utterance itself. However, some kinds of structures are more capable of being treated paren-thetically than others. These include co-ordinated/quasi co-ordinated noun phrases, tag exclamations, adverbials, relative clauses, elliptical clauses, report-ing verb groups, and amplificatory phrases. Figure 4.8 below contains some

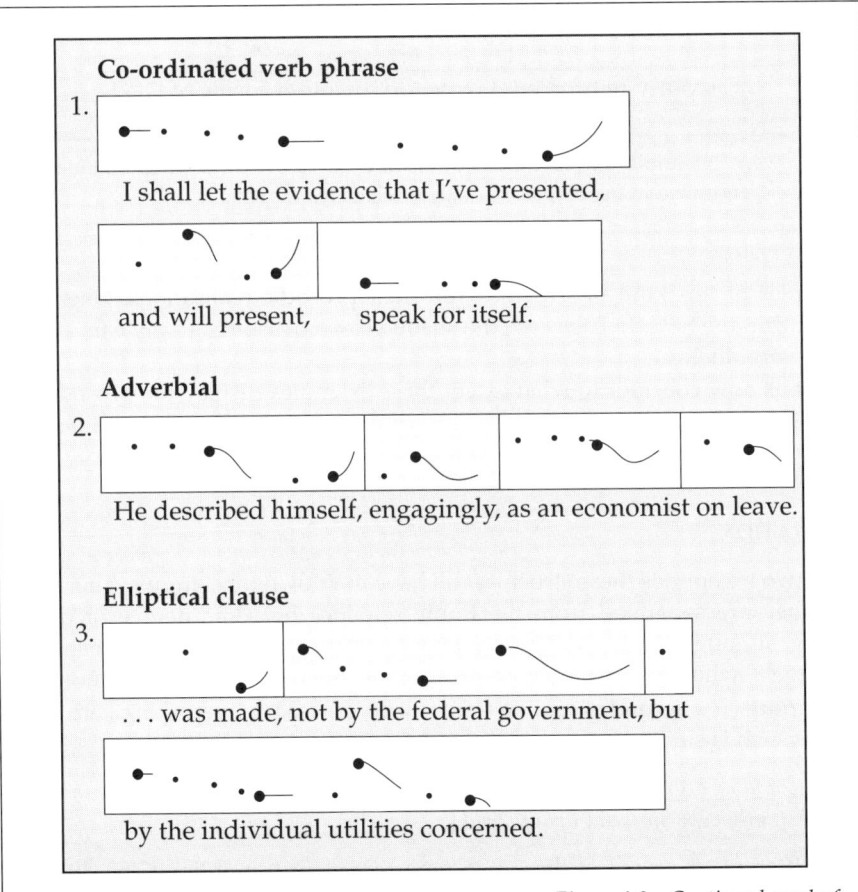

Co-ordinated verb phrase

1. I shall let the evidence that I've presented,

and will present,   speak for itself.

Adverbial

2. He described himself, engagingly, as an economist on leave.

Elliptical clause

3. . . . was made, not by the federal government, but

by the individual utilities concerned.

Figure 4.8   Continued overleaf

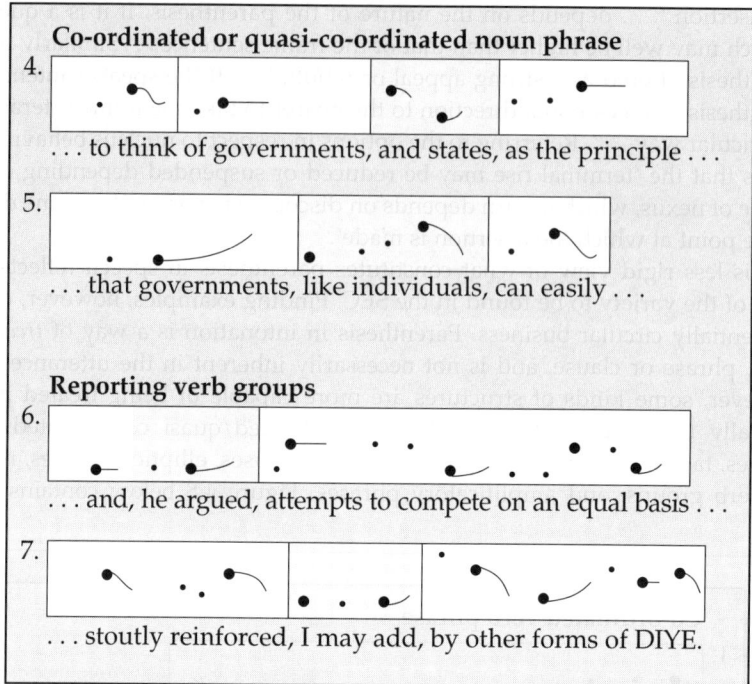

Figure 4.8 Examples of parenthesis in the SEC, text C01. Tone group boundaries are as transcribed in the corpus. Parenthetic elements are shaded.

examples of this kind of structure and their prosodic realisations, taken from text C01 in the SEC. In each case the shaded element *sounds*, to my ears at least, like a parenthetical.

Let us now consider to what extent these examples display the prosodic features suggested by Bolinger: separations (boundaries), pitch range and terminal contours.

SEPARATION

With two exceptions these structures all have their own tone groups. This means that they are separated from the frame sentence by some degree of discontinuity, although this is of course not necessarily a pause. The first exception is example 3, where the parenthesis incorporates the prehead *but* of the following tone group. The second exception (example 6) is a case of a reporting verb group and as such is similar to example 7.

‖ ↘⤴*and he argued* |
‖ ↘*stoutly rein↘forced* | *I may* ⤴*add* |

The different treatment of these two reporting clauses highlights the difficulty of defining tone groups both internally and in terms of their boundaries, and is a prime example of the problem discussed in section 3.3.2 above. Melodically these two clauses are very similar. In terms of the intonational system, however, they have been interpreted differently. This is due to the presence of a pause in example 7. (*Stoutly reinforced* (.) *I may add*) This leads the transcriber to mark a tone-group boundary, and the pitch movement which otherwise would have been regarded as one complex tone, a fall-rise, has been interpreted as a sequence of simple tones, a fall followed by a level and then a rise.[6]

PITCH

Parentheticals are assumed to be given a lower pitch than the frame sentence. This is true of two of my examples (2 and 7), but two examples (1 and 5) are in fact realised at a higher pitch, and three (3, 4 and 6) use approximately the same range as the surrounding utterance.

TERMINALS

Not all parentheticals end in a rising tone: example 5 ends in a fall.

These differences are consistent with Bolinger's view that the typical features of parenthesis, separation, lowered pitch range and rising terminal, may all be suspended. The choice is determined by the communicative function of the parenthetical utterance, whether for example as an incidental aside, an appeal, a warning, or a comparison, or a revision (Bolinger 1989: 185ff).

It is possible, of course, that those examples which do not behave with typical parenthesis intonation are simply not parentheticals. They contain structures which are potentially parenthetical, and I may hear them as such, but that is a fairly subjective analysis, and perhaps not so different from other accounts which are illustrated by equally subjectively-chosen examples. It is a pity that the only experimental study that I am aware of is also flawed, but in a different way. Kutik et al. (1983) asked subjects to read aloud a sentence containing a parenthetical clause which was inserted into a main clause and systematically lengthened (Figure 4.9 overleaf). They then examined the effect on F0 at the beginning and end of the parenthetical, and also on the declination within and around the parenthetical. They found the boundaries of the parenthetical to be marked by a sharp drop in F0 followed by a sharp rise in F0 on return to the main clause. This is indeed the 'typical' intonation of parenthesis, but we must assume that by 'parenthetical' they mean 'has the potential to be treated parenthetically', and probably asked their readers to perform it as such, which begs the question of what the subjects thought that meant. Secondly, their study was limited to one structure, a systematically lengthened comment clause, an unfortunate choice given the prosodic anomalies associated with the structure. Finally, the 'extraordinariness' of the longest item, remarked on by the authors, may lie in the extraordinary unnaturalness of the text. This is of course one of the hazards of using contrived data.

It is still possible, therefore, that the prosodic treatment of sequences which listeners perceive as parenthetical, displays much more variety than the pattern

The clock in the church, it occurred to Clark, chimed just as he began to speak.

. . ., it suddenly occurred to Clark, . . .

. . ., it only just today occurred to Clark, . . .

. . ., it had never until now occurred to Clark, . . .

. . ., it had simply never before occurred to Clark, . . .

. . ., it never in a million years would have occurred to Clark, . . .

. . ., it never in a million years would have occurred to the absent-minded Clark, . . .

Figure 4.9   The systematically extended reporting clause used by Kutik et al. (1983) to investigate the prosody of parenthesis.

represented in Figure 4.7. On the other hand, this pitch pattern is remarkably similar to the effect of onset depression (before the same kinds of structures) described in sections 4.2 and 4.3. It is possible then that the 'typical' intonation of parenthesis is simply an extreme version of this strategy of 'suspending progress', involving pitch depression at the beginning but maintaining the narrow range throughout rather than returning gradually to the range of the matrix utterance.

4.4.2   Defining parenthesis

With the exception of Bolinger, none of the accounts mentioned above suggests that 'parenthesis' itself requires definition. It is assumed by most to be a clearly identifiable phenomenon; and yet if we look at the available definitions we see that it is in fact far from simple. The following sources define 'parenthesis' mainly in terms of syntax and semantics.

> a phrase, often explanatory or qualifying, inserted into a passage with which it is not grammatically connected.   (Collins)

> 1. An explanatory or qualifying word, clause or sentence inserted into a passage with which it has not necessarily any grammatical connection . . .
>
> 2. A passage introduced into a context with which it has no connection; a digression.
>
> 3. an interval, an interlude, a hiatus.   (OED)

> There are two major kinds of relative clauses in English – those that restrict or delimit the noun phrase they modify (restrictive . . .) and those that provide additional parenthetical information (non-restrictive . . .).   Levinson (1983:183)

We can also derive indirect definitions of parenthesis from the following comments on the punctuation conventions known as parentheses (correlative commas / dashes / brackets).

> The comma is the least obtrusive correlative mark and for that reason is preferred unless there is a disruption of the syntactic structure of the clause . . . Dashes tend to give a somewhat more dramatic impression, suggesting an impromptu aside, rather than a planned inclusion. (CGEL III.20)

> Dashes or parentheses are used if the unit included in the sentence is an independent clause . . . (III.20)

> If a sentence or set of sentences is included as a digression in a paragraph, parentheses are required . . . (III.20)

The accounts of parenthetical punctuation above contain reference to different kinds of inclusion in a sentence or text: 'impromptu aside', 'planned inclusion', 'digression', 'disruption of the syntactic structure'. They reflect the variety of definitions earlier. A parenthetical utterance may or may not be a syntactic disruption. It may be planned or spontaneous. It may be semantically more or less related to the content of the matrix sentence; that is, it can digress from or add to the topic. It can be more or less central to the discourse; it can contain information which the addressee may disregard no less than the rest, but which is semantically unrelated to the frame text; it can be an aside (by the way . . . / incidentally . . .), giving the addressee the right to disregard it; or it can be self-addressed (*That reminds me, I must . . .*). As Nosek writes (1973: 100), 'Parenthesis . . . expresses a secondary communication.'

We may be able to define parenthesis in syntactic, semantic or discoursal terms, but we also need to define it prosodically. The examples I have quoted have in common that if they were deleted they would leave the rest of the utterance prosodically coherent. This says nothing about the internal prosody of the inserted element itself. A number of typically inserted items, such as comment clauses and reporting verb phrases can also occur in final as well as medial position. I mentioned earlier (section 3.1.2.1) a number of cases where an utterance ended in an extraposed element realised with a rising tone. There is a case for regarding these as final parentheses (following Svensson 1976, cited by Bolinger 1989: 185), particularly when they are realised with a narrowed pitch range, and this would be a possible explanation for the rising terminal. Reporting clauses can, of course, also occur in initial position, and in Chapter 5 (section 5.3.1, Figure 5.3) I show that these elements can also exploit an narrower pitch range than the rest of the utterance, and might therefore be considered to be 'initial parentheticals'.

It seems to me that there are two possible prosodic characteristics which might usefully be explored: firstly the prosodic coherence of the utterance *without* the parenthetical, and secondly the narrowing or expansion of pitch range of the parenthetical itself. As I will discuss in Chapter 5 (section 5.4) there is considerable evidence that the rhetorical function of individual utterances has a marked effect on pitch range. This may apply equally to the realisation of initial, final or embedded elements within an utterance. There is certainly a need for much more evidence from many different kinds of data before we can be certain that the 'intonation of parenthesis' is as invariant as is currently supposed.

4.5 Summary

In this chapter I have dealt with a number of ways in which the boundaries between text and sentence elements are modified intonationally to show relatedness. I first examined the way in which, in the spoken performance of a written text, a *depressed pitch reset* at the beginning of a (syntactic or orthographic) sentence can create a cohesive link with what has gone before. Pitch depression can also be used at the beginning of a phrase or a clause inside a sentence, and has the effect of suspending progress through an intonational sequence in order to insert additional information. It is exploited in lists, and to indicate the postmodifying function of appositional phrases and relative clauses. It is also exploited by speakers to retrospectively 'undo' an intonational closure inside a syntactic sentence. I then examined the phenomenon of *tonal parallelism* – the phonetic modification of final contours which also has a cohesive function in discourse. The cohesion arises when final contours are imitated in order to integrate 'additional' sequences into the overall intonation contour. Finally I reassessed the notion of *parenthesis*. The typical lowering of pitch at the beginning of the string is the same pitch depression which is shared with a number of non-restrictive postmodifiers. The perception of a sequence as an incidental 'aside' rather than as 'additional' information arises from the way in which the terminal contours are realised. Additional information is integrated chiefly by intonational parallelism – the matching of terminal contours. An aside is not integrated in this way: the final contour of a parenthetical is an independent choice which can be a smaller version of the previous terminal, or it can be a different contour altogether. There are in addition a number of other ways of dealing prosodically with parenthetical items. They can for example be pitched both higher and lower than the surrounding talk, depending on their communicative function. I suggest therefore that the typical prosody of parentheticals (lower, quieter, narrower) is not an independent phenomenon but an extreme case of 'suspending progress', with a specific interactional or discoursal function.

Notes

1   The following examples, however (from Cruttenden 1997), show the inadequacy of seeing the issue simply as one of 'which words to accent' and which not. The first example is straightforward:

>   (i) *(Did you have a good day?) I had a bloody* HOR*rible day.*

Here the final lexical item, by default attracting a nucleus, is 'given' and has therefore been de-accented . The speaker might, however, have responded differently:

>   (ii) *(Did you have a good day?) My* DAY *was bloody* HOR*rible.*

In this case the 'given' information (DAY) *does* receive an accent but is no longer at the end of the tone group; therefore the nucleus can fall on the 'new' information (HOR*rible*) by default.

2   Also preceded by an utterance-final low fall, syllable lengthening, vocal creak, long pause etc.

3   I owe this (reconstructed) example to Peter Roach.

4   This is similar to the tonal grammar of the IPO tradition, which distinguishes between prefix, root and suffix ('t Hart et al. 1990).

5   Gussenhoven (personal communication) accommodates reporting phrases such as this by 'copying' the last (autosegmental) tones (H or L) into the next tone-group (his 'association domain' or 'AD'). [No(H*L) | he(L) said(L).] However, in this analysis the second tone group remains anomalous since it does not contain a starred tone representing an accented syllable.

6   This touches on an important difference between the two transcribers of the SEC. Williams (BJW) consistently transcribes a pause as a tone group boundary. Knowles (GOK) transcribes a pause which co-occurs with a pitch discontinuity as a tone group boundary, but a pause which occurs inside a coherent pitch contour, such as a hesitation pause, as a caret.

CHAPTER FIVE

Paragraph intonation: local and global pitch range in discourse

In Chapter 2 I examined the notion of 'paragraph intonation', the use of pitch to signal the topical coherence of a series of utterances, much in the way a printed paragraph signals such coherence in written texts. There I concentrated on evidence for such organisation from 'beginnings' – local, topic-initial expansion of pitch range. In this chapter I shall examine further the notion of paragraph intonation, but look beyond local boundary events to evidence for global pitch features which characterise a spoken paragraph as a whole.

As a necessary background to this I must consider the status of pitch range variation in current intonational phonology. The phonology of intonation, as it is currently understood, restricts itself mainly to an account of abstract highs and lows (in the American system) or to pitch movement between these targets (the British system). The realisation (or 'scaling') of these targets – where exactly in a speaker's range a 'high' pitch accent or a 'low' boundary tone is placed, is not part of these models. The issue of pitch range is still controversial, as Ladd (1996) has pointed out in a whole chapter dedicated to the problem. There is a tendency to regard gradient distinctions of pitch height as not strictly linguistic, and to ascribe them to the paralinguistic 'ragbag'. Ladd argues very convincingly that this need not be the case. However, if we regard at least some aspects of pitch range variation as linguistic, we must consider how to incorporate them in a linguistic model. In this chapter I shall be concerned with two approaches to explaining pitch range variation: the first defines prosodic domains in terms of locally motivated events, and the other attempts to define global trends which define a given domain internally. Applying this to the intonation of text and discourse structure, we can define large-scale prosodic domains in terms of boundary events only, or we can consider whether there is also an 'internal' definition of such domains. In this way we may make some progress towards the accounting for the 'phonetic realisation of whole texts' (Johns-Lewis 1986: xxiii).

5.1   Local events or global trends?

These two approaches to modelling pitch range variation, or pitch scaling, have so far been applied primarily at the level of the syntactic sentence. They are both intended to account for the same observation, namely that there is a tendency for pitch to decline in the course of an utterance – the well-known phenomenon known as 'declination'. Declination can be seen in two ways: one is to regard it as the result of superimposing an overarching pitch framework upon the intonational string. This is sometimes referred to as the 'overlay' approach, and sees changes in pitch range as a global characteristic of a given domain. The other way to look at it is to interpret it as the result of a sequence of low level, local events.

5.1.1 Models of sentence declination

Sentence-level declination is not a recent observation. It was referred to by Pike (1945, cited by Couper-Kuhlen 1986) as 'drift', and it was later described by Crystal as a descending sequence of onsets. It is certainly true that an isolated declarative sentence uttered in a neutral manner is likely to exhibit a systematic sequence of descending pitch peaks associated with the accented syllables (Figure 1.1 reproduced in Figure 5.1(a)).

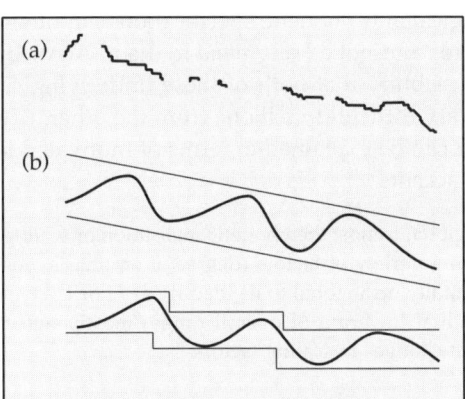

Figure 5.1 (a) F0 contour of an isolated, neutral statement, showing canonical declination pattern; (b) illustration of declination ('overlay' model and 'downstep') from Ladd (1996: 75).

While declination is readily observable there is considerable disagreement about exactly how it should be modelled. Ladd (1993) uses a musical analogy to explain the two main approaches. In one view declination could be compared to a musical tune which consists of a descending sequence of notes. In the other view it could be compared to a tune performed by an unaccompanied singer who gradually goes flat. In the first model, the falling pitch is part of the tune; in the second it is not. In the first, the 'same' notes will be at the same pitch; in the second, each successive occurrence of the 'same' note will be at a slightly lower pitch, usually imperceptibly to the listener.

The 'going flat' models posit an abstract declination line, i.e. a frame of reference to which phonologically equivalent events should be related physically (e.g. to explain their relative prominence). In an earlier review of declination studies, in which he isolates and describes the two broad views underlying the research in this area, Ladd (1984) calls this the 'frame of reference' view (later 'overlay' model) which treats declination as a slope, possibly of physiological origin, which is superimposed on an utterance over a specified domain.

Much empirical work on declination, whichever the underlying theoretical assumptions, relies on statistical information drawn from actual F0 contours.

> . . . models which are ostensibly models of a declining component or frame of reference are actually models of average trend lines. Trend lines are simply fitted to few salient points in contours – usually the obvious peaks and valleys – and the average characteristics of many such trend lines are taken to represent the decline of the phonetic frame of reference. (Ladd 1984: 56)

However, as Ladd argues, it is only helpful to model trend lines if they are fitted to points which are phonologically the same, and what counts as phonologically 'the same' will of course depend on the theoretical model.

The other view of declination, the descending tune model, is that it is 'determined by phonological and phonetic specifications', in other words a *product* of phonological features and not a *background* to them. According to Ladd we cannot rule out the possibility that both of these underlying causes are operating together, but it is very difficult to tell one from the other. Ladd is confident that most of declination can be explained in terms of motivated local adjustments to the height of pitch accents.

> Local sources for global trends: the phonetic realisation or scaling of any given H or L tone depends on a variety of factors (degree of emphasis, position in utterance, etc.) that are essentially orthogonal to its identity as H or L. Overall trends in pitch contours (e.g. gradual lowering of overall range) mostly reflect the operation of *localised* but *iterated* changes in scaling factors. (1996: 43)

The phonologically-motivated lowering of successive pitch accents is known as 'downstep', while the term 'declination' now tends to refer both to the phenomenon itself and to the 'overlay' approach to modelling it. Figure 5.1(b) illustrates the two models, overlay ('going flat') and downstep, which may account for sentence declination.

While 'downstep' can account for declination across a single utterance, and even across a single tone group, van den Berg et al. (1992) for example model it both within and between tone groups, which they call 'association domains' or ADs), the apparent higher-level declination across paragraphs has not to my knowledge been explicitly modelled in this way. But however it is modelled, there is so far no clear agreement on the domain or domains of declination itself. Clark and Yallop (1990) claim rather cautiously that: 'Declination can generally be observed over identifiable units of the intonation system, often corresponding to clauses or clause complexes' (p.285). Few analysts are explicit about the domain: most declination studies show evidence of gradual declination across a single utterance, in most cases a simple sentence, while at the other end of the scale we have the suggestions such as the following by Cruttenden (1986) that it operates across whole paragraphs – a kind of supradeclination.

> There is . . . some suggestion that it may be operating at an even higher level to produce 'paratones' in speech (particularly read speech) akin to paragraphs in written language. (Cruttenden 1986: 126–7)

5.1.2 Paragraph declination

The distinction made in the study of sentence declination between local events and global trends has similarly been made in studies of discourse intonation. Studies of spontaneous speech tend to focus entirely on local events (e.g. Brown et al. 1980, Lehiste 1975, 1979, Nakajima and Allen 1993) such as I have discussed in Chapters 2, 3 and 4. These are the so-called boundary phenomena – prosodic events, such as pitch reset, pause and low final F0, which occur at the boundary between two topical units. Studies of read-aloud speech are mainly concerned with finding global trends (e.g. Bruce 1982; Garrido 1993; Sluijter and Terken 1993, Thorsen 1985). These focus on coherent patterns, such as a gradual narrowing of pitch range, which identify the unit of discourse as a whole. Only a few studies have looked at global patterns in spontaneous speech (Douglas-Cowie and Cowie 1997, Schuetze-Coburn et al. 1991).

The most familiar model of paragraph intonation is the notion of the 'paratone', which despite some ambiguity is basically a model which defines its domain in terms of what happens at its boundaries. I shall first examine this model, and then go on to examine another notion, 'supradeclination' which is an attempt to define a discourse unit internally, based on global trends, in analogy to the sentence-level phenomenon of 'declination'.

5.2 Models of paragraph intonation

5.2.1 'Paratones'

The idea of a prosodic, paragraph-like unit based on *boundary* phenomena underlies the notion of the '*paratone*', although it actually started life as the term for a *global* pitch pattern. In a study which focuses on naturally-occurring data (both spontaneous conversation and read speech), Brown (1977) proposes the notion of the 'paratone', in analogy with the paragraph in writing, to describe intonational patterns associated with a series of related utterances. This early account of a 'paratone' is based on the behaviour of 'tonic' (nuclear) pitch contours. Brown observes in her data that each successive tonic syllable in a sentence displays a wider pitch movement than the last, and that a similar pattern is observable across a complete topical unit.

> . . . the movement of the pitch of the voice on the last tonic syllable in the sentence is greater than that on the previous tonic syllable in the same sentence. . . . If we go on to study the organisation of a whole news item we shall find that the final tonic

syllable in the complete item is marked by an even bigger pitch movement. So all
the tonic syllables of what we might call the 'paratone' after the model of 'paragraph' are grouped together. (1977: 86)

While this clearly reflects well-known patterns at the level of a syntactic sentence,
the notion that the link lies in the width of the pitch movement on the tonic, has
not to my knowledge been observed elsewhere, and is not asserted again by
Brown. In later work, Brown et al. (1980) continue to refer to 'paratones' but no
longer refer to them as units determined by the width of nuclear contours, but
instead by the presence of pauses and high pitch resets. They also point out that
these speech paragraphs are much shorter than a paragraph in writing:

> The speaker typically organises his speech into 'paratones' – a short sequence of units
> beginning with a stressed peak high in the speaker's range. These paratones are
> very much shorter than written paragraphs and, in the style of conversation dis-
> cussed here, often much shorter than those which occur in formal speech (especially
> speech that has been to some extent pre-rehearsed). In general they are only three
> or four units long. (1980: 26)

and particularly short in spontaneous speech:

> ... the organisational blocking of speech paragraphs (as manifested by pauses and
> also ... by pitch patterning) produces shorter units, even in written texts read
> aloud, than typical orthographic paragraphs. We shall find this even more strik-
> ingly the case in spontaneous speech. (1980: 54)

Perhaps in order to distinguish between short sequences with a coherent overall
pattern (similar to a major tone group in the SEC, and roughly the length of a
complex sentence) and 'speech paragraphs', larger topical units, marked by an
extra high onset pitch at the beginning, Brown et al. (1980) propose the distinction between the *'minor paratone'* and the *'major paratone'*. Both are by this time
defined in terms of boundary features (pause and high beginnings).

> We shall then distinguish between major paratones, which follow topic pauses and
> are characterised by very high peaks ... and minor paratones which follow contour
> pauses and begin with lower peaks ... (1980: 71)

All subsequent references to paratones (Brown and Yule 1983) appear to refer to
the *major* paratone, or speech paragraph.

> At the beginning of a paratone, the speaker typically uses an introductory expression
> to announce what he specifically intends to talk about. This introductory expression
> is made phonologically prominent and the whole of the first clause or sentence in a
> paratone may be uttered with raised pitch. (Brown and Yule 1983: 101)

We have now moved from the concept of a prosodic unit which has an internal
regularity (increasingly wide tonic pitch movements in the minor paratone) to
a unit which is defined purely in terms of its boundary features: low pitch and
a lengthy pause followed by a high sentence onset. Thus despite its earlier
incarnations the paratone is fundamentally a unit which is defined externally,
i.e. by prosodic events at its boundaries. It seems that the higher up one goes in

the intonational hierarchy, the harder it becomes to identify units according to internal criteria and the greater the tendency to resort to external (boundary) phenomena.

5.2.2 'Supradeclination'

To decide if there is such a thing as 'supradeclination', a gradual lowering of pitch over a topic unit (or paragraph), in analogy with the notion of declination across a single utterance, we must consider the evidence. Evidence for internal, global pitch trends across paragraphs comes mainly from controlled, experimental studies, typically using specially constructed texts read aloud. Such studies of internal systematicity of speech paragraphs have observed a systematic lowering of pitch across a read-aloud (written) paragraph. This is sometimes expressed in terms of the average F0, the initial onset height (first accented syllable), or the onset height of both topline and baseline.

One study of this kind is Sluijter and Terken's (1993) study of read speech. A five-sentence paragraph was specially designed so that the same sentence (modified by the use of connectives to make for a coherent text) could occur in four out of five positions (positions 1, 2, 4 and 5). Averaging over a number of speakers they found that while the sentence finished at the same pitch regardless of its position in the paragraph, the initial values of both the topline and the baseline were on average higher, the earlier the sentence occurred in the paragraph (Figure 5.2). This, they claim, is evidence of a global declination trend across a paragraph similar to that across an individual sentence.

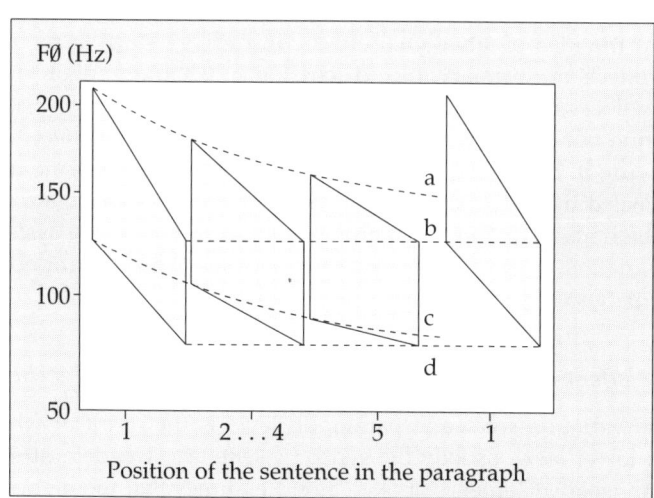

Figure 5.2   Average starting and ending pitch values (of both top-line and base-line) of sentences in initial, medial and final position in a read paragraph (from Rietveld and Van Heuven 1997, after Sluijter and Terken 1993).

A similar trend is observable in naturally-occurring data. In the corpus text SEC B04, for example, we find that the first sentence in a paragraph (news item) is on average the highest, the last is on average the lowest, and intervening sentences begin on average somewhere in between. Unfortunately, descriptions of this trend tend to be overinterpreted as meaning that in general each sentence in a paragraph will begin slightly higher than the next. In fact *average* values obscure individual patterns which are not as tidy as such trends would suggest. Although there is a tendency for a global lowering of onsets across paragraphs, individual paragraphs do not exhibit this neat regularity. They are, to put not too fine a point on it, messy, and in the next section I shall discuss one of the factors which may operate to obscure any underlying orderliness.

5.3 Looking for supradeclination in natural data: some obscuring factors

An example of the unorderliness of natural texts in comparison with the findings of Sluijter and Terken can be found in Figure 2.2. It shows that while there is a systematic topic reset on each paragraph, all subsequent sentence beginnings display no obvious regularity. Indeed, some critics suggest that the regularity observed in experimental studies is simply a function of the decontextualised reading on which such experiments are based. But as Cruttenden points out (1997: 121): 'this sort of argument, that declination only occurs in fairly "mechanical" reading styles, is in one way an argument for the usefulness of the concept. . . . it is a useful reference point for all those non-mechanical styles where textual and situational effects intrude.' This is a controversial view – those who approach intonation (and grammar) from a functional perspective would take exception to the idea of situational effects 'intruding', since in their view the situational effects are primary. (See discussion in Chapter 6.) For the moment though I will assume that there is some underlying 'default' pattern, and attempt to find out exactly what those 'textual and situational effects' are which tend to obscure it. In other words, if we assume that there is some underlying system, revealed by the experimental condition, we can investigate deviations from it in the hope of finding what else is going on – competing systems, paralinguistic variation, or simply idiosyncratic oddities, which might obscure that underlying pattern.

5.3.1 The effect of information structure on sentence declination

Some of the variation we see at paragraph level is the result of what is happening at a lower level, usually the syntactic sentence. The default declination pattern of an isolated sentence spoken aloud assumes that the highest F0 peak occurs on the first accented syllable. However, if the topic phrase shifts within the sentence the highest peak may also shift with it, in which case the first accent in the sentence may not be the highest. The default pattern may therefore arise simply because isolated sentences (especially those used in laboratory experiments) tend to start with the topic phrase, or because 'mechanical' reading tends to ignore the internal information structure of the sentence. The shifting of information structure in a sentence is the result of previous or subsequent information in a text; if there is no text other than the sentence itself this is unlikely. However, as soon as we deal with the performance of a text, i.e. coherent sequences of sentences, we must be prepared for contextually-determined changes of information structure in any one sentence, and consequently that the highest F0 peak is not necessarily the first.

This is in part due to the cumulative occurrence of anaphoric reference. As we saw in Chapter 4, items at the beginning of a sentence which refer back to previous items in the text, and are therefore to some extent 'given', tend to be downgraded prosodically. They may be deaccented altogether (more common in spontaneous speech than in prepared speech such as this news summary), or alternatively we may find that the height of the accented syllable is suppressed relative to that of the 'new' information, the 'topic expression' (Yule 1980).

There are a number of structures which will be either anaphoric or in some other way non-focal, and which may therefore delay the maximum F0 peak. These will of course vary from text to text and from genre to genre. In text SEC B04 we can identify the following:

- Reporting clauses: *Aden Radio said . . . ; A spokesperson said . . .*
- Adverbial expressions of time or place: *At a news conference . . . ; During meetings . . . ; In the Commons yesterday . . .*
- Existential *there*: *There's since been . . . ; There were fears earlier that . . .*
- Cleft sentence: *It became clear afterwards that . . .*
- Initial subordinate clause: *Although investors . . .*
- Noun phrases, particularly with a definite determiner: *The offer . . . ; The Westland chairman . . .*

Figure 5.3 shows the F0 contours of sentences containing these structures. These contours show that in each case the highest F0 value is reached *after* the initial, non-focal expression.

Compare these sentences with the sentence in Figure 5.4. This displays the canonical declination pattern, starting high and ending low. It is significant, however, that this sentence is taken from the start of a new topic, precisely where we least expect any anaphoric reference or initial non-focal information.

In Figure 5.5 (page 111) we can see how these two kinds of patterns (with and without delayed F0 peak) combine in two successive sentences. The first is topic initial: 'It will be wet and windy . . .'. The second begins with a clearly anaphoric noun phrase 'The wind and showers . . .'. The non-focal information is downgraded, meaning that the initial reset is suppressed to indicate anaphoric cohesion, and the highest F0 peak is delayed until the following verb phrase.

During the course of a coherent unit of text we must expect an accumulation of anaphoric links, and therefore it is very likely that the highest peak will be delayed in most sentences other than that which opens the topic. We can see this happening across a whole text if we graph the height of the *first* accent (allowing

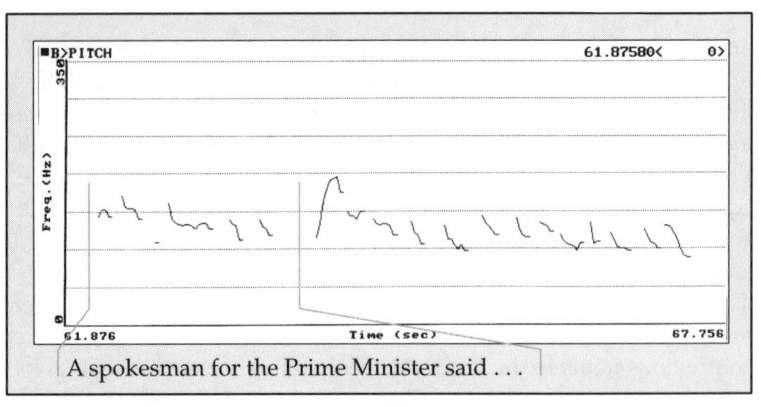

A spokesman for the Prime Minister said . . .

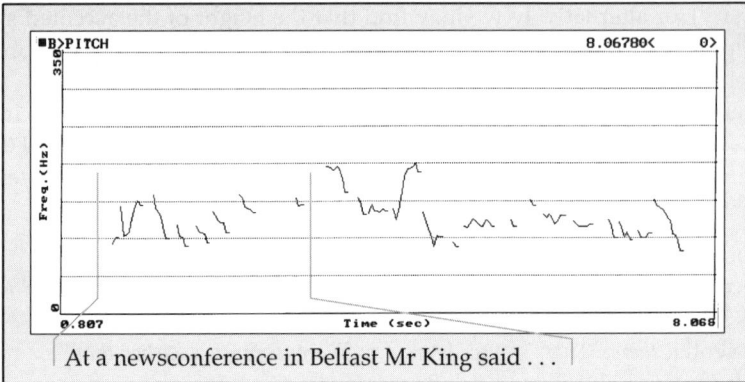

At a newsconference in Belfast Mr King said . . .

Figure 5.3 F0 contours from SEC B04 illustrating the delaying effect of initial, non-focal information on the position of the highest F0 value.

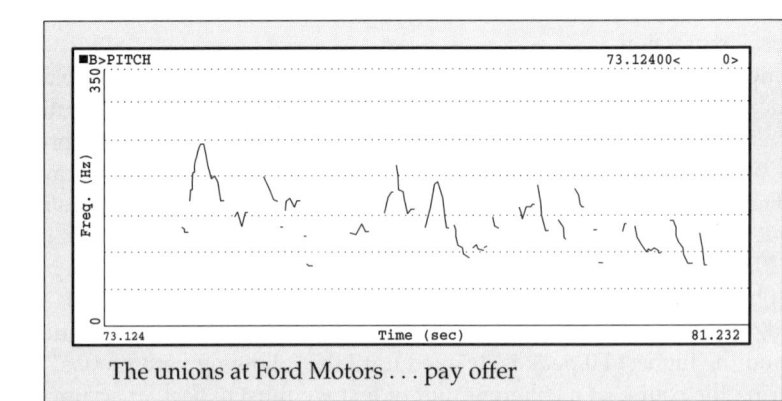

The unions at Ford Motors . . . pay offer

Figure 5.4 F0 trace of two topic-initial sentences (SEC B04) which display the canonical declination pattern with the highest F0 value in initial position.

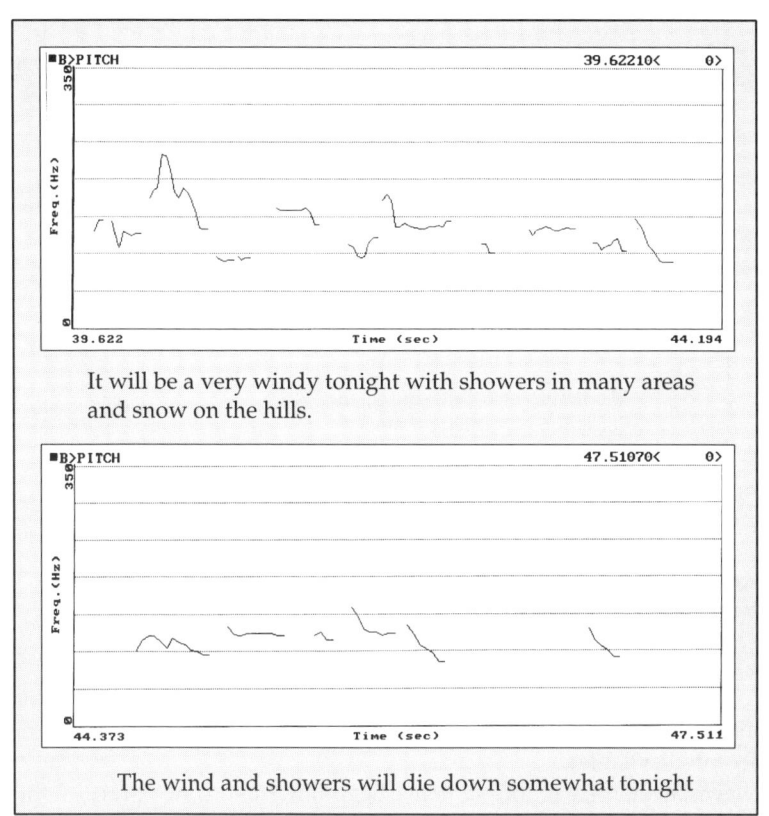

Figure 5.5 F0 contours of two successive sentences (SEC B04), showing a canonical declination pattern in the first, and a suppressed onset and delayed F0 maximum in the second. ('It will be very windy tonight with showers in many areas and snow on the hills. The wind and showers will die down somewhat tonight.')

for the fact that this might occur outside the accented syllable, see Chapter 2) against the *highest* accent in each sentence throughout the text. Figure 5.6 (overleaf) shows both measures together for each sentence in each paragraph in the text, in their order of occurrence. We see that in the first sentence of each topic, the first accent and the highest accent are identical. Thereafter the two measures diverge, and the sentence onset is lower that the F0 maximum. Where the two measures are identical *inside* the paragraph, this is motivated by the beginning of a sub-topic, related to the current topic, which is clearly marked by the speaker as a minor topic shift.

We have now some evidence of the influence of information structure on declination at sentence level. It affects the pitch height of the accents associated with non-focal information and delays the 'normal' sentence-initial reset until later. This could account for at least some of the irregularity across paragraphs

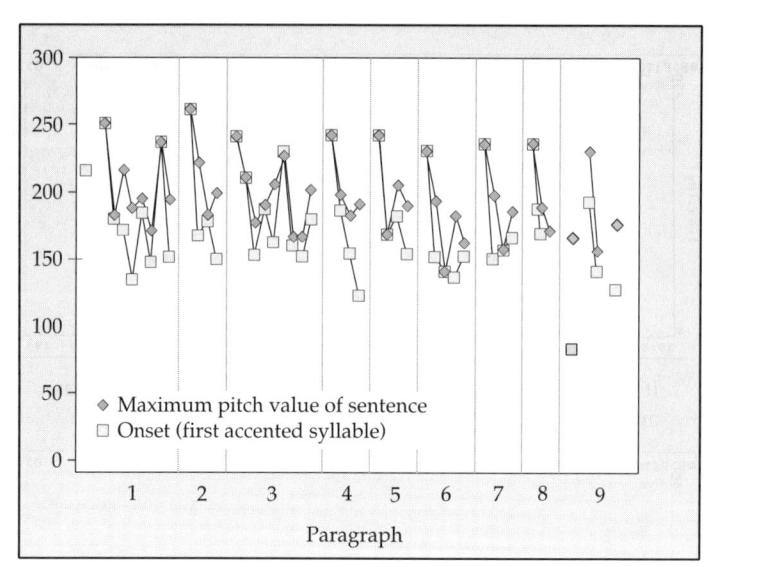

Figure 5.6 Sentence initial pitch height ('onset') against F0 maximum ('max') for each spoken sentence (major tone group) in a news broadcast (SEC B04).

when the trend is judged according to the height of the *beginning* of the sentence (first accented syllable).

However, even if we ignore sentence beginnings and concentrate on the highest pitch in each sentence irrespective of where it occurs in the sentence, there is still considerable irregularity, as we will see in the next section.

5.3.2   *Evidence for supradeclination*

While we cannot generalise from multiple performances of the same text, as Sluijter and Terken are able to do, the SEC provides the opportunity to examine read-aloud speech which is unconstrained. What do real (professional) readers do with real texts? We have already seen in Chapter 2 that they use *local* prosodic phenomena to indicate topic shifts. In the news broadcasts we saw that each news item began with an extra high pitch reset, the typical indication of a 'beginning' of a speech paragraph. News items are also separated by the predicted long pauses, so that we have a clear boundary / discontinuity signal. But these are all events which allow us to define a spoken paragraph externally, i.e. in terms of its boundaries. We can now consider whether there is any evidence of internal regularities. Do speakers also display the global pattern of declination across paragraphs which experimental studies suggest?

In order to compare my data with that in experimental studies I had to find a way of accommodating paragraphs of different lengths. For purposes of comparison I have considered the *first two* and the *last two* sentences of each paragraph (these are the positions which Swerts, Sluijter and Terken have found most predictable). One paragraph in my text had only two sentences; these were categorised as 'first' and 'last'. One had three sentences; these were categorised 'first', 'second' and 'last'.

The problem which then arises is what exactly to measure. We not only have the problem of deciding what counts as the 'same' in a paragraph, we also need to be able to compare the findings with those of experimental studies, which use chiefly acoustic measures unrelated to any underlying phonology. If we are to provide evidence for an overlay model of declination, at whatever level in the hierarchy, one should compare like with like, i.e. items which are phonologically equivalent. Since there is no phonology of the paragraph, or rather, since that is what we would like to find out, we have few pointers to what constitutes the 'same'. The most uncontroversial comparison is firstly to compare all sentence-initial accented syllables (sentence onsets),[1] then, secondly, to take into account the observed effect of information structure. I assume that the *highest* peak is in some sentences a *delayed first* peak and take the highest F0 of each sentence as the point of comparison. Finally, I will compare the *mean* F0 of each sentence, thus using a measure which avoids making any decisions about which points in a sentence to compare.

5.3.2.1 DECLINATION ACROSS SENTENCE ONSETS (THE FIRST ACCENTED SYLLABLE IN EACH SENTENCE)

The strict view of 'supradeclination' predicts a gradual and systematic lowering of sentence onsets across the paragraph. The height of the onsets (initial accented syllables) in the first and last two sentences of each paragraph are shown in Figure 5.7 overleaf, where we see that while the first onset (sentence 1) is systematically higher than others, onsets in the other positions behave less systematically, particularly that of the second sentence. Indeed, if we assume for a moment that the topic onset is a local, discursally triggered event, and exclude it from our analysis, there seems to be little regularity in the behaviour of the other onsets. Only one (number 4) of the 9 paragraphs, (here) news items, displays the strict paragraph declination predicted by experimental findings.

5.3.2.2 DECLINATION ACROSS F0 MAXIMA: THE HIGHEST F0 PEAK IN EACH SENTENCE

Figure 5.8 overleaf shows the height of the highest F0 peak of each sentence, regardless of its position in the sentence, factoring out the effects of information structure. The analysis of F0 maxima over paragraphs shows a pattern similar to that of sentence onsets. While we might expect a regular decrease in pitch height for each sentence (represented again here by the first two and last two, for the sake of comparison), we find only that the first is always the highest. In only three of the 9 paragraphs (6, 8 and 9) do we find any further sign of regular paragraph declination. (Note that paragraphs 8 and 9 only contain three and two sentences respectively, and are thus not typical.)

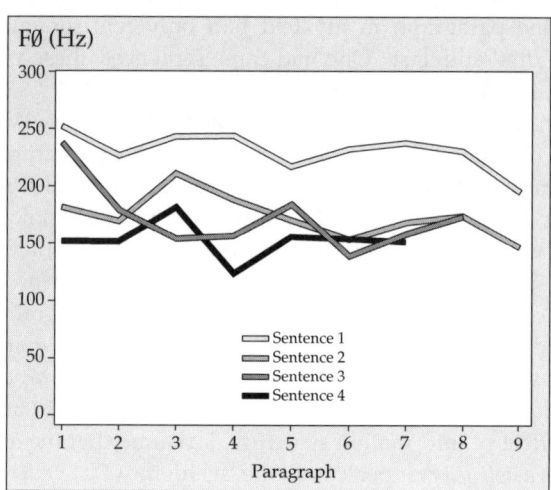

Figure 5.7 Height in Hz of the first accent in major tone groups ('spoken sentences') 1–4 (the first two and the last two in each paragraph) across 9 paragraphs (SEC B04).

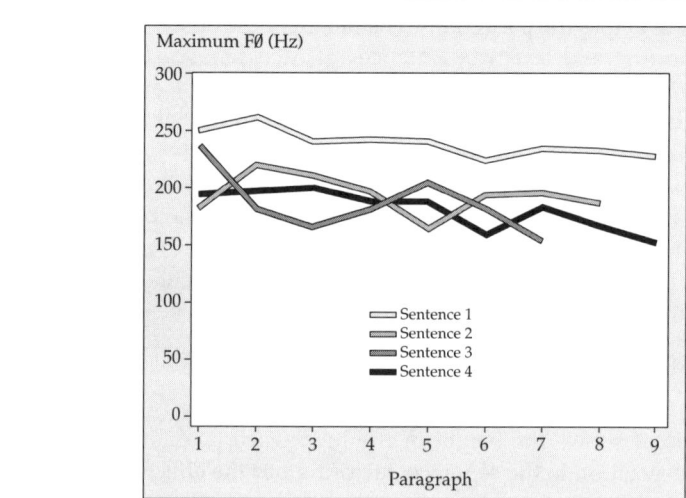

Figure 5.8 The height of the highest F0 peak of each major tone group (spoken sentence), regardless of where it occurs in the sentence.

5.3.2.3 DECLINATION ACROSS THE MEAN: THE MEAN F0 FOR EACH SENTENCE

If we wish to avoid altogether having to decide which points in a sentence are the 'same' we can take a global measure of F0 trends over an utterance, calculating the mean F0 for each sentence in each paragraph (Figure 5.9). Paragraphs 1, 2, and 7 could be said to decline systematically, although in each case the paragraph-internal sentences differ very little from one another.

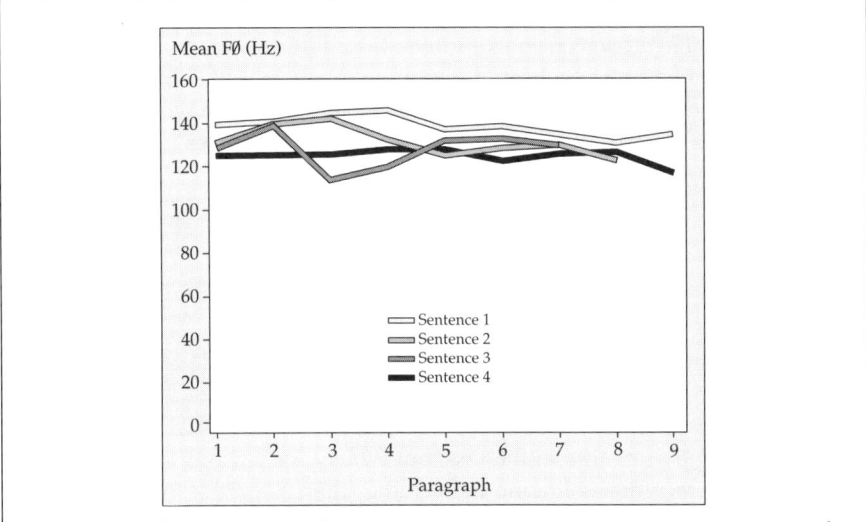

Figure 5.9 The mean F0 of the first two and last two spoken sentences in each paragraph.

The comparison with Sluijter and Terken (1993) is of course only partially possible, since their results are based on averaging over a number of speakers, any one of whom is unlikely to have performed with the regularity of the pooled results. We do have nine paragraphs compared to their one paragraph, but even so, we only find an *average* lowering across the paragraphs, but we do not find a regular lowering of onset height across any individual paragraph. Nor do we find a regular downward trend if we factor out the possible influence of information structure and selecting the maximum F0 peak in each sentence instead of the first. Comparing all three measures (Figures 5.7, 5.8 and 5.9) the only systematic finding is that the first utterance is always the highest, clearly as a result of the extra-high topic reset. If an underlying 'supradeclination' trend exists there are clearly factors other than information structure operating to 'obscure' it. One such factor is described in the next section. It is related to the discourse status of the individual sentences within the paragraph, i.e. the rhetorical relations between the sentences.

115

5.4 Pitch scaling and discourse status

The rhetorical relations between unit of discourse have been described by a number of people (see Chapter 1) and the categories used, while not identical, have similarities. Mann and Thompson (1988), for example, use terms including 'elaboration' (additional information about subject matter), 'background', 'restatement' 'solutionhood', 'concession' and 'antithesis'. The problem with this and other such models is that there is probably no closed set of such relations, and each new text will generate the need for additional categories. The alternative approach (e.g. Grosz and Sidner 1986) is to avoid specifying the semantic relations between discourse segments and simply to refer to dominance relations which hold between them (based on goals / intentions). (For a taxonomy see Hovy 1993.)

For any one text only a subset of discourse relations will be present, particularly in the rather formulaic genre of a news summary. I have identified four main categories to account for the relations between sentences in SEC B04. They are as follows:

- new topic
- additional information, same topic (paratactic relation)
- elaboration / explanation of previous sentence (hypotactic relation)
- reformulation of previous sentence.

(A similar set of categories is used by Nakajima and Allen (1993), in work discussed in section 6.2.2.)

There is one additional category necessary – metatextual comment – to account for three sentences in the text, but which, for reasons I have explained in Chapter 2, I consider as linking items rather than as part of the text itself:

> Now it's one o'clock and this is Peter Bragg in London with the Radio 4 news summary.
> And finally the weather.
> And that's the news and weather with the time just after five past one.

I will illustrate the four main categories with sentence pairs from the text. Their categorisation is of course dependent on their status in the text as a whole, and not on how they might appear in isolation.

1. new topic, 2. reformulation:
The Westland chairman, Sir John Cuckney, said the workforce was suffering because of uncertainty over the company's future. Westland had gone through an eight-month period of turbulence which had been thoroughly bad for the staff.

1. new topic, 2. addition:
Workers from the Gartcosh steelworks near Glasgow who've marched to London as part of a campaign to save the plant from closure have held a meeting with the Labour party leader Mr Kinnock.[2] But their request for a meeting with Mrs Thatcher has been turned down.

1. addition, 2. elaboration:
Liberal leader Mr David Steel described the Prime Minister's decision not to see the marchers as a slap in the face for Scotland. During meetings this morning with a

number of MPs the men said they believed the whole of Scottish steel industry would be at risk if Gartcosh closed.

These categories can be ranked in order of their position in a discourse hier-archy, or in terms of their level of embedding. A *new topic* is clearly at the top of the hierarchy. Next is *additional* information on the same topic; this is classed as paratactic since if the same relationship held between two clauses they would be regarded as co-ordinate. *Elaboration / explanation* I regard as hypotactic informa-tion which could be in a subordinate clause inside a single sentence. The fourth category, *reformulation*, is slightly problematic. Its ranking depends on whether we consider the repetition of new information to be 'new' or 'old'. It clearly ranks lower than the information which it reformulates, but not necessar-ily lower than other categories. Its salience may or may not be tied to that of the utterance it reformulates. In this text, reformulation only occurs with new information,[3] so the most appropriate ranking of salience is as follows:

1. new topic
2. reformulation
3. addition (new information, same topic)
4. elaboration

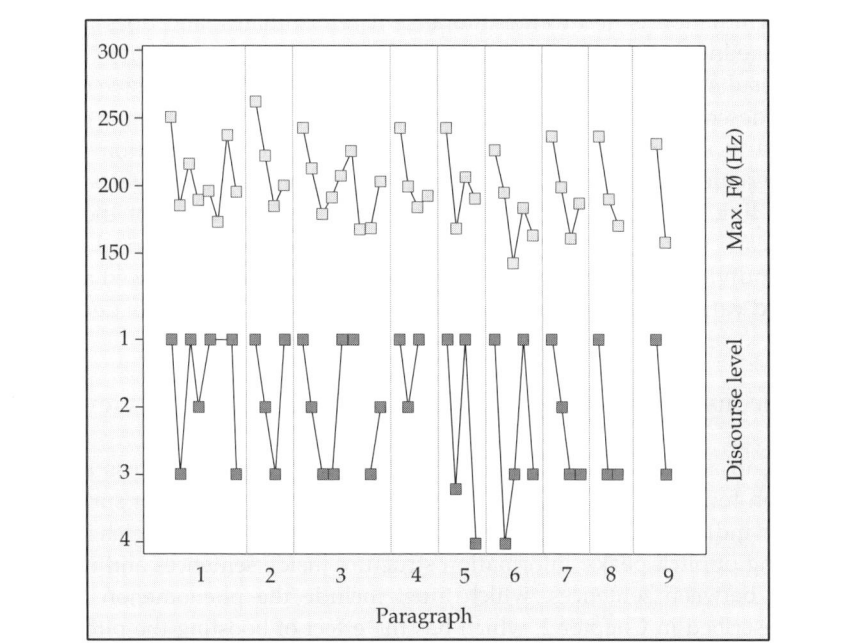

Figure 5.10   Ranked discourse categories (1–4) against the F0 maximum (the highest accent) in each spoken sentence.

Figure 5.10 shows that by plotting the F0 maximum of each sentence against the ranked discourse categories we find a positive correlation between degree of discourse salience and the scaling of the maximum F0 value. The less news / information value the sentence contains the lower the F0 maximum. In other words, when the salience of the sentence goes down, the maximum pitch of the sentence also goes down. This correlation is *not* found with the onset value, i.e. the height of the first accent in each sentence.[4]

We find, then, that in addition to the effect of information structure on pitch scaling *inside* sentences, the rhetorical relations *between* sentences have an effect on the global pitch scaling of individual sentences. A shift from a 'new' topic to 'additional but related' information seems to generate a step down in pitch, while a shift from 'background' information (e.g. elaboration or explanation) to 'new' or 'additional' information prompts a step up. Only a shift between sentences of *equal* rhetorical value ('new'–'new' or 'addition'–'addition') does not appear to have a systematic effect on scaling. The second of the two can be both higher and lower than the first. The 'reformulation' of a sentence is downgraded in relation to its predecessor, but the transition from a 'reformulation' to a 'new' or 'additional' piece of information is governed by the sentence preceding the 'reformulation'. Thus the sequence 'new'–'reformulation'–'addition' will involve a downgrading, while the transition 'new'–'reformulation'–'new' may cause downgrading or upgrading, just as the sequence 'new'–'new' (without the intervening 'reformulation') can upgrade or downgrade. This supports the view that reformulation is tied to the utterance it reformulates, and does not affect pitch range independently.

The results of this analysis suggest that the anaphorically cohesive onset depression described in Chapter 4, and the downgrading of initial sentence elements, described in section 5.3.1 of this chapter, are based on information structure *inside* the sentence, and serve a similar purpose – to signal a cohesive, backward-pointing link between two consecutive utterances. The height of the highest peak of each sentence, on the other hand, depends on the rhetorical relations *between* individual sentences. Both phenomena, however, can be seen as locally motivated variation, and occur independently of a global 'overlay' of declination.

5.5   Reconsidering paragraph declination: a composite view

In trying to account for both the global trend to declination across a spoken paragraph found by Sluijter and Terken (1993) and the absence of such a clear pattern in individual paragraphs, we have identified two factors which influence the scaling of pitch peaks: information structure inside sentences and rhetorical relations between sentences, which must include the phenomenon of 'topic reset', described in Chapter 2, which has the effect of boosting the pitch height of the first accent in a topical unit.

(i) *Information structure* can affect both the placement of accents in a tone group (a known effect of given and new) and the position of the most salient accent in the sentence, and thus the beginning of sentence declination may be delayed. This downgrading of accents on initial, non-focal sentence elements may operate together with a depression of prehead syllables to create the cohesive device described in the previous chapter. Figure 5.11(a) shows a stylised representation of a canonical sentence contour. Figure 5.11(b and c) shows how the highest pitch peak can be delayed by downgrading the pitch prominence (pitch scaling) on non-focal sentence elements at the beginning of the sentence.

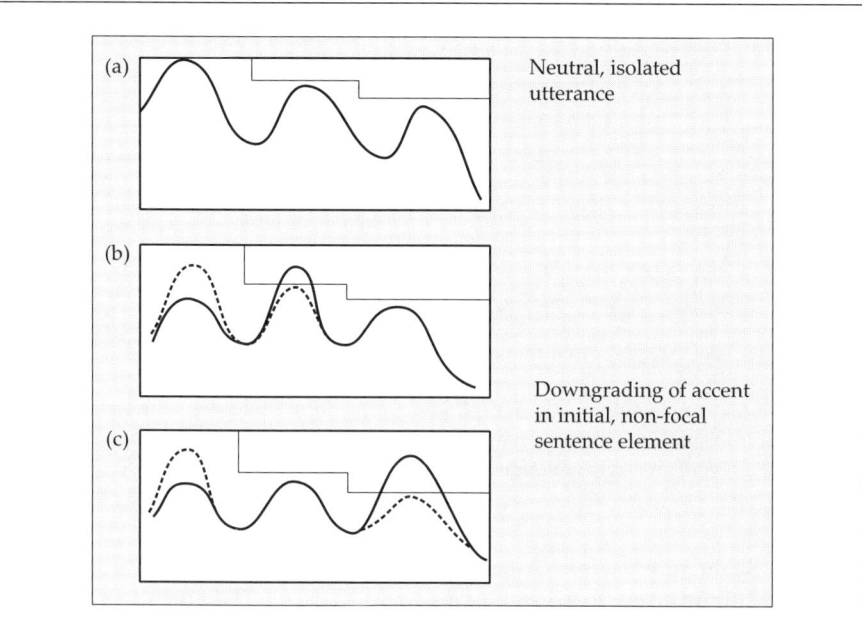

Figure 5.11   The effect of non-focal information with downgraded pitch prominence on canonical sentence declination.

(ii) *Rhetorical relations* between individual sentences, which of course also operate between clauses – usually made explicit by conjunctions – have an effect on the scaling of the pitch range of a whole sentence. A hierarchy of 'newness' can be observed. The most familiar of these is the extra high topic reset – the boosted pitch prominence of the first accent of a new topic, followed in subsequent sentences by topic continuation, topic elaboration, and topic reformulation (Figure 5.12 overleaf).

The combined effect of information structure and rhetorical relations is illustrated in Figure 5.13 overleaf, which represents an imaginary paragraph, containing four sentences. The effects of information structure occur inside the overall range determined for each sentence by its place in a hierarchy of 'newness'.

In order to account for these observations in a way which is as consistent as possible with existing models it seems necessary to make the distinction between a global 'tilt' to the realisation of an utterance or sequence of utterances, possibly of physiological origin, and the view of declination as the cumulative effect of successive local features. Sluijter and Terken's observation of an overall

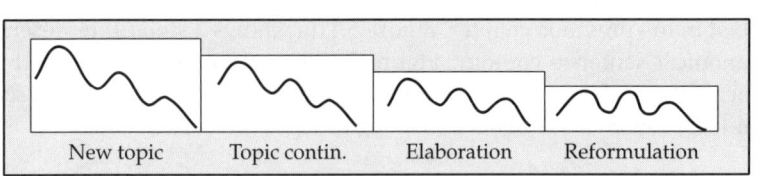

Figure 5.12 The scaling effects (expansion or narrowing of pitch range) of the rhetorical function of different sentences.

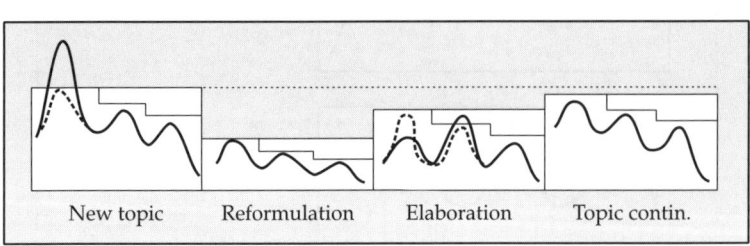

Figure 5.13 An imaginary paragraph containing four sentences, illustrating the effect of information structure on the scaling of individual accents inside sentences, and the effect of rhetorical relations on the overall pitch scaling of each sentence.

trend to declination across a paragraph can be seen as an overlay inside which the linguistically motivated scaling effects occur. The imaginary sentence illustrated in Figure 5.13 can be represented again inside such an overall declination trend (Figure 5.14). In this way the apparent messiness of individual paragraphs in naturally-occurring data can be accommodated within the clear trends observed in experimental data.

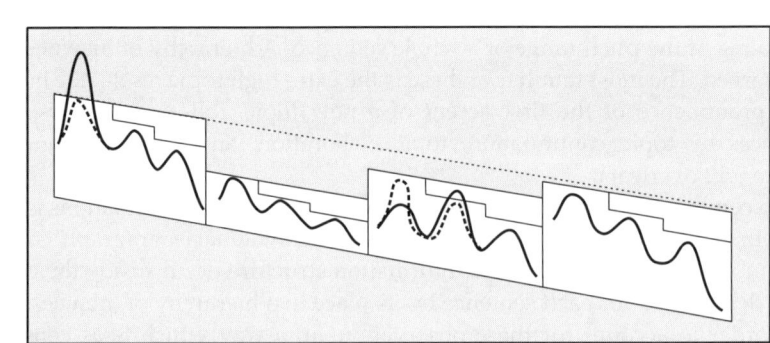

Figure 5.14 The combined effect of an overall paragraph declination and the linguistically-motivated scaling effects of rhetorical relations and information structure (illustrated in Figure 5.12).

5.6 Summary

In this chapter I have discussed the notion of paragraph intonation, the view that there is a characteristic global pitch trend across whole units of discourse ('paragraphs'), analogous to the phenomenon of declination over a single sentence. There is a widely shared intuition that there is some overall shape to a spoken paragraph, but concepts such as 'paratone', deriving from studies of naturally occurring data, have mostly been defined on the basis of strong boundary phenomena, rather than any identifiable trend which is internal to the discourse unit. I think we may assume that something like 'supradeclination' – a systematic lowering of pitch throughout a spoken paragraph – exists, with evidence both from highly controlled experimental data, and also from natural data. Nonetheless, if we take any one individual paragraph we are unlikely to find that successive sentences behave observably in such a neat way. We can therefore see 'supradeclination' as determining an 'envelope' within which linguistically motivated variation operates. I have attempted to explain how apparently unsystematic patterns across individual paragraphs may be linguistically motivated.

First of all, there are factors which affect the relative pitch scaling of consecutive sentences, and this relative scaling depends on the meaning relations between them. Some sentences introduce a new topic or sub-topic, some give new information on the current topic. Some simply elaborate on, or explain, the previous sentence. In news broadcasts, and perhaps in journalistic texts in general, a sentence may simply repeat the previous sentence in other words (reformulation). Any attempt to give a definitive list of semantic relations is over-ambitious, however, and I have restricted myself here to a limited hierarchy: from the most 'new' – the announcement of a new topic – to the least 'new' – the elaboration of previous sentences. At each transition from one point to another in the hierarchy the global scaling of the current sentence is reset to reflect its relationship to the previous one.

Secondly, there are a number of factors which affect the scaling of pitch prominences *inside* individual sentences. The common assumption that a sentence will display regular declination is based on the behaviour of sentences spoken in isolation. Sentences which form part of a coherent text, on the other hand, are influenced in their internal organisation by their co-text, and a reader's performance will be influenced by the information structure reflected in that organisation.

To summarise then, the downward trend observed by Sluijter and Terken (1993) across sentence-initial accents in a paragraph is evidence for an 'overlay' kind of declination – a gentle 'going flat' across the paragraph, but the pitch scaling *inside* that overlaid 'envelope' is a different phenomenon. It is motivated by meaning and meaning relations, and operates at a number of levels. This locally motivated scaling of individual accents and of whole intonation groups may account for much of the seemingly random variation in real texts. Any further claims to the existence of paragraph intonation must, in my view, take account of these competing effects.

121

Notes

1   I also take into account the timing of F0 peaks in relation to the accented syllable, described in Chapter 2. There we saw that the sentence-initial position of an accented syllable, especially if it is also topic-initial, has the effect of delaying the peak even beyond the syllable itself. We are therefore theoretically justified in measuring the F0 maximum *associated* with an accented syllable, but not necessarily co-occurring with it.

2   This is treated as two spoken sentences by the reader (separated by a major tone group boundary).

3   The reformulation sentence, which simply repeats the content of the first sentence in other words, appears to be a common element in the structure of news reports.

4   Spearman's rho: discourse salience with F0 = −0.679 (significant at the .01 level).

CHAPTER SIX

Intonation in conversation: structure and meaning

6.1   A theoretical framework

In the previous chapters I have described intonation patterns, or realisations of patterns, which can guide the listener through what might loosely be called 'monologues', for the most part the spoken version of a prepared or scripted text. I have treated texts as 'autonomous textual units whose internal parts stand in systematic relationship to one another' (Schiffrin 1994: 285), the components of which are analysed post hoc, and independently of how they might be embedded in surrounding talk.

These intonation patterns, particularly in the case of reading aloud, appear to be closely related to grammar. This is hardly surprising, since in the absence of an interactional context,[1] there is not much other than syntax for the reader to orient to. My description of beginnings and ends is thus closely related to grammatical units such as the clause or sentence, and, to some extent at least, to orthographic units such as the paragraph. What happens in between – the 'middles' – is largely a matter of cohesion: relations between grammatical elements – inside the sentence between smaller elements (insertions, asides, additions, elaborations) or between sentences themselves inside a higher order structural unit. However much the motivation may be semantic rather than syntactic, the appearance of a close association with syntactic structures cannot be denied.

But we now turn to how intonation is used in conversational interaction. This requires us to consider not just the *textual* influences on intonation but also the effect of the interactive context. We have seen how intonation organises 'spoken prose'. Now we must consider how it organises the collaborative event which is conversation. I am using the term loosely here, to mean an unscripted spoken text constructed between two or more participants. Typically, perhaps, we think of informal conversation between peers, but there are of course different kinds of conversation or 'activity types' (Levinson 1979: 368) which include interviews, debates and service encounters such as, for example, telephone enquiries. In contrast to such asymmetrical and often specifically goal-oriented dialogues, casual conversation is assumed to be informal, symmetrical, and have primarily the function of upholding social relations. Conversation Analysts devote much attention to this kind of interaction, while the demands of speech technology create a greater interest among speech scientists in goal-oriented, asymmetrical encounters, such as eliciting train information etc. Thus the kind of data currently being examined for the role of intonation depends very much on the perspective of the analyst. Other approaches to the analysis of conversation (Discourse Analysis, Pragmatics) go beyond closely-observed structural features of conversation, and take into account the wider context in which the talk occurs, relating language to relatively stable contextual features such as social class, region of origin, ethnicity etc. (discourse analysis) and to more ephemeral features such as social role or relative status (pragmatics) (see Thomas 1995: 185). Such analysis works on the premise that the coherence of discourse cannot be understood solely on the basis of linguistic structures and propositional meaning. The role of intonation in this wider sense of interactive meaning has so far over the years been relegated to the unsatisfactory category of 'attitudinal intonation'. I will revisit this issue towards the end of this chapter.

Despite differences, there is a shared assumption that intonation does have a role in the organising of the interaction. There remains, however, a greater divide between approaches to intonation in general, which reflects divergent views of language itself. The formal view of language underlies most current intonational phonology (see Ladd 1996). It is a fundamentally generative approach, and one which is greatly encouraged by the technology-driven context in which much of it takes place. (Much work is motivated by speech synthesis, where the only practical way to generate acceptable intonation is to derive it from a prior syntactic analysis.) The methods used are largely experimental and rely for evidence on introspection or on perceptual judgements made in an interactional vacuum. This approach in relation to *grammatical* analysis has recently been explicitly addressed by Ochs et al. (1996), who refer to work carried out in a controlled experimental environment as

> the product of largely invisible premises underlying much linguistic and psycholinguistic work at present – in which the primary organisation of language is situated at the syntactic, semantic, lexical, and phonological levels, with only the surviving, unordered 'details' – the 'residual variation' – being referred to pragmatic or sociolinguistic or interactional 'factors'. (pp.25–6)

Ochs et al. offer instead an opposing view of language, maintaining that interactional and pragmatic needs 'play a **primary and formative role**, rather than a residual one, in the organisation of . . . talk . . .' (p.26) and that grammatical structures should be '. . . revisualised as interactional structures that have their own interactional morphology and syntax within and across turns' (p.40).

This view of the role of interaction in determining the grammatical organisation of language is also reflected closely in most recent work on intonation in conversation (Couper-Kuhlen and Selting 1996), which uses the same detailed approach to data analysis as Conversation Analysts but focuses in particular on the contribution made by prosody (especially pitch and rhythm phenomena).

The Conversation Analysis (CA) framework involves a number of method-ological tenets which concern what constitutes acceptable data and what constitutes acceptable evidence. As far as data is concerned, priority is given to naturally-occurring talk as a means of reconstructing 'members' prosodic devices for achieving their conversational goals' (Couper-Kuhlen and Selting 1996: 25). This is a dramatically different view from that which claims, for example, that experimental data reveals the 'real underlying system', from which natural speech will deviate. It begs the whole question as to whether in studying dis-course intonation we are investigating its primary organisation or whether we are trying to identify 'residual variation' which, if it is factored out, will leave us with an underlying intonational phonology. Generative phonologists argue the other way round of course: that only by factoring out the underlying phonology can we identify contextual, textual, and affective influences on our exploitation of pitch.

Most importantly CA insists that the evidence for claims about interactional structures must come from the behaviour of the participants themselves. For example, if an intonation feature is claimed to indicate 'continuation', this is supported if participants refrain from taking a turn at that point, despite the opportunity provided by a pause. CA Analysts claim that '. . . participants' own handling of prosodic cues within this context . . . enables empirical proof pro-cedures for the validation of analytic categories. In other words the theory relies crucially on the way prosody is deployed in real interaction' (Couper-Kuhlen and Selting 1996: 24).

To summarise then, there are divergent views on what constitutes the prim-ary function of intonation, and indeed how to approach a more abstract model. Much current intonational phonology assumes implicitly at least that there is an underlying 'grammar' of intonation, closely related to syntax, which happens to be exploited for interactional purposes, and which is subject to contextual and textual 'interference' in the way it is realised phonetically. Conversation Ana-lysts, on the other hand, assume that intonation is primarily a signalling device fulfilling interactional needs – the need to jointly construct and negotiate verbal interaction. These functions may then happen to be exploited in scripted speech for signalling syntactic relations.

Notwithstanding the theoretical divisions, all approaches are fundament-ally structural. Conversation Analysis is concerned primarily with uncovering 'structures' in conversation – building blocks such as turn-taking rules and adjacency pairs, openings and closings etc. It is my view that these cannot be an end in themselves but are one step on the way to explaining interactional *mean-ing*, which relies crucially on an understanding of how these structures operate in a social context. The many approaches to the study of interpersonal meaning, broadly subsumed under the heading of 'pragmatics', rarely take intonation into account. The contribution of intonation to meaning still lurks unsatisfac-torily under the 'paralinguistic' or 'attitudinal' label. This is a convenient but unenlightening way of accounting for what ultimately matters most in human interaction – what people mean.

6.2   Semantic framing / topic structuring:
the units of discourse and the relationship between them

By far the most important work involved in interaction is the process of main-taining it. This requires co-operation in a number of conventions, including ordered turn-taking, observing the maxim of relevance, and seeking and provid-ing confirmation of receipt. Keller (1981) has provided a useful set of categories for classifying speaker intentions in conversation, based on a large-scale study of what he calls 'gambits'. Gambits, otherwise known as 'discourse markers' or 'conversational routines' (Aijmer 1996) are formulaic utterances, more or less syntactically independent, ranging from the very short such as *well, OK, right* to longer ones such as *The way I see it is this, Another thing is, Believe it or not, That reminds me*. Keller categorises these expressions as having a variety of functions which I have conflated as the following:

- **semantic framing:** these are expressions which show the rhetorical function of an utterance, i.e. how a contribution relates to the content of the talk. These relationships include: 'major semantic field indicators' (topic initiation, digres-sion, return to topic); subject expansion (adding, explaining, restating a point); summarising
- **turn-taking (including backchannel)**
- **attitude** (receptive, supportive, disagreeing, backing off)

Gambits are of course verbal messages to interlocutors, and a few such as *well* and *now* (Hirschberg and Litman 1987) have been studied in terms of how they are realised prosodically. Our concern here is with the possiblity that there are also prosodic messages which may accompany and reinforce or modify such expressions, but which may also substitute for them. An aside, for example, may be signalled by the expression *by the way*, but may also simply be indicated by the sudden compression of pitch range, faster tempo and decreased amplitude commonly associated with parenthesis. In the following I should like to set out some of the prosodic features, in particular those concerning pitch, which have been observed to indicate the rhetorical status of utterances, just as 'gambits' or 'routines' do it explicitly. First, however, we need to consider exactly what we mean by a spoken 'utterance'.

6.2.1   The 'spoken sentence'

Most formal attempts at modelling discourse ask the same question: 'how do we organise language into units that are larger than a sentence?' (Schiffrin 1994: viii). That leaves us, however, with the problem of what exactly we mean by a 'sentence' in the context of speech. Sometimes a cluster of criteria is used, includ-ing the grammatical, pragmatic and prosodic, to identify the spoken equivalent of sentences (Nakajima and Allen 1993 and section 6.2.2 below). However, the boundaries of such grammatical, pragmatic and prosodic units may or may not coincide (du Bois and Schuetze-Coburn 1992). We have already seen (Chapter 3) that even in the oral performance of written texts readers do not always map their spoken units (major tone-groups in the SEC) exactly onto orthographic sentences. The hierarchy of intonation units is therefore something to be investigated in its own right, starting with the smallest unit which is assumed to be the tone-group (intonation unit) 'a stretch of speech bounded by a single coherent intonation contour ' (du Bois and Schuetze-Coburn 1992: 229). It is rare, however, for such a small unit to be perceived as a complete 'spoken sentence', and a way of seeing how these are grouped together to form a larger unit is described in the following investigation of declination in spontaneous speech.

Schuetze-Coburn et al. (1991), in a study of spontaneous American English speech, found that declination operates across several tone-groups or 'intonation units' (IUs). '. . . declination is not necessarily reset at each IU boundary, but . . . commonly extends over a sequence of two or three (and occasionally more) IUs' (p.227). They question the assumption, prevalent in experimental literature, that an intonation unit equals a sentence, and that the basic declination domain is the intonation unit. That this is not so is hardly a surprise to anyone who has worked with naturally-occurring data, but is nevertheless problematic for some intonational phonology.

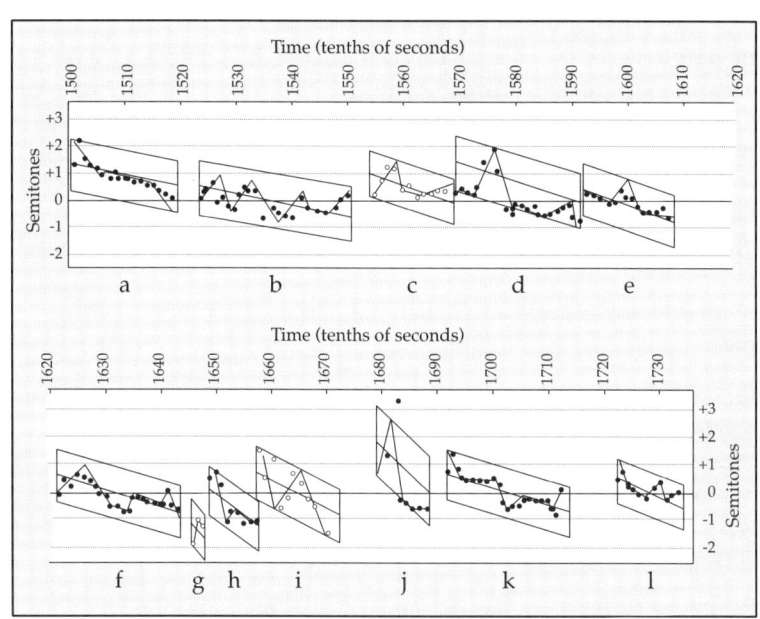

Figure 6.1   After Schuetze-Coburn et al. 1991: A study of declination in spontaneous speech: In this study, declination was calculated in such a way as to normalise across speakers. F0 plots were stylised and divided into sections sharing a common declination line, which was based on a calculated average F0. This only took account of fairly large pitch variation – small changes were ignored. A parallelogram grid was constructed with a height = +/−1 standard deviation from midline. Outliers were disregarded.

> . . . declination in normal Americal English conversation frequently extends beyond the scope of standard prosodic phrasing. The adequacy of the 'intonational phrase' as the primary domain for declination is thus called into question.　　　(p.231)

The study reveals that Declination Units (DUs) are nearly always longer than intonation units, i.e. contain one or more IUs. (See Figure 6.1 on previous page.) This is very reminiscent of Brown's minor paratone (see Chapter 5) – a domain larger than a tone group but not necessarily as large as a topical unit. In fact it is also similar to the major tone group of the SEC. The declination unit as described by Schuetze-Coburn et al. is thus close to what we might call a 'spoken sentence', and gives us an independent acoustic measure of what is otherwise an elusive building block in the hierarchy of units in spoken discourse.

6.2.2　Meaning relations between 'spoken sentences'

A more eclectic approach to identifying the 'spoken sentence' is taken in a study by Nakajima and Allen (1993). This is a study which provides statistical evidence of how pitch variation can indicate the relations between successive 'sentences', signalling to the listener whether a sentence contains a continuation of the previous topic, an elaboration, or initiates a new topic.

Their data reflects the typical concern of speech technologists with simple goal-oriented encounters, naturally enough, since this is the kind of interaction which they hope to be able to simulate. It consists of simulated telephone conversations (speakers had no visual contact and communicated by microphones and headphones), and covered a very restricted topic domain (getting advice on how to transport manufactured goods to a specified city by a certain date). In total they used approximately one and a half hours' speech from six sessions.

They divide their data into Utterance Units according to the following principles:

- Grammatical principle (where there could be a full stop, or before a sentence conjunction)
- Pragmatic principle (Unit should correspond to a speech act)
- Conversational principle (Unit boundary if speaker changes)
- Prosodic principle (pause longer than 750 ms – to exclude search/repair pauses)

They then classify the boundaries between one utterance and the next on the basis of the the the semantic relationship between them. They arrive at four main boundary classes as follows: (Each class contained a number of sub-classes which have been omitted here.)

- Topic shift [TS]
- Topic continuation [TC]
- Elaboration [ELB]
- Speech act continuation [AC]

These classifications reflect closely those described in Chapter 5 (section 5.4).

Nakajima and Allen's findings show that each boundary class can be identified on the basis of a combination of three measures: the pitch at the beginning of the utterance, the pitch at the highest point in the utterance, and the pitch at the end of the utterance.

1. Utterance beginning: this is the F0 of the pre-head, or in their terms the 'onset' – the F0 at the beginning of the first stable part of the F0 contour, whether or not it is associated with a stressed syllable. The height of the 'onset' above the baseline of an utterance is shown to be related to its discourse status: onset height declines from Topic shift (TS is markedly higher than the others) to Topic Continuation to Elaboration, which is similar to Speech Act Continuation (TS > TC > ELB ≈ AC). This shows that even the beginning of the pre-head gives some indication of the topic status of the utterance – important for automatic speech recognition (ASR) when the phonological status of parts of the F0 contour is not known, and the system has to rely simply on the acoustic signal.

2. The highest pitch: the authors measure the relationship between two utterances in terms of the *'peak F0 ratio'* = the highest F0 of one sentence divided by the highest F0 of the preceding sentence. This is also found to vary according to the nature of the transition, but discriminates slightly differently. It produces a stronger discrimination than onset height between ELB and AC: 'speech act continuation' maxima are higher than 'elaboration' maxima. The authors claim that since continuation is co-ordinate and elaboration is subordinate, co-ordinate utterances are less suppressed than subordinate ones. This measure, however, does not discriminate strongly between TC and AC.

3. End of utterance: this measure discriminates least between the utterance boundaries – further evidence for the relative stability (and therefore probably physiological origin) of utterance endpoints. The only high utterance-final F0 is found where the next utterance is, in their terms, a continuation of the same speech act.

Nakajima and Allen's findings can be represented in a stylised fashion (Figure 6.2 overleaf), showing the way in which pitch range is exploited to reflect the rhetorical relationships between successive utterances. These observations of interactive data (albeit artifically constrained to simulate human-machine interaction) in fact only deal with the rhetorical relationships inside turns, not across turns. It is therefore not surprising that they reflect the same intonational responses to discourse relations in read speech, described in Chapters 4 and 5, and strongly support the idea that the relations between successive utterances are reflected primarily in the degree of pitch expansion above the base line. Closely anaphorically related utterances are realised in a compressed range, while topic initial utterances show the most marked upward expansion.

Studies such as this one are motivated by the need in ASR to identify the relationship between successive utterances in real time on the basis of local prosodic

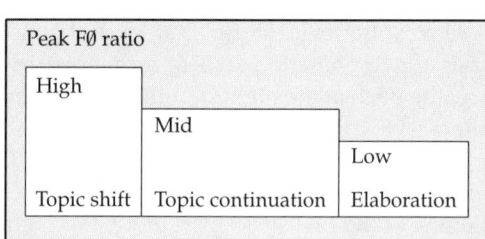

Figure 6.2   The difference in pitch range, in terms of peak F0 ratio, between different kinds of utterance in dialogue (based on the findings of Nakajima and Allen 1993).

signals.[2] The next study is more concerned with post hoc observations of more global changes in the course of a conversation.

6.2.3   *Meaning relations between discourse moves*

In the previous two sections we have looked at the intonation of the 'spoken sentence' and the rhetorical relationships between them. We now move to a study of the intonational correlates of larger units of discourse (Douglas-Cowie and Cowie 1997). In contrast to the study described in the previous section, which concentrated mainly on local indications of inter-unit relations, i.e. those phenomena located at the boundaries between units, this study is of global pitch effects – pitch range characteristics of whole constituent units of discourse.

Douglas-Cowie and Cowie (1997) describe the systematic exploitation of pitch range or register over the course of recorded telephone conversations. This is a study of features of intonation which are sustained across discourse and which the authors refer to as 'intonational settings'. It examines 16 business phonecalls, between university secretaries and outside callers, in which only the secretaries' voices were recorded. The calls were analysed into basic units of discourse which reflected functional categories based on the model of Sinclair and Coulthard (1975) and its later developments (e.g. Coulthard 1992, Francis and Hunston 1992). These units are assumed to be continuous and non-hierarchical, i.e. a linear arrangement of functional 'moves'. The units identified and analysed were: openings, transactions, preclosures and closures (a few others were also identified but were too infrequent for useful statistical analysis). The results of the analysis show that these conversational moves typically take place in a 'tonal space' (to use Ladd's term) which varies from compressed to expanded pitch range. Since speakers' baselines tend to be fairly constant, these tonal spaces are normally created by widening the pitch range upwards. (See Figure 6.3.)

As the authors point out, these findings are unlikely to be unique to phonecalls, but their categorisation of constitutents leaves the whole body of a conversation (in between opening and closing moves) unanalysed. We do not know whether the components *inside* this middle section can also be identified by characteristic pitch range 'settings'.

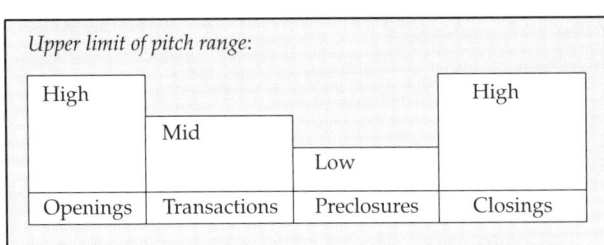

Figure 6.3   The pitch ranges exploited in the course of telephone conversations, based on the findings of Douglas-Cowie and Cowie (1997).

The authors suggest that the dimensions which they observe may relate to patterns of interaction in a wider sense, and that exploitation of pitch range may relate in some way to the speaker's degree of engagement with the message, with the interlocutor or both. This link between pitch range and engagement is referred to by Tench (1996: 123): 'The general characteristics of the departures from normal pitch range seem to display the speaker's relationship to the listener. With a wide range, the speaker is warm and open towards the listener . . . with a narrow range, the speaker is cold towards the listener and may well not be interested in any response.' This interpretation of a speaker's feelings and intentions is in my view too narrow. Nonetheless, it may indeed be true that the apparently greater involvement associated with high pitch is more hearer-oriented, which would be appropriate for the more phatic and formulaic sections of a conversation such as openings and closings, while the lower range could suggest a more neutral, proposition-oriented attitude. Whether this is interpreted as 'warm', 'cold' or 'indifferent' is a separate issue, depending on the expectations of the participants.

One disadvantage of this particular study is that (for good ethical reasons) we have no knowledge of the pitch patterning across the speakers involved. Do speakers co-operate in shifting from one range to another? Who initiates the shift? What happens when a shift is not successfully negotiated? These are questions which might usefully be addressed if the promising approach described in the study were applied to conversation more generally.

6.2.4   Summary

This section has been concerned with the intonation of units of conversation above the sentence. We considered first the notion of the 'spoken sentence' and then looked at two studies of how the relationships between such sentences or utterances is reflected in the realisation of boundary features at the transition between them. Finally we examined a study of larger units of conversation – and the way in which global intonation characteristics are related to the function of these units. This way of decomposing discourse into its constituent parts is based on their contribution to the talk, whether in terms of the semantic relationships between utterances, or the functional relationships between longer stretches of talk. There are clearly other structures, however, which are of prime importance in conversation and these will be discussed in the next section.

6.3 Turn-taking

In addition to looking at spoken discourse from the point of view of its coherence in terms of function and content, we can also look at the way in which the interaction itself is organised. Studies of conversation show that it is a highly structured activity and that participants in a conversation follow tacit conventions in a co-operative way. Taking turns at speaking is one of these conventions, and requires of participants that they recognise when they may or may not take a turn. In order to do this, participants must be able to respond to a number of signals. They must first of all be aware of certain conventions that dictate, for example, that a question requires an answer, that a summons requires a response, and that a greeting requires a greeting. But they should not only know *why* they should take a turn, but also *how* it is done smoothly.

In the following I will describe some studies of how intonation can provide cues to smooth turn-taking in addition to semantic and syntactic signals.

6.3.1 Smooth turn-taking

Early studies of intonation cues to the end of a turn include Yngve 1970 (cited in Cutler and Pearson 1986), Duncan 1972, Beattie, Cutler and Pearson 1982, Cutler and Pearson 1986). Production correlates of end-of-turn include pause and changes in pitch and amplitude, but this does not necessarily tell us what is used by listeners as a perceptual cue. Yngve shows that pauses are *not* used as a turn-taking cue, not surprising since most turn exchanges occur with no intervening pause. Cutler and Pearson aimed to establish first of all the existence of 'perceptually effective turn signals' (1986: 143), and secondly what these might be. They explicitly do not address the production question of what speakers actually do in natural conversation, since reading aloud experimental utterances is clearly not 'natural conversation'. They feel justified, however, in dealing with perception, since the listeners 'at least have a task which approximates the normal case. . . . The very premise of this study . . . is that such judgements must regularly be made in the course of normal everyday conversation' (1986: 143–4).

Limiting their study therefore to the issue of perception, Cutler and Pearson constructed five dialogues which were read aloud in two versions by ten speakers. In each dialogue there was a pair of sentences which made sense in the context in whichever order they were spoken. In each version of each dialogue one of the sentences was turn-final, the other turn-medial. These ten sentences, two in each of five dialogues, were the subject of analysis. They were then judged in isolation according to whether they were perceived as 'final' or 'medial'.

The intonation feature which correlated most highly with the perception of turn-final utterances was what they called 'downstep' (a 'tonic syllable starting significantly lower than the previous syllable'), and correlating most highly with turn-medial utterances was 'upstep' (a 'tonic syllable which starts on a higher pitch than the previous syllable') (p.149). The authors find no other features which correlate significantly with listeners' perceptions of turn-medial and turn-final utterances. They remain 'in no doubt that this feature was used by . . . listeners as a basis for categorising utterances as turn-final or turn-medial' (p.150).

Cutler and Pearson equate their 'downstep' feature with Crystal's 'drop' or 'low drop', and their 'upstep' as Crystal's range of 'booster' (Crystal 1969: 144–5). 'Upstep' and 'downstep' respectively also correspond closely to the 'high' and 'low' falls described by Cruttenden (1986, 1997). In the experiment described in Chapter 3 (see Wichmann 1991b) a low fall similar to the 'downstep' or 'low drop' was consistently perceived to sound most final. Cutler and Pearson's work therefore confirms the general principle set out in Chapter 3, which is that the lower the starting point of a fall, the more final it will sound. It is therefore not surprising that a low fall constitutes a strong turn-ceding signal[3] (see Figure 6.4).

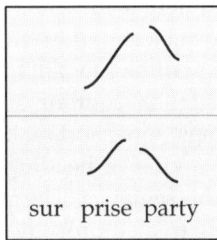

Figure 6.4 Two contours (high and low fall) identified as turn-final and turn medial (after Cutler and Pearson 1986).

6.3.2 Topic control: creating conversational space

We have seen that there are certain signals given by speakers that they may cede the floor. Sometimes, however, it is important to keep the floor. One of the advantages of having a turn at speaking is that one has control over the topic of the talk. Speakers are therefore obliged to not only take a turn but keep their turn if they are to develop or change a topic. Often the tacit agreement in casual conversation that speakers should take frequent turns militates against speakers having the extended turn needed to develop a topic or tell a story. In order to do this they need to create 'conversational space' (Schiffrin 1987: 16). The strategies needed to do this depend very much on the nature of the interaction and the roles of the participants.

6.3.2.1 NON-COMPETITIVE TALK

There are some kinds of talk in which one speaker explicitly, or implicitly, has the right to an extended turn. This is the case for example in interviews, the purpose of which is to elicit talk from the interviewee with as little prompting as possible from the interviewer(s). Another example is the radio phone-in, where callers are often expected to make their contribution without too much prompting, although topic control remains the prerogative of the journalist. In each case we are therefore able to observe how speakers organise their own turns in a non-competitive environment, i.e. without undue fear of interruption.

A common way of projecting a long turn, and thus controlling the topic, is for speakers to suggest a number of points they would like to make. This can be done more or less explicitly: by saying *There are two (three, four etc.) points I would like to make,* or simply by starting with *first of all / firstly / in the first place* etc. In example (1) the speaker has adopted the second strategy by starting with *number one,* and in a subsequent contribution with *one.* There is each time a low falling contour on the word *one.*

(1) Radio Phone-in (R4 18.2.97 9.05am)
   (*a*) *Now | number ⌍one | let's make it perfectly plain | one can have . . .*
   (*b*) *⌍One | the function of the coroner's court is to decide . . .*

The prosodic device being used here is the same as that described in Chapter 2, where news readers realise the subject noun phrase of a new topic (news item) as a complete utterance, ending with a low fall to the baseline. It is the strategy referred to there as using a citation contour as an intonational 'opener'. By isolating the first element of a new topic and realising it as a complete utterance the speaker is presenting it as a kind of heading or title which is syntactically incorporated into the rest of the sentence. The phrases *number one* and *one* in example (1) above are also being treated prosodically as titles or headlines, turning them in conversational terms into 'openers'.

This is not the only way of realising these phrases. It would in fact be perfectly possible to end the phrase on a rising contour (*⌐one . . . number ⌐one*) suggesting perhaps a list of two or at the most three, and also suggesting relatively short list items. The marked topic projection, or 'opener' intonation of the phrase each time it occurs suggests to the listener a rather longer and more complex list of items to be mentioned. In the event the caller doesn't get very far since the interviewer interrupts and takes back the floor. This bid for space is unsuccessful.

6.3.2.2 COMPETITIVE TALK

Television or radio interviews with politicians might be assumed to fall under the same category of asymmetrical discourse as radio phone-ins or job interviews, and to a certain extent this is true. The nature of the event requires, for example, that interviewers will ask questions and politicians will answer them, and not vice versa. There is also a view, not universally held, that interviewers should show a certain deference to their interviewees – they should preferably not interrupt them and should allow them to say what they want to say. In practice we have a common (if controversial) culture in the British media of highly combative political interviews where the rules of the game involve a battle for turn and topic control. The interviewer's aim is to elicit answers to preferably uncomfortable questions on behalf of the public, while the politicians' aim is to say what they would like the public to hear. In such a situation, the notion of topic control is crucially important. In the following I will give some examples of how the citation contour, in its discourse organising function, is used for this purpose. They are all taken from a BBC interview[4] between John Humphrys (JH), an assertive (or aggressive, depending on one's view) journalist, and Michael Howard (MH), the then British Home Secretary.

Example (2)[5] shows an undisputed turn and topic change. MH cedes his turn using a low falling terminal contour. JH takes his turn and signals a topic shift, lexically – using the discourse marker *right*, and also prosodically – by giving it a falling contour. The effect is to close off the previous strand of discourse and mark the opening of a new topic, or at least a new slant on the current one.

(2) MH   *Now that is a change which would not have happened if we hadn't had a conservative government and it's making a difference in bringing guilty people to justice and convicting them in the courts of this country* **all the ↘time.**

   JH   **↘Right** | *you got that through when you had a decent majority*

Example (3) shows MH being interrupted in a brief bid for the floor by JH who uses a falling tone on *deal* in *no but let's ↘DEAL with that*, albeit a rather tentative, truncated fall. Perhaps for this reason, MH successfully regains the floor and immediately projects ahead using a citation contour ending in a low fall on *let's remember what we're ↘DEALing with*, echoing the words of JH's interruption. This contour creates 'conversational space' for the speaker, so that even a pause at the end of it is not exploited by JH to take the floor again. (Square brackets indicate overlapping speech.)

(3) MH   . . . *are not to do with entering [people's homes and all that sort of thing*
   JH   *[No but let's* **↘deal with that** *[because . . .*
   MH   *[absolutely*
         but **let's remember what we're ↘dealing with** *(.) Most of the most of the powers are used to track people's property . . .*

In example (4) the same pattern is used, this time by JH, having successfully won the floor from MH. The words *let me quote you if I may* are treated prosodically as a complete utterance, even though it becomes immediately clear that the sequence is grammatically incomplete at that point. Again this is an opening device which successfully makes space for the speaker to hold a lengthy turn and control the topic.

(4) JH   **let me quote you if I ↘may** | *Lord Alexander, Conservative Peer, very disting . . . former chairman of the Bar Council, all the rest of it. 'This' he said, and I quote, 'is one step down the slippery path to a police state.'*

The above examples show how the speakers use prosody to create space for themselves when they have got the floor. By realising the opening sequence with a citation contour the speaker is marking it as an 'opener', in other words he is projecting a major unit of discourse to come.

135

6.3.2.3   INFORMAL CONVERSATION: SUSPENDING TURN-TAKING

The obvious asymmetries present in the activity types described above are generally absent in ordinary casual conversation, where we may assume equal rights to take turns, and an absence of constraints on the type of turn (e.g. questions, answers). Turns tend to be relatively short unless one participant is engaged in a narrative of some kind, and this requires special conditions to be established. Schiffrin points out that 'if a storyteller is to situate and complete the story, turn exchange has to be temporarily suspended . . . to gain a turn long enough for a story, speakers can project an anticipated turn length through strategies which manipulate several levels of discourse' (1987: 16). In the following conversational data we find one such long turn which stands out against the rest of the interaction in the course of domestic talk between two sisters and their respective husbands. (The data is referred to here and elsewhere as Sister Talk.[6]) The kind of story-telling devices quoted by Schiffrin, however (*y'know what happened?* or *A funny thing happened the other day*) are not present. Instead, the long turn here is projected prosodically by means of applying a complete citation contour, ending in a low fall, to the first sentence. The talk is about air travel. In response to her husband's comment that having to show various documents at frequent intervals is a *constant damn nuisance*, the speaker disagrees, and her turn begins as follows: *Well it isn't really when you got a system*. This is realised with a high pitch reset (higher than the surrounding talk) on *isn't* and a low fall on *system* (Figure 6.5).

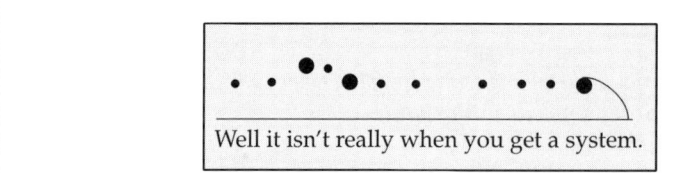

Figure 6.5   Pitch contour of an intonational opener in casual conversation.

The cue gains cumulative effect because it is repeated three more times on subsequent utterances; additional salience is of course also achieved by lexical repetition, a powerful rhetorical device in itself.

Well it isn't really when you got a system (.)
you've got to have a system (0,7)
and I think I have that system (0,8)
from long experience (0,5) [mm]

Compared with the brief turns and frequent speaker changes until this point, this turn is indeed remarkably long. The entire turn, directed apparently at the speaker's sister who is shortly to fly to Australia, is as follows: (pause length, or backchannel from other participants is in brackets).

Well it isn't really when you got a system (.)
you've got to have a system (0,7)
and I think I have that system (0,8)
from long experience (0,5) [mm]
You've got to know where your passports are
you've got to know where your (.) tickets are [mm]
and where your boarding cards are (0,8)
and if you can't put your ha /
I'd l – like to keep one side of my handbag for only those articles (0,6) [mm]
s and then (.)
I hopefully i /
Johnny's got a pocket
a – a breast pocket in his shirt
so you slip the boarding cards into
then they're easily pulled out (.) [yeah]
otherwise I just have to hold them in my hand (1,1)
because :er (0,8)
you don't want to go fumbling for those when you're going through (0,9)
[no]
but anyway you'll find it's as easy as pie (1,1)
easy as pie dear

Schiffrin suggests that using a device to project a long turn is necessary in order to 'enlist from the hearer the tacit agreement to bypass many potential turn transition points' (1987: 16). This seems to be the case in the above talk. There are several such potential transition points but in each case the other participants are either silent or just offer backchannel responses. Since there is no explicit story preface or opener it is presumably the use of intonation which has such a powerful blocking effect on subsequent turn taking.

Couper-Kuhlen and Selting (1996) cite a similar example of a long turn (part of a radio phone-in programme) but suggest that an alternative analysis, taking into account prosodic signals, might more properly represent it as a sequence of shorter turns, between which the other participants choose to forego their own 'turns'. Their evidence for this is that there is a point inside their 'long turn' where topic completion, syntactic completion and a fall (to low) in the intonation contour coincide. These together constitute a strong completion cue,[7] and the authors claim that the pause at this point, before the same speaker continues, is actually an indication that the other speaker declines to take the offered turn. The subsequent talk, which begins with a high pitch reset, also confirms retrospectively, in their view, that the previous talk was complete and that a new turn is beginning. Couper-Kuhlen and Selting therefore analyse the long turn in their data as a multi-unit turn which 'grows into its ultimate shape as a result of on-the-spot decisions made by participants in the process of negotiating talk' (p.31). This analysis rightly takes into account the dynamic nature of talk. If we apply this analysis to the Sister Talk quoted above, we might also see it as a multi-unit turn during which the other participants choose not to take possible turns.

The strong 'intonational opener' at the beginning is in my view a possible explanation *why* they chose not to take turns. It is thus not quite appropriate to call it an 'on-the-spot' decision, which suggests (perhaps unintentionally) an unmotivated local choice. The choice, if such it is, may have been made earlier in the discourse, and may depend on a number of factors which can be internal or external to the talk. In the Sister Talk data I am claiming that the intonational opener may have suspended normal turn-taking, but there may of course be other contextual reasons in addition, of which I am not aware. In Couper-Kuhlen and Selting's data the motivation not to take a possible turn may well be found in the type of talk – a phone-in – where turn-taking conventions operate which are different from those in casual conversation. The hosts in these programmes elicit or suppress talk from participants depending on time constraints, interest to listeners and other factors which are a function of the type of programme.

Clearly, then, the motivation to take or not take possible turns depends on the speaking rights of individual participants in a particular speech event. In phone-ins and similar situations, such as interviews, 'normal' turn-taking may mean that a speaker (e.g. the interviewee) is *expected* to take longer turns. This means that the current speaker can legitimately produce a number of 'paratones', each ending in a low fall and a pause, and the interlocutor can legitimately choose not to take a turn at that point. In casual conversation, such as Sister Talk, turns are generally short and speaking rights are assumed to be equal, so some blocking device such as an 'intonational opener' may be needed to suspend the normal turn-taking.

I have attempted to show here how the signposting of text and discourse structure can be performed by intonation, both in conjunction with explicit markers in the text – discourse markers, openers, conversational 'routines' (Schiffrin 1987, Aijmer 1996), and also in their absence. In conversational interaction the 'intonational routine' of the citation contour can be further exploited as a means of creating conversational space for the speaker, temporarily suspending normal turn exchange.

6.3.3 Communication checks

Some contributions to a conversation are not intended as an independent contribution but to encourage the current speaker to continue. Such 'backchannels' can include nods, and verbal responses such as *mmmhh, yes, right, oh, oh yes* etc., or verbal echoes, repetition and reformulation of current utterances.

A study of one such 'token of recipiency' is that by Local (1996) on the realisation of the word *Oh*. By making very detailed observations of the segmental and prosodic features of each token, Local builds up a description of different types of *Oh*, one of which, occurring alone with no subsequent talk by the same speaker (a 'free-standing news receipt'), is characterised by falling pitch ending low in the speaker's range, often with lengthening and vocal creak, sometimes with an initial glottal stop but never a final one. *Oh*-tokens realised in this way appear to terminate a sequence of 'telling', meaning the recipient is now adequately informed and no more telling is necessary. Local insists that the pitch pattern – the falling contour – is on its own not a determining feature of its interactional function. However, all the *oh*-tokens with a falling contour have the effect of either closing or curtailing the talk, and it is tempting to see that at least some degrees of finality are being suggested by these falling contours. The minute detail captured in these analyses leaves plenty of opportunity, however, for alternative possibilities to be investigated. Is the presence or absence of a glottal stop the determining perceptual cue to the function of the *Oh*? Or is it the vowel quality which is distinctively different for different kinds of *Oh*? These are the kinds of questions which can usefully be followed up in a controlled experimental environment. As is often pointed out in relation to turn-taking cues, simply establishing a list of phonetic correlates does not tell us what is perceptually relevant to the listener.

Supportive 'tokens of recipiency' or 'continuers' (Müller 1996: 131) are 'designed to fit into gaps in ongoing talk' rather than overlapping with it, but despite the convention that only one person speaks at a time, conversation also contains many examples of overlapping, simultaneous speech. Some of these have the same function as backchannels. Edelsky (1981) pointed out, for example, that an interruption can be made either to take a turn or to express solidarity with the current speaker, creating the so-called 'collaborative' floor.

Of course, some utterances are constructed in such a way that they are vulnerable to overlap. One such case is 'early closure' (see Chapter 3) – for example before a sentence adverbial, or before an end-of-sentence 'routine' such as *and that sort of thing, and stuff,* often treated prosodically as a nuclear tail – a sequence of unstressed syllables after the nucleus, trailing off in amplitude. It is possible that any utterance-final elements which are treated as non-focal are sensitive to overlap in this way, and that simultaneous speech in such cases is the result of misreading turn-ceding cues rather than not bothering to wait for one. This has been studied for German (Auer 1996) but not to my knowledge for English.

So far I have illustrated how intonation reflects some of the 'rules' of interaction – orderly turn-taking and backchannelling. The next section will deal with the way in which speakers use intonation to break, bend or exploit rules to show the degree of compliance with other speakers. This is, in my view, a welcome step towards investigating the *meanings* which are conveyed by intonation.

6.4 Co-operation, affiliation, disaffiliation

One assumption we make about conversation is that in principle participants co-operate. Of course this is not always the case – questions are not answered, summonses are not responded to, and backchannel feedback is withheld if a participant so chooses. This is, of course, independent of intonation, but intonation can play a subtle role in indicating non-compliant behaviour.

An obvious example is the competitive interruption, the attempt to take a turn before the current speaker has ceded the floor. French and Local (1986) examined natural conversation in an attempt to show the difference between turn-competitive and non-competitive interruptions. They found that competitive interruptions are 'markedly raised in pitch and loudness' (p.164). When both raised pitch and loudness are present in an interruption, the current speaker modifies his or her speech prosodically, indicating a willingness to relinquish the floor or, presumably by further raising pitch and loudness, the intention to continue.

There are times when verbal responses are realised in a way which constitutes not so much encouragement or support for the current speaker's talk but a challenge to it. Backchannelling, for example, is essential to the maintaining of interaction, but speakers may choose to do apparently conflicting things: provide the required 'yes, I'm listening' responses but at the same time discourage the other speaker in some way (signalling disaffiliation while observing interactional rules). This distinction can be crucial to the understanding of the discourse processes but is one which cannot always be made on the basis of the orthographic transcription alone. Sometimes its identification lies in the prosody and not in the words.

In the following I will describe a number of studies of these subtle modifications, most of which identify prosodic strategies which combine pitch and timing (rhythm).

6.4.1   Pitch modification

6.4.1.1   NON-SUPPORTIVE BACKCHANNELS

Supportive verbal responses can include words like *yes, right*, and also repetitions, as in example (5) below, again from the radio interview previously cited.[8] The orthographic transcription suggests supportive backchannel responses, but in fact they sound highly competitive. The word *right*, spoken with a rising tone, could be heard as encouragement meaning 'yes I understand, please continue'. Similarly, the word *precisely*, using the same 'tonal space' as the current speaker, could sound supportive, and the echoing of the current speaker's own words with *reviewing* could be heard as collaborative. Here, however, the speaker uses a falling tone (also spoken here very rapidly) and the effect is very different. The sense of closure conveyed by the way the words are spoken, whether *right*, *precisely* or *reviewing*, does not imply support. On the contrary, it suggests an attempt to end the current speaker's topic and turn. The interruptor is on the one hand co-operating by giving backchannel responses, on the other hand using the intonation that implies closure of the current topic and projects forward to a new topic. The tenacity of the politician in the face of this might not be shared by a less experienced (or more sensitive) interviewee. (Overlapping speech in this example is indicated by square brackets.)

(5) MH   . . . *we're going to put the exercise of these powers on a proper statutory basis*
[*with a completely new safeguard, and independent commissioner, who is*

JH [↘*right*

MH *to be a serving or former high court judge who will have responsibility for reviewing and*
    [monitoring the way in which the police use these powers [and

JH *[re↘viewing | pre↘cisely*   *[pre↘cisely*

MH *quashing and quashing an authorisation if he thinks that it has been given [improperly and er outside the scope of the act*

JH [↘*right*

6.4.1.2 SPEAKER-HEARER ORIENTATION: THE NOTION OF PITCH CONCORD

Compliant behaviour: Brazil's model of intonation (Brazil 1985) also referred to in Coulthard (1985) includes the notion of 'key'. Brazil claims three significant 'keys': high, mid and low, and claims that these set up constraints across speaker turns. The key of 'termination' (the starting point of a (falling) nuclear tone) puts constraints on the key of the next turn. In compliant behaviour Brazil assumes a pressure towards pitch concord, at least after mid and high terminations.

high termination expects high key
mid termination expects mid key
low termination permits high, mid and low key

The termination keys are similar to the idea of high mid and low fall (Chapter 3), starting at different heights in the speaker's range, relative to what has gone before (here Brazil is not more specific). I will therefore show Brazil's ideas both as he represented them and also in the more familiar tadpole transcription (Figure 6.6).

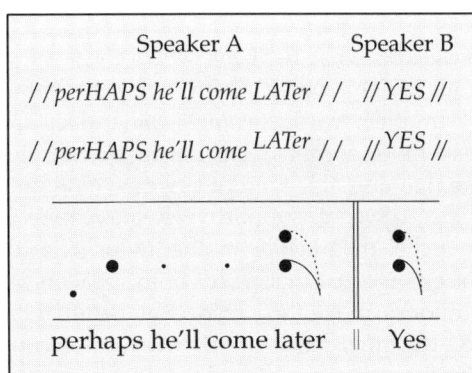

Figure 6.6 Two imaginary performances of 'perhaps he'll come later', with the most 'compliant' responses according to Brazil.

One of the weaknesses of Brazil's published work is the illustrative nature of his data. We have little evidence of whether speakers generally behave in the way he predicts. The examples he gives, however, are intuitively convincing, such as in Figure 6.7, quoted in Coulthard (1985). The suggestion that key concord is typical of compliant behaviour is not inconsistent with example (5) above. The backchannel responses with a falling 'citation' contour tend to sound non-supportive because they are spoken in a low key after a high or mid termination by the current speaker.

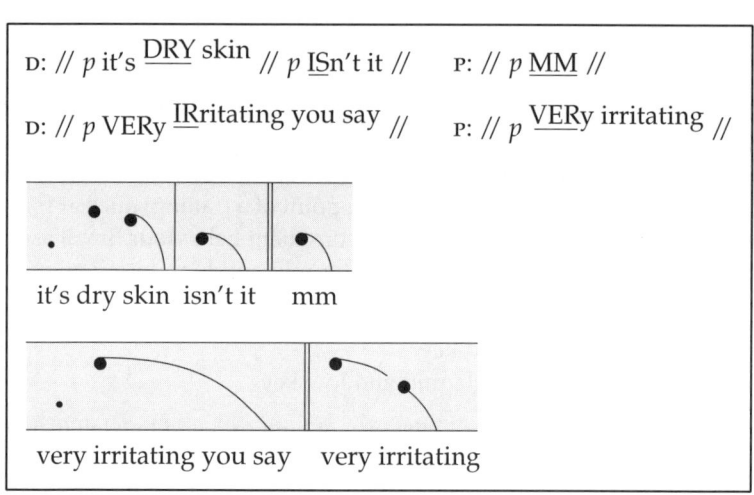

D: // *p* it's <u>DRY</u> skin // *p* <u>IS</u>n't it //   P: // *p* <u>MM</u> //

D: // *p* VERy <u>IR</u>ritating you say //   P: // *p* <u>VER</u>y irritating //

it's dry skin isn't it   mm

very irritating you say   very irritating

Figure 6.7 Brazil's example of doctor-patient interaction: 'It's dry skin isn't it' (cited in Coulthard 1985: 116). Brazil gives this as an example of compliant behaviour indicated by pitch concord.

Non-compliant behaviour: So what happens when speakers are not compliant? How is such behaviour understood by other participants? Brazil's notion of 'key' is a relative concept. In other words, the *high, mid* and *low* must be understood in terms of the speaker's own range, and not in any absolute terms. Couper-Kuhlen (1996) shows that only this kind of key matching (in her terms 'relative register matching') is perceived as supportive. Relative register matching occurs when one speaker matches the pitch of another by using a corresponding point in his or her own voice range. In other words both speakers are using a pitch the same number of semitones above their respective habitual base-lines. Absolute register matching, on the other hand, occurs when the second speaker imitates the same absolute pitch as the first, regardless of where it occurs in his or her own voice range (Figure 6.8). Couper-Kuhlen claims that the verbal and melodic imitation of prior talk can both have a supportive function – in the case of relative register matching – and present a negative comment in the case of absolute register matching. The closer the melodic imitation the more we feel that the speaker is distancing himself or herself from the other 'voice'. Exact imitation is perceived as 'mimicry' and to be thus mocking the other speaker.

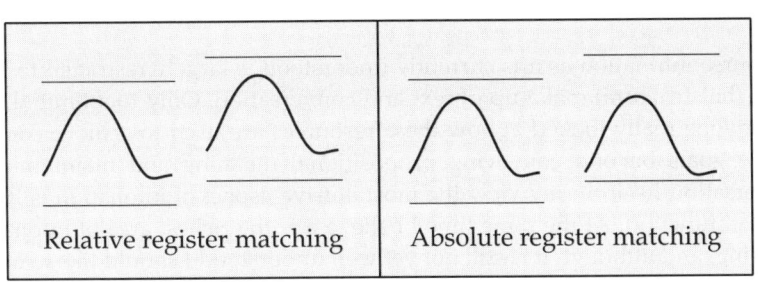

Figure 6.8 Illustration after Couper-Kuhlen (1996) showing relative and exact register matching: (a) relative register matching; (b) absolute register matching.

6.5 Summarising intonation resources in conversation

In this chapter I have tried to integrate various accounts, scattered in the literature, of what intonation resources are available to speakers in an interactive context.

In some cases the choice of contour, e.g. in RP a fall rather than a rise, can contribute to the structure of interaction. This is mainly due to the 'closing' and 'continuing' effects of the contours, making a falling tone a more likely signal of turn finality than a rise (unless of course associated with a question). In the main, however, it is clear that the most important way in which intonation contributes to conversational interaction is not in features of pitch direction but of pitch range.

At the local level we have seen that an extra high accent can indicate the beginning of a new topic. The counterpart to this is in the extreme finality suggested by an extra low final fall. The pitch range of an entire utterance also signals the rhetorical relationship between that utterance and the surrounding text. Pitch range (taking into account the range of the individual speaker) also appears to be important across turns. Echoing the final contour of one speaker by another is perceived as supportive only as long as the second speaker does not shift from relative register matching to absolute register matching. The latter is perceived as 'mimicry' and as a negative contribution. Finally, we have seen that entire sections of conversation can display global pitch range which serves to distinguish the sections functionally from one another.

One of the most important features of intonation analysis in the CA framework is that it considers much more than simply pitch. There is important work on the function of rhythm in turn-taking (Couper-Kuhlen 1993) and also on how non-rhythmic backchannels can have a disaffiliating effect (Müller 1996). Local's (1996) work on *Oh*-tokens (see section 6.3.3 above) captures both segmental and prosodic variation, claiming quite rightly that in order to know what is important we must look at everything that is there, and not at an unmotivated subset of what is there.

143

6.6   Attitudinal intonation: interaction and intonational meaning

Discourse intonation as it is currently understood is largely restricted to identi-fying the structural make-up of text and conversation. Only to a limited extent has anyone really looked at how these resources are used to achieve commun-icative goals beyond conveying propositional meaning and maintaining the conversation itself. In my view the most elusive aspect of intonation is its 'atti-tudinal' function. At the same time I believe it is the richest area of intonational meaning, and although it is still not yet well understood I should like to address it here.

There is a long and honourable tradition in intonation research of providing attitudinal labels to explain the perceived, imagined or predicted effect of intona-tional features used in a particular context. The profusion of labels has so far been the main problem, along with the assumption that every label must refer to something different, or even to anything at all. I am by no means the first to suggest that this mass of labels is unhelpful. O'Connor made the same point over a quarter of a century ago.

> This topic [attitudinal intonation] is bedevilled by the lack of agreed categories and terms for dealing with attitudes; they have been characterised here by terms such as 'conspiratorial, awe, concern, perfunctory' etc., etc., more with an eye to identifying them to the reader than to classifying them in an orderly scheme, and until some method of dealing with attitudes is developed along very much more scientific lines than is possible at present, we shall not even be able to tell whether this language and that are similar or different in the number or nature of attitudes they mark.   (O'Connor, 1973: 270)

If we look at even the most recent publications on intonation, for example Tench (1997), there seems to have been little progress on this front. And yet we all know intuitively that intonation can express something which we loosely term 'attitude'. One of the problems lies in distinguishing 'attitude' from other kinds of affective meaning such as 'emotion'. In fact the two are frequently assumed to be synonymous, or at least overlapping. Crystal (1995: 249) notes that an import-ant function of intonation is 'attitudinal', but he does so under the heading 'emotion':

> Emotion: Intonation's most obvious role is to express attitudinal meaning – sarcasm, surprise, reserve, impatience, delight, shock, anger, interest, and thou-sands of other semantic nuances.

An attempt at bringing some order into this complex issue was made by Couper-Kuhlen (1986: 185–7), who suggested a possible distinction between emotion and attitude, emotion representing a speaker state (*He is (feeling) happy, sad, . . .*) and attitude representing a kind of behaviour (*He is being condescending, friendly . . .*). Since then some progress has been made in the description of the prosodic correlates of emotion (e.g. Murray and Arnott 1996), but little in accounting systematically for perceived attitudes, and I think it is useful to try to refine the framework.

While Couper-Kuhlen's distinction between emotion as speaker state and attitude as speaker behaviour is useful, there are some attitudes which are not to do with behaviour but which are better described as opinions, beliefs or knowledge about something (*He is critical of . . . , impressed by . . .*). These are attitudes towards propositions, a 'psychological attitude towards a state of affairs' (Leech 1983: 106). This kind of propositional attitude is in itself affectively neutral, but the kind of labels we associate with it reflect the emotions aroused by that opinion, belief or knowledge. The labels associated with the expression of propositional attitudes seem therefore to be closely allied to those associated with emotion. They also have in common the fact that emotions can be felt and opinions held whether or not another person is present. Attitude defined as 'speaker behaviour' on the other hand cannot be present independently of interaction. To put it simply, you can be happy on your own, and disapproving on your own, but you cannot be condescending on your own.

I will therefore categorise as 'expressive' intonation, those intonational characteristics which appear to convey both pure emotion, and emotion arising from beliefs, knowledge and opinion. 'Attitudinal' intonation, on the other hand, is in my view any aspect of intonation (including expressive intonation) which in a given context reflects a certain speaker behaviour, as intended by the speaker, or as perceived by the receiver, or both. I believe that this kind of attitude is part of speaker meaning. To understand it and to establish the role of intonation in communicating it, we must see it as a part of pragmatics.

Expressive intonation reflects . . .	and . . .	Attitudinal intonation reflects . . .
emotion	**propositional attitude** Opinion, belief, knowledge about a person or issue	**speaker behaviour** intended and/or perceived in relation to a given context
He is (feeling) . . .	I am . . .	You are being . . .
happy	*critical*	*condescending*
angry	*impressed*	*friendly*
sad	*disapproving*	*rude*
. . .	. . .	. . .

Knowles (1987: 205–6) rightly suggests that 'it is extremely unlikely that there are any attitudes which are conveyed uniquely by intonation . . . It is possible that intonation patterns that are regarded as attitudinally marked use the intonation system in an unexpected way, and possibly in conjunction with other linguistic patterns.' This view is consistent with a pragmatic approach to meaning, the kind of approach which is context-dependent. Speaker meaning, in so far as it deviates from the surface meaning of an utterance, is generated in a systematic way, usually when there is a perceived mismatch between the content of an utterance and the context in which it is conveyed. I assume that at least *some* intonationally conveyed attitudes are also conveyed by some kind of mismatch, for example between the intonation and the message, or between the intonation and the context. Some attitudes, of course, are not conveyed by mismatch. Sometimes we say what we mean. The response *wonderful!* with a smile and a high fall to a friend's announcement that he is to become a father needs little explanation. The wide pitch range is a typical expression of strong feeling (here, given the meaning of 'wonderful', it conveys pleasure – the same pitch contour on *no!* might express a very different emotion); the expression of pleasure can be interpreted as a positive attitude towards the proposition contained in the message, and this in turn is likely to be inferred by the receiver as implying a positive attitude, such as 'friendly' or 'supportive', towards himself.

Many intonationally conveyed attitudes, however, in particular negative ones, are the result of some kind of mismatch. In the situation I just described, the response *wonderful!* with a narrow pitch range and no smile would indicate that the speaker meant something else, although any implied or inferred meaning would depend on the situation. Clearly, if we are to investigate mismatches we must first have a clear idea of what constitutes a 'match'. It must be possible to assign to a particular intonation pattern, or some aspect of intonational behaviour, a 'normal' or 'expected' meaning which then has the potential to be exploited in an unexpected way, either intentionally, generating a prosodic implicature, or unintentionally, generating an inference on the part of the receiver. These implied or inferred meanings are in my view the key to many cases of perceived 'tone of voice' or attitude. However, until we are in a position to identify a 'normal' association between intonation, text and context we are not in a position to identify any deviation from that norm.

Many of the observations I have made in this book are of normal, or unmarked, relationships between intonation and text. Conversation analysis, on the other hand, is in addition concerned with the relationship between intonation and interaction, and it seems to me that one area of such research which currently promises to contribute much to our understanding of attitudinal meaning in intonation is the study of 'affiliating and disaffiliating' behaviour. Here we see the beginnings of a study of how intonation contributes to speaker meaning, by observing what happens when speakers appear to be uncooperative. (I am using the word 'cooperative' here in the Gricean sense of maintaining regularities in interactional behaviour rather than in the sense of 'being nice'.) Of course, some apparently uncooperative behaviour is unintentional. Participants may mishear, fail to hear, be distracted or physically unable to respond in a cooperative way. Since conversational principles are to some extent culture-specific, there may also be a cross-cultural reason for perceived uncooperativeness. In the main, however, we must assume that if speakers flout shared principles they do it for a purpose. Thomas (1996: 1) observes that 'people do not always or even usually say what they mean. Speakers frequently mean much more than their words actually say.' If this is the case, however, we need to explain how it is that we manage to communicate. The answer lies in the study of linguistic pragmatics, and what I would like to discuss here is the way in which we can, and should, include intonation in the linguistic system which speakers exploit to make meaning.

The investigation of the intonation of co-operative behaviour, and by extension unco-operative behaviour, is useful because it can explain participants' responses. If we know that co-operative backchannel responses are both 'in time' and 'in tune' with the current talk (Müller 1996), we can begin to explain participant responses when backchannels are out of tune and out of time. What this appears to mean interactionally is: *I am no longer interested in maintaining this interaction.* How this message is interpreted, however, will depend on the context. In some contexts it might be perceived as a polite way of closing the conversation, in other contexts it might feel extremely impolite. If I am speaking in a professional capacity to someone with higher professional status (such as the vice-chancellor) I would see it as his or her right to bring our meeting to a close. However, if we are meeting socially, where the difference in professional status is irrelevant, I might perceive the message as rather offhand. In other words, the same prosodic behaviour can have different effects in different situations.

Pragma-linguists do not to my knowledge attempt to make a list of all possible implicatures. They simply identify the mechanisms whereby they are generated. Many of the 'attitudes' which refer to behaviour are, in fact, descriptions of inferences by the listener rather than implicatures intended by the speaker, and linguists are just as unlikely to consider listing all possible inferences on which listeners can draw. In the same way, I would regard it as futile to attempt a comprehensive list of attitudinal effects associated with intonation and equally futile to look for their acoustic correlates.

If we apply pragmatic analysis to that subset of 'attitudes' which I regard as implied or inferred speaker meaning, we can begin to re-evaluate some of the impressionistic comments found in intonation literature. For example, Brown et al. (1980) consider the low endpoint of a terminal contour (falling tone) to be an important finality signal. 'Not-low terminals' (e.g. rises, mid falls), on the other hand, are associated with 'more to come'. She claims that 'Not-low is also associated with a range of affective meanings including deference, politeness, vulnerability . . .' (p.30). This is not difficult to account for. Extreme finality means 'that is the end of the matter' – a powerful statement which is only appropriate in situations where the speaker has the 'right' (whether given by social role (e.g. interviewer), social status, age, or other factor) to control the discourse. The expression of non-finality, on the other hand, effectively lays the power to control the discourse with another participant – hence the perceived 'deference', and if this is thought to be appropriate by participants, 'politeness'. Vulnerability also reflects an unequal power relationship, but on the scale of 'weak to strong' rather than 'high status to low status'. When power lies with the stronger, the weaker is by definition vulnerable. All these labels, then, simply refer to the effect in different contexts of the same intonational behaviour, namely ceding control of the discourse to another participant.

Of course, different people may make very different inferences from the same interaction, depending on their beliefs about the nature of the context. So for example, if a political journalist is described as an 'aggressive', 'combative' interviewer, we have evidence that in some way he is breaking a rule held to be true for that listener about the roles of the participants and their relative rights and status. Those who believe that politicians should be deferred to will perceive the journalist's attempts to control the discourse (see section 6.3.2.2) as inappropriate, and use such negative descriptions. Those who believe otherwise will interpret the behaviour positively as 'assertive' or 'determined'.

There is far more to be done to investigate the prosody of interaction. We know as yet only fragments of the system which speakers exploit. In my view it would be far more useful to concentrate research efforts on looking for correlates of more systematically definable contextual factors, such as those dictated by participant roles and activity types, which *explain* the interpretation by participants, rather than looking for correlates of the interpretations themselves.

Notes

1 Of course reading aloud does not occur in an interactional vacuum – we must assume an audience even if it is only the reader herself (see Brazil 1992), but the interpersonal element is far outweighed by the prosodic orientation to the text itself.

2 If similar pitch relations were shown to operate *across* turns, any ASR system trained to respond to pitch height would of course have to find a way of normalising across speakers.

3 This applies, of course, only to RP. A study of turn ceding in Ulster English has been described by Wells and Peppé (1996).

4 'On the Record' (19.1.97).

5 Conversation analysts would require more data here in order to provide the crucial evidence of subsequent participant behaviour.

6 I am indebted to Elizabeth Couper-Kuhlen, University of Konstanz, for the permission to use this data.

7 The authors also take account of rhythmic cues (see section 6.5).

8 'On the Record' (19.1.97).

Appendix I

Prosodically transcribed version of text B04 (a news broadcast) from the Spoken English Corpus.

016 SPOKEN ENGLISH CORPUS TEXT B04
BBC News
Broadcast notes: Radio 3, 1.00pm, January 14th, 1986
Transcribed by GOK

`now it's ·one o'ˎclock | and ·this is ¯Peter ·Bragg in ¯London | ↑with the _Radio ·3 `news ·summary || the ¯board of ·Westland ˎhelicopters | have ¯made _clear | that ·they `won't ·put the ‸ `Anglo-·Euro·pean `rescue ·bid for the ˏcompany | to their ˎshareholders | `even if the ‸ `rival Aˇmerican ·bid | ˎfails || the ˇshareholders ·meeting | ¯called to ˇvote on the A·merican ·offer | was ad`journed this ˏmorning | until `Friday as ˎplanned || the `Westland ´chairman | Sir _John ˇCuckney | ·said ‸ the `workforce was ˎsuffering | be·cause of the un`certainty | over the ˏcompany's ˎfuture || ´Westland | had ·gone through an ¯eight ·month ˏperiod | of ˎturbulence | which had been ·thoroughly `bad for the ˎstaff || Sir ˇJohn said | the ¯board | would have a ¯number of conˇtingency ·plans | `ready | in ·case they ¯didn't suc_ceed | in ·winning e¯nough su_pport | for the Aˎmerican ·offer || it be·came ¯clear _afterwards | that the Euroˇpean ·bid | was `not aˎmong those ·options || and the ¯Prime _Minister | is ex¯pected to _face | ¯further _criticisms | of the ¯government's _handling | of the ´Westland a·ffair | during `question ·time | in the ˎCommons | this afterˎnoon || the ´trade | and ˏindustry ·secretary | Mr `Leon ˇBrittan | ·said ‸ he's `not ·planning to reˎsign | over his ·Commons _statement | ˎyesterday || the con↑¯fede_ration | of ¯British ˎindustry | has ¯said | the `Chancellor should ·use the ˇbudget | to ¯try | to ¯bring _down | unem`ployment | ·rather than ‸ to ·make ·widespread ˎtax ·cuts || ↑in its recommen`dations to the ¯Chancellor | the `CB¯I ·says | a ¯thousand ·million ˎpounds | should be ·spent on ¯job creaˎtion ·measures || it ·says ‸ unem¯ployment | could be ¯cut | by a ¯third of a ˎmillion | over ¯two ˎyears in this ·way || the ¯CB_I ·says ‸ if there ˇis money a·vailable for ·tax cuts | it should ¯go on _raising aˎllowances | ·rather than re¯ducing the _basic ·rate of ˎincome ·tax || the ↑ˇbuilding so·cieties | have re¯ported | a ¯good ˎmonth | in Deˎcember || al`though in·vestors with¯drew | more than `four thousand ·million ˎpounds | ¯even _more | ˇnew ·money | was inˎvested || to ·give the so·cieties a ¯net ·income | of `eight ·hundred and ˎsixty-·five

| _million ˎpounds ‖ ·that's the ˇhighest ·figure | for ˋany ·month | in ⁻nineteen ·eighty-ˏfive ‖ the ·secretary ´general | of the ˇbuilding so·cieties a·ssoci·ation | Mr ·Richard ˇWeir | ·såid the ⁻outlook for ˎJanuary | was _less enˏcouraging | but there was ·no imˇmediate ·need | for an ˋincrease | in ˎinterest ·rates ‖ and the ⁻Bank of ˎEngland | has ˇindicated that it ·wants | ˇbank ·interest ·rates | to ˋstay at their ·present ·level | for the _time ˎbeing ‖ there were ˋfears ˎearlier | that ˎinterest ·rates | might ·have to ˋrise | and ˎthis ·brought a ⁻fall | of ·more than ⁻eighteen ˎpoints | in the Fiˎnancial ·Times ˎshare ·index ‖ but ·prices re⁻covered ·somewhat | ·after the _Bank of ·England's ˎsignal ‖ at ´noon | the ⁻FT ˎindex | was ´down | ⁻11.ˎ8 | at ⁻one ˎthousand | and ·ninety _seven | eˎxactly ‖ the ↑⁻unions | at ⁻Ford ˎmotors | ·say ˰ the ⁻company's ˇhourly ·paid ·workers | a˗ppear to have reˎjected | a ⁻two year ˎpay ·offer ‖ the ˋchief ·union neˇgotiator | Mr ·Mick ˎMurphy | ·said ˰ the ˇfirst indi·cations were | that a ⁻clear maˎjority | had _voted aˎgainst ‖ the oˎfficial re·sult of the ·ballot | will ⁻not be a_nnounced | until ˋFriday | when ⁻union _leaders | will deˋcide ·whether to ·call for ˰ for ˋstrike ·action ‖ the ´offer | de·scribed by ˎFord | as ˇfinal | would ⁻give ˋpay ·rises of be·tween | ˋthir·teen and a ˇhalf | and ⁻fif·teen point ˋseven per ·cent | ·over _two ˎyears ‖ ⁻workers from the Gartˇcosh | ˋsteel ·works | near ˎGlasgow | who've ⁻marched to ´London | as ·part of a camˋpaign | to ·save the ·plant from ˇclosure | have ⁻held a ·meeting with the ˇLabour ·party ·leader | ·Mr ˋKinnock ‖ but their reˋquest for a ·meeting with ·Mrs ⁻Thatcher | has been _turned ˎdown ‖ the ˇLiberal ·leader | Mr ·David ˎSteel | de⁻scribed | the ˎPrime ·Ministers de_cision | ˇnot to ·see the ·marchers | as ˰ a ⁻slap in the ·face for ˎScotland ‖ during ⁻meetings this ˎmorning | with a ⁻number of MˎPs | the ˋmen ·said they be⁻lieved | the ⁻whole of ·Scottish ˎsteel ·industry | would be at ˎrisk | if _Gartcosh ˎclosed ‖ the ↑ˋPrime ·Minister of ·South ˎYemen | who's in ˎIndia | has postˋponed a ·trip to ˎChina | ·after the a_ttempted ˋcoup ˰ in his ·country ‖ a ⁻spokesman for the ·Prime ·Minister ·said | ˋno infor·mation had been re·ceived from ˎAden | for the _past two ˎdays ‖ he de⁻scribed the situ·ation _there as ˰ _abˎnormal ‖ ·Aden ´Radio | ·said ˏyesterday | that the ˋleaders of a ˎplot | to aˋssassinate the ˎPresident | had been ˎexecuted ‖ there's ˇsince been | ˋuncon·firmed re_ports of ˎfighting ‖ the ⁻Northern ˇIreland ·secretary | Mr ⁻Tom ˎKing | has ⁻said | that the ˋforth·coming ˇbyelections | ·caused by the ·resig·nation of ˎfifteen ˇunionist M·Ps | will ˋnot ·change | the ·government's su⁻pport | for the _Anglo-·Irish aˎgreement ‖ at a ˋnews ·conference in ·Bel⁻fast | Mr ˇKing ˰ ·said | there was ˋno way that the ⁻byelections | could _overturn a ·vote in ˎparliament ‖ the a⁻greement | was e⁻stablished ‖ and _would go ˎforward ‖ he ·said he was a⁻vailable for ˋtalks with poˎlitical ·leaders | in the ˎprovince ‖ the Con↑ˇservative ·party ·chairman | Mr ·Norman ˎTebbit | has ·had an opeˊration | at ·Stoke ˇMandeville ·hospital | in ˎBuckinghamshire | for ˋinjuries he ·received in the ⁻Brighton ˎbomb a·ttack | ·fifteen ˎmonths a·go ‖ a ⁻spokesman _said | ˋeverything had _gone ˎwell | and Mr ⁻Tebbit | _spent a ·comfortable ˎnight ‖ he's ex·pected to ⁻stay in ˎhospital | for _up to ·two ˎweeks ‖ and ˏfinally the ˎweather ·forecast ‖ it will be ⁻very ˎwindy | with ⁻showers | in ´many _areas | and ⁻snow ˰ on the ˎhills ‖ the ·wind and ⁻showers | will ·die ˎdown ·somewhat | toˎnight ‖ and that's the ·end of the ·news and ´weather | with ↑the _time | ˎjust ·after _five past ˎone ‖

Appendix II

Prosodic transcription conventions used in the SEC (see Knowles, Wichmann and Alderson 1996 pp.28–29 for a detailed account).

|	Minor tone-group boundary
||	Major tone-group boundary
˄	Caret
ˋ	High fall
ˏ	Low fall
ˊ	High rise
ˎ	Low rise
‒	High level
_	Low level
˅	High fall rise
˅	Low fall rise
ˆ	Rise fall
·	Stressed but unaccented
↑	Up arrow
↓	Down arrow

References

Abercrombie, D. (1965) *Studies in Phonetics and Linguistics*. Third impression 1971. London: Oxford University Press

Aijmer, K. (1996) *Conversational Routines in English*. London: Longman

Allen, J. (1995) *Natural Language Understanding*, 2nd edn. Redwood City, CA: The Benjamin / Cummings Publishing Company, Inc.

Allerton, D.J. and Cruttenden, A. (1974) 'English sentence adverbials: their syntax and their intonation in British English'. *Lingua*, 24, 1–30

Altenberg, B. (1987a) 'Some Functions of the Booster in Spoken English'. In Lindblad, I. and Ljung, M. (eds) *Proceedings from the Third Nordic Conference for English Studies*. Stockholm: Almquist and Wiksell

Altenberg, B. (1987b) *Prosodic Patterns in Spoken English*. Lund, Sweden: Lund University Press

Altenberg, B. (1990) 'Predicting text segmentation into tone units'. In J. Svartvik (ed.) *The London-Lund Corpus of Spoken English: Description and Research*. Lund, Sweden: Lund University Press

Andersson, L.G. (1975) 'Talaktsadverbial'. *Nysvenska Studier*. 25–47

Armstrong, L.E. and Ward, I.C. (1931) *A Handbook of English Intonation*, 2nd edn. Cambridge: Heffer and Sons

Auer, P. (1996) 'On the prosody and syntax of turn-continuations'. In Couper-Kuhlen, E. and Selting, M. (eds)

Beattie, G. (1983) *Talk*. Milton Keynes: Open University Press

Beattie, G.W., Cutler, A., Pearson, M. (1982) 'Why is Mrs Thatcher interrupted so often?' *Nature* 300, 744–747

Van den Berg, R., Gussenhove, C. and Rietveld, A. (1992) 'Downstep in Dutch: Implications for a model'. In Docherty, G. and Ladd, D.R. (eds) *Papers in Laboratory Phonology II: Gestures, Segment, Prosody*. Cambridge: Cambridge University Press. 333–359

Bolinger, D. (1986) *Intonation and its Parts*. London: Edward Arnold

Bolinger, D. (1989) *Intonation and its Uses*. London: Edward Arnold

Brazil, D. (1985) Phonology: Intonation in Discourse. In Van Dijk, T. (ed.) *Handbook of Discourse Analysis Vol. 2 Dimensions of Discourse*. London: Academic Press

Brazil, D. (1992) 'Listening to people reading'. In Coulthard, M. (ed.) *Advances in Spoken Discourse*. London: Routledge

Brazil, D., Coulthard, M. and Johns, C. (1980) *Discourse Intonation and Language Teaching*. London: Longman

Brewer, R.F. (1912) 'Speech'. In Blackman, R.D. (ed.) *Voice Speech and Gesture. A practical handbook to the elocutionary art*. Edinburgh: John Grant

Brown, G. (1977) *Listening to Spoken English*. London: Longman

Brown, G. and Yule, G. (1983) *Discourse Analysis.* Cambridge: Cambridge University Press

Brown, G., Currie, K.L. and Kenworthy, J. (1980) *Questions of Intonation.* London: Croom Helm

Bruce, G. (1982) 'Textual aspects of prosody in Swedish'. *Phonetica 39,* 274–287

Bruce, G. (1997) 'Models of intonation – from the Lund horizon'. In Botinis, A., Kouroupetroglou, G. and Carayiannis, G. (eds) *Intonation: Theory, Models and Applications.* Proceedings of a European Speech Communication Association (ESCA) Workshop, Athens, Greece: ESCA and University of Athens

Butterworth, B. (1975) 'Hesitation and semantic planning in speech'. *Journal of Psycholinguistic Research* 4, 75–87

Carletta, J., Isard, A., Isard, S., Kowtko, J., Doherty-Sneddon, G. and Anderson, A.H. (1995) 'The Coding of Dialogue structure in a corpus'. In Andernach, J.A., van de Burgt, S.P. and van der Hoeven, G.F. (eds) *Proceedings of the Ninth Twente Workshop on Language Technology: Corpus-based approaches to dialogue modelling.* Universiteit Twente, Enschede

Chafe, W. (1979) 'The flow of thought and the flow of language'. *Syntax and Semantics. Vol. 12: Discourse and Syntax.* Academic Press, Inc.

Chafe, W. (1980) 'The deployment of consciousness in the production of a narrative'. In Chate, W. (ed.) *The Pear Stories.* New York: Ablex

Chafe, W. (1992) 'Prosodic and functional units of language'. In Edwards, J.A. and Lampert, M.D. (eds) *Talking Data.* New Jersey: Lawrence Erlbaum

Chafe, W., du Bois, J.N. and Thompson, S.A. (1992) *Corpus of spoken American English.* Unpubl. manuscript, Linguistics Department, University of California, Santa Barbara

Clark, J. and Yallop, C. (1990) *An Introduction to Phonetics and Phonology.* Oxford: Blackwell

Coulthard, M. (1977), (1985) *An Introduction to Discourse Analysis* (new edition). London: Longman

Coulthard, M. (ed.) (1992) *Advances in Spoken Discourse Analysis.* London: Routledge

Couper-Kuhlen, E. (1986) *English Prosody.* London: Edward Arnold

Couper-Kuhlen, E. (1993) *English Speech Rhythm. Form and function in everyday verbal interaction.* Amsterdam and Philadelphia: Benjamins

Couper-Kuhlen E. (1996) 'The prosody of repetition: on quoting and mimicry'. In Couper-Kuhlen, E. and Selting, M. (eds)

Couper-Kuhlen, E. and Selting, M. (eds) (1996a) *Prosody in Conversation.* Cambridge: Cambridge University Press

Couper-Kuhlen, E. and Selting, M. (1996b) 'Towards an interactional perspective'. In Couper-Kuhlen, E. and Selting, M. (eds)

Croft, W. (1995) 'Intonation units and grammatical structure'. *Linguistics 33,* 839–882

Cruttenden, A. (1986), (1997) *Intonation,* 2nd edn. Cambridge: Cambridge University Press

Crystal, D. (1969) *Prosodic Systems and Intonation in English.* Cambridge: Cambridge University Press

Crystal, D. (1995) *Encyclopedia of the English Language.* Cambridge: Cambridge University Press

Crystal, D. and Davy, D. (1969) *Investigating English Style.* London: Longman

Cutler, A. and Pearson, M. (1986) 'On the analysis of prosodic turn-taking cues'. In C. Johns-Lewis (ed.) *Intonation in Discourse.* London: Croom Helm

Douglas-Cowie, E. and Cowie, R. (1997) 'Macrostuctures in prosody: the case of phonecalls'. In Botinis, A., Kouroupetroglou, G. and Carayiannis, G. (eds) *Intonation: Theory, Models and Applications.* Proceedings of an ESCA workshop Athens, Greece pp.103–106

du Bois, J.W. and Schuetze-Coburn, S. (1992) 'Representing Hierarchy: Constituent structure for discourse databases'. In Edwards, J.A. and Lampert, M.D. (eds) *Talking Data. Transcription and coding in discourse research.* London: Lawrence Erlbaum Associates

Duncan, S. (1972) 'Some signals and rules for taking speaking turns in conversation'. *Journal of Personality and Social Psychology* 23, 283–292

Edelsky, C. (1981) 'Who's got the floor?' *Language in Society.* Vol. 10

Esser, J. (1988) *Comparing Reading and Speaking Intonation* (in co-operation with A. Polomsky). Amsterdam: Rodopi

Fang, A. and Huckvale, M. (1996) 'Synchronising syntax with speech signals'. In *Speech, Hearing and Language: Work in progress* Vol. 9, 11–26

Fox, A. (1984) 'Subordinating and Co-ordinating Intonation Structures in the Articulation of Discourse'. In Gibbon, D. and Richter, H. (eds) *Intonation, Accent and Rhythm. Studies in Discourse Phonology.* Berlin: de Gruyter

Francis, G. and Hunston, S. (1992) 'Analysing everyday conversation'. In Coulthard (ed.) *Advances in Spoken Discourse Analysis*

French, P. and Local, J. (1986) 'Prosodic features and the management of interruptions'. In C. Johns-Lewis' (ed.) *Intonation in Discourse*. London: Croom Helm

Gårding, E. (1982) 'Prosodic expressions and pragmatic categories'. *Working papers 22*, 117–135. Dept. of Linguistics, University of Lund

Garrido, J.M. (1993) 'Analysis of global pitch contour domains at paragraph level in Spanish reading text'. In D. House and P. Touati (eds) *Working papers 41*, 104–7. Dept. of Linguistics, University of Lund

Grosz, B. and Hirschberg, J. (1992) 'Some intonational characteristics of discourse structure'. In *Proceedings of the International Conference on Spoken Language Processing, Banff, Canada.* pp.429–432

Grosz, B.J. and Sidner, C.L. (1986) 'Attentions, intentions, and the structure of discourse'. *Computational Linguistics* 12 (3): 175–204

Gussenhoven, C. and Rietveld, T. (1991) 'An experimental evaluation of two nuclear tone taxonomies'. *Linguistics* 29, 423–449

Hadding-Koch, K. and Studdert-Kennedy, M. (1964) 'An experimental study of some intonation contours'. *Phonetica* 11, 175–185

Halliday, M.A.K. (1967). *Intonation and Grammar in British English.* The Hague: Mouton

Halliday, M.A.K. and Hasan, R. (1976). *Cohesion in English.* Longman: London

't Hart, J., Collier, R. and Cohen, A. (1990) *A perceptual study of intonation.* Cambridge: Cambridge University Press

Hirschberg, J. (1993) 'Studies of Intonation and Discourse'. In House, D. Touati, P. (eds) *Working Papers 41*, Dept. of Linguistics, University of Lund

Hirschberg, J. and Litman, D. (1987) 'Now let's talk about "now": identifying cue phrases intonationally'. In *Proceedings of 25th Annual Meeting of the Association for Computational Linguistics.* 1987 ACL: Stanford, Ca.

Hirschberg, J. and Pierrehumbert, J. (1986) 'The intonational structuring of discourse'. In *Proceedings – 24th Annual Meeting of the Association for Computational Linguistics.* Columbia: NY

Hobbs, J.R. (1990) 'The Pierrehumbert-Hirschberg theory of intonational meaning made simple'. In Cohen, P.R., Morgan, J. and Pollack, M.E. (eds) *Intentions in Communication.* MIT Press: Cambridge Ma, London

House, J. and Wichmann, A. (1996) 'Investigating peak timing in naturally-occurring speech: from segmental constraints to discourse structure'. In *Speech, hearing and language: work in progress.* Volume 9 pp.99–117. University College London, Department of Phonetics and Linguistics

Hovy, E. (1993) 'Automated discourse generation using discourse structure relations'. *Artificial Intelligence*, 63, 341–386

Johns-Lewis, C.M. (1986) 'Prosodic differentiation of discourse modes'. In C.M. Johns-Lewis (ed.) *Intonation in Discourse*. London: Croom Helm

Keller, E. (1981) 'Gambits> Conversational strategy signals'. In Coulmas, F. (ed.) *Conversational routine. Explorations in standardized communication situations and prepatterned speech.* The Hague: Mouton

Kingdon, R. (1958) *The Groundwork of English Intonation.* Longman: London

Knowles, G. (1975) 'Scouse: the urban dialect of Liverpool'. Unpublished PhD thesis. University of Leeds

Knowles, G. (1987) *Patterns of Spoken English.* London: Longman

Knowles, G. (1991) 'Prosodic labelling: the problem of tone group boundaries'. In Johannson, S. and Stenstrom, A-B. (eds) *English Computer Corpora.* Berlin: de Gruyter

Knowles, G., Wichmann, A. and Alderson, P. (eds) (1996) *Working with Speech.* London: Longman

Knowles, G., Williams, B. and Taylor, L. (1996) *A corpus of formal British English Speech: The Lancaster/IBM Spoken English Corpus.* London: Longman

Kreiman, J. (1982) 'Perception of sentence and paragraph boundaries in natural conversation'. *Journal of Phonetics* 10, 163–175

Kutik, E., Cooper, W. and Boyce, S. (1983) 'Declination of fundamental frequency in speakers' production of parenthetical and main clauses'. *Journal of the Acoustical Society of America 73*, 1731–1738

Ladd, D.R. (1980) *The Structure of Intonational Meaning.* Bloomington, London: Indiana UP

Ladd, D.R. (1984) 'Declination: a review and some hypotheses'. *Phonology yearbook 1*

Ladd, D.R. (1986) 'Intonational phrasing: the case for recursive prosodic structure'. *Phonology Yearbook 3*, 311–340

Ladd, D.R. (1990) 'Metrical representation of pitch register'. In J. Kingston and M. Beckman (eds) *Papers in Laboratory Phonology I.* Cambridge: Cambridge University Press

Ladd, D.R. (1993) 'On the theoretical status of "the baseline" in modelling intonation'. *Language and Speech* 36, 435–451

Ladd, D.R. (1996) *Intonational Phonology.* Cambridge: Cambridge University Press

Ladd, D.R. and Terken, J. (1995) 'Modelling intra- and inter-speaker pitch range variation'. *ICPhS 13* (Stockholm), vol. 2: 386–389

Leech, G.N. (1983) *Principles of Pragmatics.* London: Longman

Lehiste, I. (1975) The phonetic structure of paragraphs. In Cohen, A. and Nooteboom, S.G. (eds) *Structure and Process in Speech Perception.* N.Y.: Springer Verlag

Lehiste, I. (1979) 'Perception of sentence and paragraph boundaries'. In Lindblom, B. and Oehmann, S. (eds) *Frontiers of Speech Communication Research.* London: Academic Press

Lehiste, I. (1980) 'Phonetic characteristics of discourse'. *Acoustical Society of Japan, Transactions of the Committee on Speech,* April 1980, 25–38

Levinson, S.C. (1979) 'Activity types and language'. *Linguistics* 17 (5/6), 365–399

Levinson, S.C. (1983) *Pragmatics.* Cambridge: Cambridge University Press

Local, J. (1996) 'Conversational phonetics: some aspects of news receipts in everyday talk'. In Couper-Kuhlen, E. and Selting, M. (eds)

Local, J.K., Kelly, J. and Wells, W.H.G. (1986) 'Towards a phonology of conversation: turn-taking in Tyneside English'. *Linguistics* 22, 411–437

Mann, S.C. and Thompson, S.A. (1988) 'Rhetorical Structure Theory: Towards a functional theory of text organisation. In *Text 8* 3, 243–281

McArthur, T. (1992) *The Oxford Companion to the English Language.* Oxford: Oxford University Press

Menn, L. and Boyce, S. (1982) 'Fundamental frequency and discourse structure'. *Language and Speech* Vol. 25 Part 4

Mittwoch, A. (1977) 'How to refer to one's words: Speech act modifying adverbials and the performative analysis'. *Journal of Linguistics* 13, 177–189

Müller, F.E. (1996) Affiliating and disaffiliating with continuers: prosodic aspects of recipiency. In Couper-Kuhlen, E. and Selting, M. (eds)

Murray, I. and Arnott, J. (1996) Synthesising emotions in speech: is it time to get excited? *Proceedings of ICSLP*, pp.1816–1819

Nakajima, S. and Allen, F.A. (1993) 'A study on prosody and discourse structure in cooperative dialogues'. *Phonetica,* 50, 197–210

Nosek, J. (1973) 'Parenthesis in modern colloquial English'. *Prague Studies in English,* 15, 99–116

Ochs, E., Schegloff, E.A. and Thompson, S. (eds) (1996) *Interaction and Grammar.* Cambridge: Cambridge University Press

O'Connor, J.D. (1973) *Phonetics.* Middlesex, England: Penguin Books

O'Connor, J.D. and Arnold, G.F. (1961) *Intonation of Colloquial English.* London: Longman

Palmer, H.E. (1922) *English Intonation, with systematic exercises.* Cambridge: Heffer

Passoneau, R. and Litman, D. (1993) 'Intention-based segmentation: human reliability and correlation with linguistic cues'. In *Proceedings of ACL-93 Ohio State University. Association for Computational Linguistics*

Perera, K. (1989) 'The development of prosodic features in children's oral reading'. Unpublished PhD dissertation. University of Manchester

Pickering, B. (1996) 'Distributional features of TSMs in the SEC'. In Knowles, Wichmann and Alderson (eds) pp.109–128

Pickering, B., Williams, B. and Knowles, G. (1996) 'Analysis of Transcriber Differences in the SEC'. In G. Knowles, A. Wichmann and P. Alderson (eds) pp.61–86

Pierrehumbert, J.B. (1980) 'The Phonology and Phonetics of English Intonation'. Unpublished Ph.D. Thesis, Massachussetts Institute of Technology

Pierrehumbert, J. and Hirschberg, J. (1990) 'The meaning of intonational contours in the interpretation of discourse'. In P.R. Cohen, J. Morgan and M.E. Pollack (eds) *Intentions in Communication.* Cambridge Ma, London: MIT Press

Pike, K.L. (1945) *The Intonation of American English.* Linguistics 1, Ann Arbor, Michigan: University of Michigan Publications

Propp, V. (1968) *Morphology of the Folk-Tale* [1928] transl. from the Russian. 2nd edn. Bloomington: Indiana UP (cited in van Dijk 1977)

Quirk, R., Greenbaum, S., Leech, G. and Svartvik, J. (1985) *A Comprehensive Grammar of the English Language.* London: Longman

Reichman, R. (1985) *Getting Computers to Talk Like You and Me. Discourse Context, Focus and Semantics (An ATN Model).* Cambridge, Massachusetts: MIT Press

Rietveld, A.C.M. and Van Heuven, V.J. (1997) *Algemene Fonetiek.* Bussum, Holland: Coutinho

Roach, P. (1994) 'Conversion between prosodic transcription systems: Standard British and ToBI'. *Speech Communication* 15: 91–99

Sacks, H., Schegloff, E.A. and Jefferson, G. (1974) 'A simplest systematics for the organisation of turn-taking in conversation'. *Language,* 50: 696–735

Schaffer, D. (1984) 'The role of intonation as a cue to topic management in conversation'. *Journal of Phonetics* 12: 327–344

Schegloff, E.A. (1982) 'Discourse as an interactional achievement: some uses of "uh huh" and other things that come between sentences'. In D. Tannen (ed.) *Analyzing Discourse: Text and Talk.* Washington D.C.: Georgetown University Press pp.71–93

Schiffrin, D. (1987) *Discourse markers.* Cambridge: Cambridge University Press

Schiffrin, D. (1994) *Approaches to Discourse.* Oxford: Blackwell

Schuetze-Coburn, S., Shapley, M. and Weber, E.G. (1991) 'Units of intonation in discourse: A comparison of acoustic and auditory analyses'. *Language and Speech,* 34, 207–234

Silverman, K., Beckman, M.E., Pitrelli, J., Ostendorf, M., Wightman, C., Price, P., Pierrehumbert, J. and Hirschberg, J. (1992) 'ToBI: a standard for labelling English prosody'. *Proceedings, Second International Conference on Spoken Language Processing* 2: 867–70. Banff, Canada

Sinclair, J. and Coulthard, M. (1975) *Towards an Analysis of Discourse: The English used by Teachers and Pupils.* London; Oxford University Press

Sluijter, A. and Terken, J. (1993) 'Beyond sentence prosody: paragraph intonation in Dutch'. *Phonetica*, 50, 180–188

Stark, H.A. (1988) 'What do paragraph markings do? *Discourse Processes* 11, 275–303

Svartvik, J. (ed.) (1990) *The London-Lund Corpus of Spoken English: Description and Research.* Lund, Sweden: Lund University Press

Svensson, J. (1976) 'Report indicators and other parentheticals'. In F. Karlsson (ed.) *Papers form the Third Scandinavian Conference of Linguistics.* Turku: Text Linguistics Research Group, Academy of Finland. pp.369–380

Swerts, M. (1994) 'Prosodic features of Discourse Units'. PhD Dissertation. Technical University Eindhoven, Institute for Perception Research, Eindhoven

Swerts, M. and Geluykens, R. (1993) 'The prosody of information units in spontaneous monologue'. *Phonetica* 50, 189–196

Swerts, M. and Veldhuis, R. (1997) 'Interactions between intonation and glottal pulse characteristics'. In Botinis, A., Kouroupetroglou, G. and Carayiannis, G. (eds) *Intonation: Theory, Models and Applications.* Proceedings of a European Speech Communication Association (ESCA) Workshop, Athens, Greece: ESCA and University of Athens

Swerts, M., Wichmann, A. and Beun, R-J. (1996) 'Filled pauses as markers of discourse structure'. In *Proceedings of the International Congress on Spoken Language Processing (ICSLP).* Philadelphia, USA

Taylor, L. (1996) 'The correlation between punctuation and tone group boundaries'. In Knowles, Wichmann and Alderson (eds)

Tench. P. (1996) *The Intonation Systems of English.* London: Cassell

Thomas, J. (1996) *Meaning in interaction: an introduction to pragmatics.* London: Longman

Thorndyke, P.W. (1977) 'Cognitive structures in comprehension and memory of narative discourse'. *Cognitive Psychology* 9: 77–110

Thorsen, N.G. (1985) 'Intonation and text in standard Danish'. *Journal of the Acoustical Society of America* 77, pp.1205–1216

Trim, J.L.M. (1970) 'Some continuously variable features in British English intonation. *Proceedings of the 10th International Congress of Linguistics.* Bucharest: Editions de l'Academie de la Republique Socialiste de Roumanie

Turnbull, G. (1995) 'Children reading aloud'. Unpublished undergraduate dissertation, University of Central Lancashire

van Dijk, T. (1977) *Text and Context. Explorations in the Semantics and Pragmatics of Discourse.* London: Longman

van Dijk, T. (1982) 'Episodes as units of discourse analysis'. In: D. Tannen (ed.) *Analyzing Discourse* Georgetown U.P.

Wells, B. and Peppé, S. (1996) 'Ending up in Ulster'. In E. Couper-Kuhlen and M. Selting (eds)

Werlich, E. (1983) *A Text Grammar of English.* Heidelberg: Quelle und Meyer

Wichmann, A. (1987) 'Stylistic Variation in Prosody: A Preliminary Study of the Spoken English Corpus'. Unpublished MA Dissertation, Lancaster University

Wichmann, A. (1990) 'A manner of speaking'. Lancaster Papers, 70, Lancaster University

Wichmann, A. (1991a) 'Falls: variability and perceptual effects'. In *Proceedings of ICPhS91* Aix-en-Provence. 5, 194–197

Wichmann, A. (1991b) 'Beginnings, Middles and Ends'. Unpublished PhD dissertation, Lancaster University

Wichmann, A. (1991c) 'A Study of Uparrows in the Lancaster/IBM Spoken English Corpus'. In Johannson, S. and Stentstrom, A-B. (eds) *English Computer Corpora.* Berlin: de Gruyter

Wichmann, A. (1993) 'F0 troughs and prosodic phrasing'. In D. House and P. Touati (eds) *Working Papers 41* Dept. of Linguistics, University of Lund

Wichmann, A. (1996) 'Prosodic style: a corpus-based approach'. In Knowles, Wichmann and Alderson (eds)

Wichmann, A. (1998) 'Using intonation to create conversational space: projecting topics and turns'. In Renouf, A. (ed.) *Explorations in Corpus Linguistics*. Amsterdam: Rodopi

Wichmann, A. and Knowles, G. (1995) 'How determinable are intonation units'. In *Proceedings of ICPhS95* Stockholm, Sweden

Wichmann, A., House, J. and Rietveld, T. (1997) 'Peak displacement and topic structure'. In Botinis, A., Kouroupetroglou, G. and Carayiannis, G. (eds) *Intonation: Theory, Models and Applications*. Proceedings of a European Speech Communication Association (ESCA) Workshop, Athens, Greece: ESCA and University of Athens

Wichmann, A., House, J. and Rietveld, T. (forthcoming) 'Discourse effects on tonal peak timing in English'. To appear in Botinis, A. (ed.) *(forthcoming)* Cambridge: Cambridge University Press

Williams, B. (1987) 'Wordstress assignment in a text-to-speech synthesis system for British English'. *Computer, Speech and Language*, 2, 235–272

Williams, B. (1996) 'The formulation of as intonation transcription system for British English'. In Knowles, Wichmann and Alderson (eds) *Working with Speech*. Longman: London

Yngve, V. (1970) 'On getting a word in edgewise'. *Papers from the 6th Regional Meeting, Chicago Linguistic Society*, 567–578

Yule, G. (1980) 'Speakers' topics and major paratones'. *Lingua 52*, 33–47 North Holland

Index